TEACHING WITH
poverty
and equity
IN MIND

ERIC JENSEN

TEACHING WITH
poverty
and equity
IN MIND

ascd

Arlington, Virginia USA

2800 Shirlington Road, Suite 1001 • Arlington, VA 22206
Phone: 800-933-2723 or 703-578-9600 • Fax: 703-575-5400
Website: www.ascd.org • Email: member@ascd.org
Author guidelines: www.ascd.org/write

Penny Reinart, *Chief Impact Officer;* Genny Ostertag, Managing Director, *Book Acquisitions & Editing;* Allison Scott, *Senior Acquisitions Editor;* Julie Houtz, *Director, Book Editing;* Miriam Calderone, *Editor;* Thomas Lytle, *Creative Director;* Donald Ely, *Art Director;* Georgia Park, *Senior Graphic Designer;* Cynthia Stock, *Typesetter;* Kelly Marshall, *Production Manager;* Shajuan Martin, *E-Publishing Specialist*

All web links in this book are correct as of the publication date below but may have become inactive or otherwise modified since that time. If you notice a deactivated or changed link, please email books@ascd.org with the words "Link Update" in the subject line. In your message, please specify the web link, the book title, and the page number on which the link appears.

PAPERBACK ISBN: 978-1-4166-3056-2   ASCD product #120019   n5/22
PDF E-BOOK ISBN: 978-1-4166-3057-9; see Books in Print for other formats.
Quantity discounts are available: email programteam@ascd.org or call 800-933-2723, ext. 5773, or 703-575-5773. For desk copies, go to www.ascd.org/deskcopy.

Library of Congress Cataloging-in-Publication Data

Library of Congress Cataloging in Publication Control Number: 2021061999

31 30 29 28 27 26 25 24 23 22   1 2 3 4 5 6 7 8 9 10 11 12

TEACHING WITH poverty *and* equity IN MIND

Preface

More than a decade ago, I wrote a book called *Teaching with Poverty in Mind: What Being Poor Does to Kids' Brains and What Schools Can Do About It*. Why have I decided to follow up with this new volume, expanding on the subject of supporting students who live in poverty? For you to understand it better, you'll want to read a brief (and true) story about a kid. This young boy's life changed at age 2, when his mom walked out. Tears gushed liquid pain down his face. Divorce is always tough on children, and the boy felt like he had just been hit by a bus. Unfortunately, his father had no idea how to raise his three kids. Four years of "take any babysitter you can find" (some of them would have been arrested in today's world) motivated his dad to remarry for the first of three times.

This boy's first stepmother was violent, alcoholic, and abusive. Without hesitation, his oldest sister found safety living with the next-door neighbors for seven years. His other sister moved into the garage, where she lived with no bathroom.

The stepmother made life a living hell for her new stepchildren. This kid never, ever went into the kitchen when she was there, because that's where the knives were kept. Marital fights were common, and so was broken glass and blood.

The boy's father felt trapped in a bad marriage. He worked during the day, then was off to night school, and added weekends with the National Guard. The boy was often locked out of his own house, and he snacked from a bag of Purina dry dog food in the garage between meals. From 2nd through 10th grade, his daily mindset at home and at school was "Just one more day. I can do this."

To help him escape his hellish home and get away to safety, his dad moved him (with his "garage" sister) out of the house. He lived with his uncle (and attended a new school), then with his grandmother (attending another school), and then independently (at yet another school). After each move away, his unstable stepmother would promise to "be good," and they would move back home. The cycle of violence repeated itself again and again. Moving around was the norm, not the exception; this kid went to three elementary schools, four middle schools, and two high schools (nine total schools and 66 teachers).

This kid was never taught social-emotional skills, and because he was never at any school long enough, he developed few friendships. Neither his father nor his stepmother ever said "I love you" or gave him a hug. Trust me, that really messes up a kid.

He was often truant and sent to the office for discipline issues. Why? In class, this kid usually sat in the back making wisecracks, feeling stressed, and wondering, "What is it going to be like when I get home? Will I get hurt again?" For him, home was unsafe and a source of chronic stress. I would guess that most of his teachers were pretty sure he was going nowhere and would amount to nothing.

Yet somehow, all of this felt "normal." Why? His peers were experiencing the same thing. He had three friends, and two of them had abusive fathers. By age 20, he had been arrested twice and had almost dropped out of school.

Maybe you're asking, "Is there a point to this story? Why are you telling me about this kid's upbringing?"

The kid I have been describing was myself. In the widely publicized Adverse Childhood Experiences (ACE) survey, nearly half of all school-age kids in America have at least one childhood risk factor (e.g., divorce, abuse, drugs, parental incarceration, alcohol, mental illness). When you have four or more adverse childhood experiences, you pass a threshold for being at a particularly high risk of adverse physical and mental health outcomes (Felliti et al., 1998). I can check *seven* factors (out of ten). I don't expect sympathy, credit, or blame. I didn't choose my parents, my neighborhood, my DNA, or my upbringing. It is what it is: crappy luck.

I am also not telling you I grew up in poverty; *I didn't.* My story is relevant because I do know (firsthand) a bit about growing up with adversity. I also grew up with white privilege, meaning I never experienced racism and daily microaggressions based on my ethnicity. There was no generational or historical trauma in my world, as many people of color experience.

If you're wondering how my two older sisters turned out, they struggled. Between them, they've had four marriages and four divorces. Two children were abandoned; both sisters have often been depressed; one contemplated suicide. They have lived in poverty much of their lives. I have seen firsthand the impact of their adverse childhood experiences.

It took me 25 long years (starting after high school) to turn my life around. Can I take credit for that? Yes and no. I was lucky enough to meet high-quality adults who became my role models. That helped me pivot and change my life.

I also had to go head-to-head with my own attachment disorder, antisocial personality disorder, attention deficit disorder, physical trauma, and chronic stress. I had to learn how to be around people, to trust them, and to quit lying. Over time, I learned social skills, emotional skills, and self-worth. Once I started to work on myself, making a living and having a life became easier for me. With tools, I had hope.

I could not have written this book any earlier in my life. There is so much I simply did not know when I wrote *Teaching with Poverty in Mind* in 2009, and I had not dealt with the trauma and healed myself enough to write this book. I still have much to learn, and I am growing every year. As soon as I feel like I have risen to a new plateau, I become humbled again. As the book moves forward, I'll walk you though my growth.

I often share a message with teachers and students I work with: "Life's not fair, but you *always* have a choice." You have choices in the jobs you interview for, the job you accept, the attitude you bring to work, the decisions you make at work, the people you call friends, the foods you eat, whether you do or don't have children, the person who becomes your partner, and how you spend your time on this planet.

At work, you choose whether you greet students with a smile and warmth every day or not. You choose whether you are an ally or an adversary to your students. You choose whether you work on yourself daily or stay the same. The teachers who are perceived by students as adversaries usually dislike their jobs. The teachers who believe in their students, support them, and have faith in them are perceived as allies. Yes, luck does play a part in life, but your choices do, too. You do have a choice. Every day.

Now, you may say to me, "Eric, you are privileged and have no idea what it's like living on a teacher's salary." Actually, I do know. First, I taught middle and high school in San Diego for seven years (wages under $15,000 per year). And here's a memo: San Diego was (and is) a very expensive city. But I simply made the decision to live cheaply. For seven years, I never paid more than $50 a month for housing. I lived in a laundry room for two years, paying just $25 a month. In college, I had a food budget contest with my college roommate. I won it, spending just under $14 ... for a month of food! (Yes, I ate mostly oatmeal and potatoes.) I was a caretaker for a professor's property for five years and lived in a 15-foot travel trailer for $50 a month. My point is, *you would be surprised at what you can do*. It may be better than you think you can do. You always have a choice.

Over the years, I have faced many of the same demons that I am asking you to face. I struggled with my identity, the stories I chose to share, my implicit biases, my lack of self-care, and the difficulty of setting an intention for each day. In this book, you'll learn how I grappled with these challenges and came to deal with them.

This book is about how you might approach and succeed with students from adversity. The next time you have a kid in your class who appears unmotivated or is acting out, remember this: *I WAS one of those kids,* and I took it personally when a teacher judged me and refused to help me succeed. Never wait for a kid to show potential; they all have it.

I have continued on a path of growth since I wrote *Teaching with Poverty in Mind,* and I'll never stop. This new book has different points of view, stronger evidence, and a wider perspective on the issues. This book will show you why and how you can love your job. I am also hoping that as you read this book, you'll enjoy learning how to foster *a better version of you.*

Acknowledgments

It took me decades to write this book. No, I'm not a slow writer. The reality is that many influential people in my life gave me micro-nudges over the years. Each nudge has shown up in this book. I knew at the time that each of these people had much to teach me. But I am embarrassed to admit, I may have accidentally left some of them out. I'm sorry for that. Any omissions are accidental.

I have drunk deep from the well by reading, meeting, and listening to my favorite educational leaders, such as Lionel Allen, Ronald Ferguson, Michael Fullan, Zaretta Hammond, Robyn R. Jackson, Yvette Jackson, Baruti Kafele, Ibram X. Kendi, Anthony Muhammad, Pedro Noguera, Dylan Wiliam, and Ereka Williams.

I am also blessed to have colleagues to learn from. Many amazing teachers are featured in this book (privacy was preserved), and if you are one of them, thank you. Colleagues who have contributed to this work include Jim Ewing, Bryan Harris, Shauna King, Eric Larison, Liesl McConchie, and LeAnn Nickelsen.

I am indebted to the sources for many of the background ideas, processes, and tools in the book. My shortlist of researchers, thinkers, and writers includes Peter Attia, James Clear, Patrick Edblad, Huda Essa, John Hattie, Daniel Kahneman, Robert Marzano, Shane Parrish, Kerry Patterson, Naseem Taleb, Richard Thaler, and Chris Voss.

I am blessed in my long-time friendship with Harry Pickens. He's been a role model and friend who has made unique contributions to my life. I would be less of a person without having met him over three decades ago.

I am also grateful for the committed, patient, never-ending support of both Allison Scott and Miriam Calderone.

Finally, my wife Diane has been my best supporter, and I am over-the-top grateful for that.

Introduction

This book may be unsettling for you. You'll be addressed as if you're sitting right across from me and we're having a conversation.

We are going to start with a lie.

The lie is one of the most damaging, inexcusable, and widespread lies of the last 100 years. The lie has ruined millions of lives. The lie has cost our economy trillions of dollars. This lie has changed the course of education, and hence America's economy, social structure, and culture.

You have been told many lies as an educator. It's time to set the record straight. Because when you become more aware of what's hurting you and your students, you'll likely choose to grow, change, and get better results in the classroom. Or, you'll quit. That halfway in-between zone is not going to make it for you anymore.

Here's the lie: "All students deserve a high-quality public school education." As a nation, we superficially espouse this lofty ideal—and then fail to back it up with better pay for our teachers, reliable funding, realistic policies, and action. We can get rah-rah about meritocracy, hard work, and earning your way "up the ladder," but this lack of follow-up on our supposed values has become comfortably accepted by too many.

Countless students have been misled about opportunities and subjected to lower expectations. Many have found that their culture is unwelcome at school, have faced discrimination, and have been excluded from gifted classes. Millions of students of color have been assigned less-skilled, less-experienced, and undertrained teachers, often with a temporary certification. Innumerable students from poverty have been steered away from challenging or lucrative career opportunities because of perceptions of weaker character or intelligence.

Most of us in education are guilty. The good news is that times are changing. I am hoping you are reading this book because you are considering being part of the change. But why change, and why change now?

When teachers succeed with middle-income and upper-income students, they will assign a *positive impact* to their role. In fact, in surveys, most teachers say they are doing a "pretty good job." They believe they work hard to help their students succeed, and sharing credit for that success seems justified. Who could blame them?

But what happens when you ask teachers about the *negative impact* of their role in a school with students from poverty? There is rarely a self-assigned responsibility for disparities in academic outcomes. Instead, most teachers have a narrative to explain students' lack of academic success. Many teachers use "code speak" to describe why their proficiency scores, engagement responses, and discipline numbers are lower with poor students. Some teachers will play the sympathy card: "Bless their hearts. They come from poor families; you can just guess what that's like." Many use the character card: "He's just not motivated," or "She's got an attitude that won't stop." Some teachers play the bad-seed behavior card: "Well, you know his father's in prison, so the apple doesn't fall far from the tree." Still other teachers play the "times have changed" card: "Our student body has changed; kids used to be better disciplined, speak English, and work hard. Nowadays, it's all different." If this is how staff members at your school speak to one another, your students may have a bleak future.

Roughly half of students who start school in the United States will struggle. These students often experience some form of marginalization: They live in poverty, they are students of color, they are immigrants, they are English learners, or they have special needs. The majority of these students will start school below grade level, and somehow, after 13 years of school, most will not have become proficient in reading, writing, or problem solving. They will have fallen behind their peers of higher socioeconomic status. Too few ever catch up.

So there you have it: plenty of reasons to explain why students from poverty will always struggle in school. But if it's inevitable, why did I write a new book on teaching students from poverty? You'll find out as you explore each of the nine chapters in this book.

Before I introduce each chapter, keep in mind that I have chosen to exclude many of the basics of teaching. This book assumes you already know how to plan lessons, set up your room, handle transitions, and design and conduct useful formative assessment. If not, there are other books that cover those topics well. This book is designed to fill in the gaps that are unique to teaching students from poverty and takes a fresh approach with equity in mind. I hope you find this approach to be valuable.

The book is organized around core equity questions. The first chapter is about discovery; it asks you to "Start with Yourself." Chapter 2, "Conscious Connections," gives you three critical relationship levels to reach with your students. Chapter 3 explains how to "Raise the Roof" by fostering high expectations in ways that matter most.

Chapter 4 explores "Equitable Environments" as one of the core paths to your success. Chapter 5, "Rousing Relevance," introduces you to what matters most in students' school experiences; relevance and engagement are pretty high on most students' lists. Chapter 6 has you "Scaffold Scorekeeping." You'll learn how to provide high-quality feedback in ways that will work for every student. In Chapter 7, you'll learn how to move "From Discipline to Coaching." This chapter shows you a simple three-part path to fostering better behaviors. You'll learn the secrets to de-escalation and other classroom climate challenges.

In Chapter 8, "Cognitive Climbers," we'll explore the powerful accelerated learning tools that I've used for decades to help educators become amazingly good at teaching. You'll get reminders of how to build equity in every class. The last chapter is "The Emerging You." The core tenet here is that change is not easy, but it is doable. You'll learn how to reset your brain for a new path forward, and you'll discover what tools and resources you will need to be a successful teacher.

As an educator, you likely value learning and growing. Every chapter in this book will be putting those values on the line. This book is about growing *you*. We will start with a bit of unlearning, clearing debris, and dispelling myths.

1

....

Start with Yourself

Student Questions
➤ *"Who is my teacher, and what does my teacher believe?"*
➤ *"Does my teacher respect and support me, or will I be marginalized again?"*

This first chapter is focused on you. Now, you may be tempted to push back and say, "Wait a minute, I just wanted some strategies for my classroom." But pause for a second. How has that "grab and go" approach been working out for you and your students? Are your students reaching grade-level proficiency every year? Do you love your work? Do you achieve high inclusion and engagement with every student, every day? Do your students grow at a rate at or above your high expectations? Is classroom discipline a nonissue for you? Do your students love being in your class?

These are far from rhetorical questions. The experiences above not only are possible, but also commonly happen with high-performing Title I teachers. There are teachers who get more than a year and a half's worth of learning gains every year.

Now, if you can already answer a strong "Yes" to every one of those questions, feel free to give this book to someone who needs it more than you do. But if you're like most teachers, your "No" answers might be ready for an update.

You noticed some student questions at the start of this chapter. You'll see such questions throughout the book. One of the book's messages is that unless your teaching answers the questions your students care about most, you'll lose them. They will disconnect, and your school year will not go well.

Each chapter will assist you in better answering the student questions at the start of that chapter. The focus of this book is on *what students need.* Why? That message is at the core of equity.

Today is the first day of the rest of your teaching career. Let's begin with a different approach. Your topics in this chapter are:

- Start with Yourself
- The Impact of Poverty on Your Students
- How Your Brain Works Against You
- Emerging Equity Tools to Embrace

As in each of the other chapters, this one includes several sections at the end to help you reflect on the information and move forward on your growth journey:

- Chapter in a Nutshell
- Revisit the Student Questions
- Before the Next Chapter

We'll begin with a shift in how you learn and prepare. I'm sure that before you begin each class, you have made your preparations and you know just what you intend to do. You have asked the usual questions: "Have I got this? Is this handled, and is that taken care of?" But it's possible that you've failed to include the most important questions—the questions that your students care about the most.

In this first chapter, we'll be holding up a mirror. Each school year, your new students are asking, "Who are you?" It's time we explore what you believe, assume, and subsequently act on. Has your school added "grit" to the curriculum? Do you know that kids from poverty often show more grit than their teachers do? Low-income 8th grade students will end up graduating from high school at a 78 percent rate, which is increasing annually (Atwell, Balfanz, Bridgeland, & Ingram, 2019). But during the same five-year span, only 56 percent of new teachers will stay in the profession (Ingersoll et al., 2018). Seems like students have grit already.

After five years in school, the majority of students from poverty read below the 4th grade level. Most students eligible for free or reduced lunches are at a basic reading level or below (Nation's Report Card, 2019). This is a critical benchmark. As if that's not bad enough, in the next eight years, the majority are still below grade level in reading proficiency. We can sugarcoat that any way you'd like, but collectively, we are failing our students. As you read this chapter, you'll see in a whole new way why this is happening.

For starters, do you understand poverty? Is it a federal guideline for income earned by a family of four? Is it an aggregate of chronic risk factors? Maybe you've lived in poverty and have your own understanding of it. We all know it's not an assured destiny, nor is it an automatic, predicted lifetime outcome. And although there are many sensible policy suggestions, there's simply a lack of political will to implement most of them. For the moment, let's narrow our focus to what you have strong influence over right away, at your workplace.

Start with Yourself

In any learning experience for their own students, successful teachers will typically start out with discovery. Let's do the same thing here and find out what you already know about the impact poverty has on your students. Figure 1.1 lists 10 statements, and you will decide whether each is true or false. Grab a pen or pencil and mark your responses. Take this seriously, because you'll want to find out where you stand and discover what you already know about poverty.

Figure 1.1   10 Discovery Questions About Poverty

(T/F)   1. The neighborhood that kids live in and the classroom teachers they have in school are two of the biggest influences on students' lifelong success.

(T/F)   2. Children from low-income families start school with smaller and less-complex vocabularies than their middle-income or high-income peers. There's a 30-million-word gap.

(T/F)   3. Students from poverty have typical brain development. They just fall behind because of lack of motivation or parental support. Unfortunately, once a student from poverty enters school one to three years behind, there is little hope.

(T/F)   4. Even if you're poor in the United States, you're still doing pretty well. Poor people often have cell phones, name-brand shoes, and big-screen TVs.

(T/F)   5. The U.S. education system is mostly equal and fair, partly because we live in a meritocracy (a system based on effort and achievement).

(T/F)   6. Poor people value education about the same as middle-income people do.

(T/F)   7. It's cheaper to be poor. Poor people don't have to pay for a lot of things that middle-income and wealthy people have to pay for.

(T/F)   8. Most poor people are unmotivated and lack ambition. They are more likely to be substance abusers than middle-income and wealthy people are.

(T/F)   9. African Americans in poverty have higher rates of suicide, depression, and drug use and lower rates of college attendance and completion than those in any other racial or economic category.

(T/F) 10. Poor people get more government handouts than nonpoor people do.

Debrief Time

The answers to the quiz are in Appendix A. If you got 9 or 10 correct, congratulations! If you got 8 or fewer correct, join the club. Maybe you know less about poverty than you thought you did. Did you discover that some of your beliefs may not be true? Take four minutes and do a quick write. Just offload what's on your mind. You can also do this assignment verbally or share with a partner. There will be more opportunities to grow your awareness, knowledge, and skill sets as you move forward.

The Impact of Poverty on Your Students

There are, of course, many ways to define poverty. I typically define poverty as the presence of multiple adverse risk factors leading to economic, emotional, social, cultural, and biological disadvantages that are multiplied by systemic classism and racism. *But poverty is still best defined by each and every person,* one by one. There are more than 30 million adults in the United States living in poverty (U.S. Census Bureau, 2020), but each person's story is unique. Remember, some poor people live a blessed life, full of gratitude, health, and love. They live within their means with an intact family. Many nonpoor people may dream daily of a life that good. As Nobel Prize–winning economists Abhijit Banerjee and Esther Duflo observe, we need "to stop reducing the poor to cartoon characters and take the time to really understand their lives, in all their complexity and richness" (Biswas, 2019, para. 11). We cannot and should not make generalizations about poor people.

The real truths about poverty can typically elude even the most dedicated social scientists. Poverty is not defined by the opinion of a researcher who writes an article, blog, or book (like this one). It is not defined by someone who grew up in poverty, and then shares their life story and wants to generalize it to every student. It is not defined by one community in one part of the country. (Should we pick rural, urban, or suburban?) And it is certainly not defined by broad-stroke Department of Labor statistics.

To add to the challenge, addressing poverty in your classroom is different from addressing race, although there are correlations between the two. Understanding that the experience of poverty can be exacerbated by racial injustice is critical. Many teachers are unaware that most public schools discriminate against people of color. Nationally, our schools have facilitated significant inequity, and it's time for that to stop. The U.S. Census found that in the United States in 2019, "the share of Blacks in poverty was 1.8 times greater than their share among the general population. Blacks represented 13.2% of the total population in the United States, but 23.8% of the poverty population. The share of Hispanics in poverty was 1.5 times more than their share in the general population. Hispanics comprised 18.7% of the total population, but 28.1% of the population in poverty" (Creamer, 2020). Although the overrepresentation of Blacks and Hispanics living in poverty is a critical concern, poverty is not solely a racial issue. Non-Hispanic Whites made up 41.6 percent of all people in poverty in the United States in 2019, whereas Blacks made up just 23.8 percent and Hispanics made up 28.1 percent (Creamer, 2020). Although the reasons may be different, all of us have a stake in the process of teaching with poverty and equity in mind.

Typically, the greatest challenges for many teachers are in working with those who are different from themselves. Keep in mind that poverty refers to socioeconomic class only (not gender, geography, or ethnicity). However, achievement gaps for students of color give us additional incentives to acknowledge and change our practices. To become amazing, we'll be starting down the path of equity and using several important processes to succeed. Three of the most common paths that we use to learn about equity are

1. The stories we are told and share.
2. The experiences we've had.
3. The research we read, watch, and share about poverty.

So, can we generalize *anything at all?* What does the research tell us? One way to understand poverty is through the adverse effects of early life experiences—that is, the dual impact of *threat* and *deprivation* (McLaughlin, Weissman, & Bitrán, 2019). Those two forces impact a child's cognitive, emotional, and social development in multiple ways.

The *threat* may be a debilitating or recurring trauma in the form of bullying; home, street, or school violence; internalized pressure from negative stereotypes; or careless and threatening teachers. The *deprivation* may include the loss of a parent (for instance, through divorce, incarceration, or death); loss of an *agile* parent (for instance, through depression, cancer, or heart disease); loss of residence (for instance, via eviction); loss of respect (for instance, via racism); loss of safety (for instance, via unsafe housing or public transit commutes); or lack of high-quality schools, nearby access to affordable food, affordable health care, or high-level social contacts.

Another pathway to understand the lives of people living in poverty is through the Adverse Childhood Experiences (ACE) studies. These studies show clear links between poverty and childhood adversity (Hughes & Tucker, 2018; Raphael, 2011; Schweiger, 2019). The original ACE study was one of the largest research inquiries into childhood adversity and corresponding adult health outcomes. The study began as a partnership between Dr. Robert Anda at Atlanta's Centers for Disease Control (CDC) and Dr. Vincent Felitti at Kaiser Permanente in San Diego. More than 17,000 adult Health Maintenance Organization (HMO) members took a detailed physical exam and answered a list of questions about their childhood experiences. The beginning of the survey asked, "Did this happen to you before the age of 18?"

The survey questions included topics on abuse, neglect, divorce, incarceration, drug addiction, violence, mental health, eviction, and more. The ACE study tells us that there are correlations between childhood adversity and later health, cognitive, and social issues (Felitti et al., 1998). As you know, correlations are different from causality, so we are going to be cautious. For one thing, studies suggest there's commonly a risk in using subjects' self-reports of early childhood; there is evidence in studies of both underreporting and overreporting (Hardt & Rutter, 2004).

But given the size of the study, it's still well worth our attention. Here are some of the student responses that often correlate with adverse childhood experiences:

- **Chronic and acute stressors** can lead to the possibility of greater impulsivity, on-off motivation, worse short-term and long-term memory, increased misbehavior in the classroom, less-reflective thinking and writing, and higher absenteeism.

- **Lack of access to mentors and inspiring adult connections** can lead to less hope, weaker motivation, lack of life skills, and lack of encouraging role models.
- **Substandard medical, emotional, and mental health resources** mean less access to good food; lack of a healthy, supportive family structure; an increased potential for hearing issues; a decreased likelihood of vision care; and a decreased likelihood of immunizations.
- **Lack of experienced, high-quality teachers in Title I schools** can lead to lower expectations of the value of education, less likelihood of high school graduation, and increased hopelessness.
- **Unsafe neighborhoods and housing instability** can increase tardiness at school. High crime in unsafe neighborhoods means students may have to take time-consuming detours around a police scene. In addition, students may not have reliable transportation. If their families are evicted or moving, students will bring stressors to school. Exposure to violence can happen in a neighborhood, at school, or at home. Students may normalize violence or have extreme responses to the trauma of it.
- **Social and emotional skills** not suited for classrooms might show up as poor behaviors, inappropriate responses to teacher requests, lack of empathy leading to disciplinary issues, and weaker social and personal relationships.
- **Less exposure to critical connections** means that many families in poverty lack access to networks of financial and medical professionals. These families often lack access to high-speed internet and computers, as well.
- **Continuous exposure to classism, racism, or other biases** may evoke mistrust of authority; bitterness, anger, or resentment because of the disrespect felt at every social or institutional turn; and loss of academic hope.

As you might guess, the more adversity a student has in childhood, the greater the risks the student faces in school and adulthood. The risks include lower grades, poor health outcomes, mental health issues, legal problems, suboptimal social-emotional skills, and less income mobility. A large, recent survey with nearly a quarter of a million subjects (Merrick, Ford, Ports, & Guinn, 2018) revealed that adults in the United States have the following percentages of ACEs:

- 38 percent have zero adverse experiences.
- 24 percent have one adverse experience.
- 13 percent have two adverse experiences.
- 9 percent have three adverse experiences.
- 16 percent have four or more adverse experiences.

This tells us that ACEs are common but not universal; over 60 percent of adults have had one or none. How many did you have? Many healthcare professionals have told me that anyone with four or more ACEs will likely have severe difficulties as an adult. As you might guess, the ACEs listed above are largely missing from many teachers' lives. Students from poverty might be in a situation that many middle-class educators can't even wrap their heads around.

How Your Brain Works Against You

How do you react to the research about adverse childhood experiences? Maybe you say to yourself, "Oh, that explains it. Bad things at home mean the kid's going to have issues at school. Tell me something I don't know." That's a common response. But there's a problem with that instant takeaway. When you hear or read of a study, remember this: Nearly every study is about correlations, and proving causality is very difficult. Studies are about the details. As a shortcut, our brain wants to jump to the bottom line. That's a bias. Why should you care?

The original ACE study has generated more than 70 subsequent scientific articles, so it is easy to predict doom and gloom for kids from poverty. Yet it is critical to know that *zero* of the ACE survey participants were asked about strengths, resources, or resilience (Leitch,

2017). Those factors *can mitigate the effects of adversity*. Trauma-informed approaches also mitigate adverse experiences (Ortiz, 2019). It is easy to misinterpret ACE studies. In short, the story of adversity in childhood is complex. The bias is to think you're helpless. You're not (unless you start believing everything you hear).

Keep in mind that for some students, living in poverty has forged a powerful sense of character and resilience, with a never-quit determination. Such students can teach you a lot about grit. My question to you is, do you believe it is possible for *every student* to grow and succeed? Maybe you find it hard to believe it is possible for every student. Would I change your mind if I told you how many engineers, leaders, scientists, authors, or Nobel laureates came from poverty? Or would you say, "Those are just outliers"? That's a bias. How many outliers do you need in order to believe in your students? Because if you need more than one, maybe you just don't want to believe.

If you do have a problem believing that all students can succeed, you are not alone. It's a result of your brain trying to help you cope in a world that your biology left you unprepared for. So, what are the brain's tendencies, how did they develop, and what do they have to do with you teaching students from poverty?

Your System 1 Brain Can Help You Survive

Early human tribes likely spent a good portion of the day doing what you take for granted: surviving. Survival steered our species toward select and crucial skills: finding food, early procreation, maternity, escaping from predators, raising families, and forming tribal bonds (Kenrick, Neuberg, Griskevicius, Becker, & Schaller, 2010). To survive, your brain uses a series of quickly learned tools. Why?

If a predator is approaching, you have mere seconds to assess the risk, choose a survival strategy, and take action. "Think fast or die" was the survival mantra encoded in our early brain. Nobel laureate Daniel Kahneman calls it our *System 1* or *reactive* brain (Morewedge &

Kahneman, 2010). Decades ago, educators referred to this as the *reptilian brain.*

The System 1 part of your brain enables you to absorb quick bites of information and make fast generalizations. It often establishes a set of attitudes, or biases, toward groups of people, places, and things. Those biases may be designed to keep you alive, but remember that surviving is different from thriving. Because speed can keep you alive, your brain uses shortcuts to cut out the time-consuming process of thinking, analyzing data, listening to opposing points of view, gaining consensus, and sharing the decision. The predator would have eaten you a long time ago in that thoughtful scenario.

Your brain generates cognitive biases so quickly you rarely notice it. In fact, researchers have identified more than 175 cognitive biases (Benson, 2016). Here are five common biases you may have experienced:

1. **Bandwagon effect:** We tend to join in with what many others are doing. ("Ten other schools are doing this in our state; let's do it!")
2. **Blind spot bias:** We are often unable to notice our weaknesses ("I would know it if I had those cognitive biases.")
3. **Confirmation bias:** We tend to see anything that confirms what we already believe in. ("Yes! This example confirms exactly what I was saying earlier.") This bias gives us the feeling of pride and validation (Darley & Gross, 2000; Hart et al., 2009).
4. **Familiarity bias:** If we have already heard of an idea before, it is easier to be biased in favor of it or to dismiss it. ("This idea's as old as my grandma. We've all heard it before; we should move on.")
5. **Stereotype bias:** We often judge others by the gender, social, or ethnic group they are in ("That kid's like the rest of those people. Not a drop of motivation.")

A starting bias to remember is the *blind spot bias* (see above). That's the inability to notice and reveal your own weaknesses because you feel you would already know about them (Pronin, Lin, & Ross, 2002). Any time you catch yourself denying that you have a bias, pause. That defense just might be your worst bias of all.

Throughout this book, you'll find yourself uncovering one bias after another. When that moment happens, relax; we all have them.

Why is this brain-based background relevant to you? As I said, we all have biases. Some biases are helpful and save us time. But others distort our perception of reality and become destructive. Biases are rarely "fixed," but they can be altered, diminished, or reinforced. Educators who succeed with students from poverty have different, more constructive biases than those who struggle. Fortunately, there are solutions to solve this big bog of biases, and they lie in our "System 2" brain (see Figure 1.2).

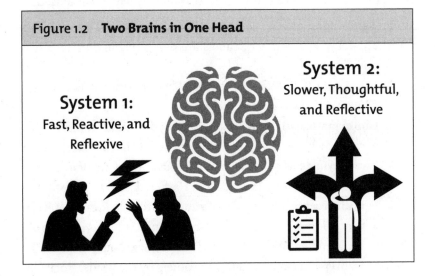

Figure 1.2   **Two Brains in One Head**

System 1:
Fast, Reactive, and Reflexive

System 2:
Slower, Thoughtful, and Reflective

Your System 2 Brain Can Help You Thrive

Eventually the System 1 brains of the emerging Homo sapiens (roughly 160,000 to 200,000 years ago) began to develop into the brains we have today (Roebroeks & Soressi, 2016). Over the millennia, the human brain has added greater complexity as the world changed. Our brain added the capacity for more sophisticated life skills, such as reflection, language, and cognitive problem solving, which Dr. Kahneman calls our *System 2* brain. These emerging pathways enabled us to form larger tribes, boost communication skills, improve planning, and gain better predatory and defensive options. Tribes and cultures grew, moved, and then expanded. They clashed with others for resources again and again. There were "in-groups" and "out-groups" with subsequent warfare.

Over time, our brain's newly adaptive survival tools allowed us to make conscious changes. If you're serious about growing yourself, these are what it takes to make success happen. The "grab and go" mentality (using System 1) only gets you more of the same. For many, the biases created by System 1 thinking are about stereotypes related to gender, race, or ethnicity. But that's just the tip of the bias iceberg. The good news? You'll learn how to flip that bias. Yes, *you can do it,* and it will change the way you think and act. Let's start fresh with a term you've heard a lot lately: *equity.*

Emerging Equity Tools to Embrace

If you teach students from poverty, the single solution that can change everything for you is equity. Equity refers to the mindset, policies, and approaches used to ensure that every student gets what they need to succeed. Equity is different from equality. Equity requires giving more to those who need it most, so that students have a greater chance of successful outcomes. Equity is not a new curriculum or assessment. Equity fosters antidiscrimination, antisexism, and antiracism. Equity also includes the policies, systems, and structures that may be in place in the classroom or school. In sum, equity is a framework for understanding your role at work in ways that will help every one of your students succeed. See Figure 1.3 to better understand equity at a personal, social, and systemic level.

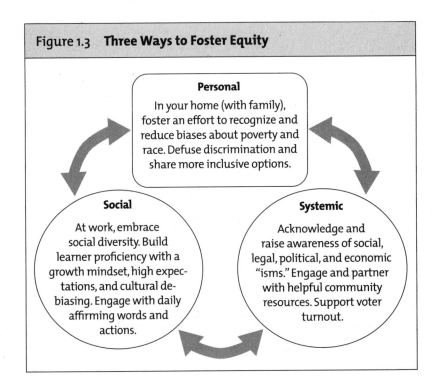

Figure 1.3   Three Ways to Foster Equity

Personal

In your home (with family), foster an effort to recognize and reduce biases about poverty and race. Defuse discrimination and share more inclusive options.

Social

At work, embrace social diversity. Build learner proficiency with a growth mindset, high expectations, and cultural de-biasing. Engage with daily affirming words and actions.

Systemic

Acknowledge and raise awareness of social, legal, political, and economic "isms." Engage and partner with helpful community resources. Support voter turnout.

The lack of equity is what started most of the problems, and for that reason, equity is the solution to most of the problems. Equity means you are doing whatever it takes for students to succeed. Make the choice to embed equity in every single facet of your work, and you'll mitigate enough potential student risk factors so that students will thrive, every day. Let's be very clear about this: Equity is a path, but it is not just another item for your daily to-do list. Equity in your school works best when it is based on a strong foundation.

What does it look like, sound like, and feel like to your students? Many staff members at Title I schools may complain about their students but fail to develop the insights, expertise, or daily habits to make changes. Equity is learning to be empathetic and to act on student needs. Until you can wrap your head around the world that your students live in, you'll always struggle. This book will share mindsets, tools, and action steps to help you grow in your engagement with equity. You can download a handy, simple equity graphic organizer at www.jensen learning.com/equity-resources.

Finally, what's in your path preventing you from being amazing is not genes, talent, or an education. It's your own brain. Sometimes your brain's biases, stories, and identities can help; other times they can hurt. In this chapter, you learned why and how your brain's System 1 tendencies of bias and distracted intentions often work against you. The good news is that brains are highly malleable, and you can pivot to a new choice any day of your life (see Figure 1.4.). Your System 2 brain is more than capable of change. Let's start with what equity steps we will need to take to succeed.

This book will introduce growth paths that may potentially become life-changing and powerful for you. Even better news? Each path is modifiable to best fit you, your classroom, and your students. They will allow you to enhance your personal and professional life. One or two tools will be introduced in each chapter, and any one of these is powerful for helping you be amazing in your life. However, they are

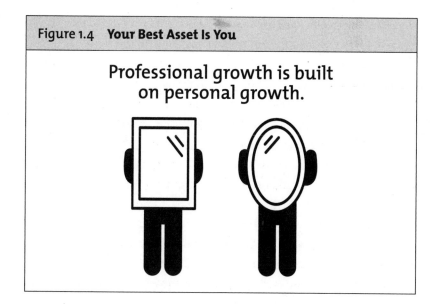

Figure 1.4   **Your Best Asset Is You**

Professional growth is built on personal growth.

insufficient individually to make the miracles we're after, so stay with us on this path.

I'd suggest starting with just one tiny but powerful step: *authentic intention.* For years, I felt like the most intention-less person on the planet. I rarely focused on a single task for long. I would jump from one idea to another. Not much got finished, and what was finished was rarely done well. I remember blaming it on my ADHD. In fact, I failed to even ask myself, "What on earth *am* I intending at the moment?"

Over the years, I discovered that unless I focus authentically and intentionally, write things down, and make lists for almost everything, I am a basket case. You may have students who seem distracted and unfocused. Do you have a bias against those students? My personal turning point was to realize there were others like me. I started to reflect on all the students whom I had thought less of because they seemed scattered and devoid of intention. I felt ashamed, but over time, I learned to forgive myself. I decided the best course was to help other kids just like me. That's why I became a teacher focusing on skills for underperforming students.

Authentic intention is defined as a directed thought to perform a determined, specific task in a specific location at a specific time. Intention could be a stated or written goal ("I will affirm the value of a different student every day, in person, at the door before they leave, starting next Monday."). Intentional thought guides one into an action (Bonilla, 2008). Intentions are regarded by many researchers as a directed thought for a predicted gain, but we often intend the wrong things, intend nothing at all, or get distracted. Intention is usually a necessary difference-maker for growth.

One study found that subjects' success in habit forming was partly driven by the level of involvement of the part of their brains that supports goal-directed intention (Zwosta, Ruge, Goschke, & Wolfensteller, 2018). Strong intention suppresses irrelevant distractions which, in turn, helps the brain focus on the task at hand (Eryilmaz et al., 2017). In fact, intention is in the *top three* interventions that form new habits

(Mergelsberg, Mullan, Allom, & Scott, 2020). (The other two interventions are the *type of habit* and the *specific behavior chosen*.) In short, there's clear evidence that intentions matter.

Chapter in a Nutshell

This chapter is about you, the teacher, and how your equity mindset can make the difference for your students. Equity is the belief, commitment, and actions that help students get what they need to succeed at school. In other words, if a student walked to school barefoot, and continually had blisters, would you point fingers and blame the mayor, the uneven sidewalks, and the potholes in the streets (the environment)? Or would you help that student get a pair of shoes?

Poverty is not the reason for underperforming students. Students who struggle are the result of a mismatch between the students' needs and the response provided by the teachers and the school. *The lack of compensatory equity is our challenge to meet.* Successful schools enhance existing assets, build new skills, shift expectations into high gear, build community, show respect, and open opportunity doors. Struggling schools fail at these missions. The difference is you.

Revisit the Student Questions

At the start of each chapter, you will see several equity questions that students may ask about you and your class. These questions come from five aggregated surveys of more than one million students. The sources used to gather these student questions are listed in Appendix B. Notice that equity questions are all about what students need. Other questions will be answered within each of the upcoming chapters.

Here are the student questions for this first chapter:

➤ *"Who is my teacher, and what does my teacher believe?"*

➤ *"Does my teacher respect and support me, or will I be marginalized again?"*

Your students care about those two questions as much as or more than you care about *your* questions. Most teachers' questions about teaching are about themselves. They have the words *I, me,* or *my* in them: *How should I set up my classroom? How can I make this process easier for me? What's my plan for this semester? What software, books, programs, or activities will I use this year? How will I implement our new discipline policy? What is the latest tech that I could use in my classroom?* and on and on. The student questions above suggest that students care as much about the question "Who are you?" That's where this book fits in.

Before the Next Chapter

Write a list of things you intend to do differently in your classroom over the next 30 days. These are things that you are thinking of changing after reading this first chapter. You might end up with multiple intentions. Once you have done that, rank them in order of priority. Use the criteria of "urgent and important" for the top of the list, maybe listing just your top two intentions. A couple of examples might be the following:

- "Choose my intentions daily for work and home life."
- "Be an ally and advocate for the students who struggle the most!"

Next, add the place and time you'll complete the intention. Those added critical details are called *implementation intentions* and are highly effective (Milne, Orbell, & Sheeran, 2002). Always pair your constructive professional changes with personal changes. That's why you'll make two tiny (but powerful) changes this chapter. Your new intentions might read like this:

- **Professional:** "Every day, once I arrive in my classroom, I will select a different student whom I will be an amazing ally for. I will connect with empathy and joy. I will support this student with one piece of positive feedback today."

- **Personal:** "Later in the day, as soon as I arrive at home and park my car, I pause. I review my home intentions ('Leave my work at work and bring kindness and joy as an ally for my partner, family, or roommate') before going through the front door."

Review your top intentions every morning. If you hear a voice in your head saying, "I don't have time for more new stuff!", recognize that that voice is expressing your "time bias," which consistently makes iffy estimates. After all, most teachers seem to have plenty of time for reteaching. You *do* have time to make crucial changes. After two weeks, you can add to, subtract from, or modify your intentions. Reading these daily will help them serve as your guiding North Star for this next segment of the change process.

If you want to see what really matters to you, pause and look at how you spend your time as you read this book. You can "borrow" knowledge, reading or listening from others, but the delegation of habits (showering, eating, sleeping, working out, brushing teeth, changing clothes, and thinking) is impossible. *You* make the choice to change your habits and grow. Be different. Think, plan, and embed the affirming answers to the student questions at the start of every chapter. The next action step is all yours. We will add to your growth each chapter. In this chapter, it's all about intentions and equity. Go ahead and start with your intentions; your students are waiting.

2

Conscious Connections

Student Questions

➤ *"Is my teacher an ally or an adversary?"*

➤ *"Does my teacher see, hear, and respect me with empathy and show that they care about how I am doing?"*

It's likely you have heard, "Build relationships with your students." As a beginning teacher, I heard that, too, but I had no idea *how to* connect. I had poor eye contact, rarely smiled, and failed to give enough positive feedback. What's worse, I had zero empathy skills. Empathy is partially genetic and partially learned. I had issues in my own personal relationships that influenced the relationships (or lack of relationships) with my students. No one had ever modeled empathy for me or taught me what to do. How well do you think I did with building close relationships with my students? I am ashamed to say, I was awful.

What changed for me? My eureka moment came when I was reading a "brain book." In one chapter, it talked about the impact of early childhood abandonment and trauma. Because my parents had divorced and my mom had left when I was 2, I leaned in and read closely. The book suggested that a child's brain can be traumatized by a parent leaving that child. Later, as an adult, I was fearful of any relationship that seemed to be getting serious. It turns out my brain had been saying, "You'll get hurt again, like you did when your mom left you!" For me, that was a huge wake-up call. My brain was trying to help me avoid pain and sending me a message: "Women who love me will leave me." But my brain was also working against me as a teacher.

Before we begin learning from an expert teacher, reread the two critical questions at the beginning of this chapter. At the start of each school year, students are asking these questions. If they don't get a positive answer quickly, students say to themselves, "Another boring class with a teacher who couldn't care less." They may shut down on you before the first hour is up.

But maybe you're willing to be different. Maybe you're willing to orchestrate an amazing start to the year. The single place where you get the biggest return on your time and effort is in the relationships you build with your students. Our topics for this chapter are:

- The Teacher You Wished You Had
- Connections to Poverty
- You Go First: Check Your Biases
- Engaging Relationships on Three Levels
- Emerging Equity Tool to Embrace

Let's begin by looking at a teacher who builds relationships with students that make all the difference.

The Teacher You Wished You Had

It's day one of school. Our teacher has a class in which 100 percent of her students live in poverty. When students enter the classroom, they see the name of the class up front: *Honors Biology*. What's the first thing that runs through each student's mind when they see the class title?

If you predicted squinted eyes, tilted heads, and looks of confusion or dread, you're right. This teacher is sharp and has situational awareness, checking out every arriving student. She notices one student who looks particularly confused, and she goes up to him just as he asks, "Am I in the right class?"

Most teachers would say, "Let me check the roster." Sorry, that's the wrong answer. The student is not just asking if he is on the roster. On a deeper level, the student is saying, "I'll bet it's hard to succeed in an honors class. Do I have what it takes? Will my teacher help me succeed? Do I *really belong here?*"

The savvy teacher in our scenario, though, has a deep understanding of her students from many years of experience. She answers the question "Am I in the right class?" by saying, "Welcome! Of course, I'd love to have you in my class; find a seat!" Why that answer? First impressions matter! She is affirming, "I care about you, and you belong!"

She will later check the roster to confirm whether the student is in the correct class. If a student is missing from the roster, she never sends that student to the office to get to the correct class. That sends the wrong message. School should be a place where students feel like they belong, like they're more than a number that gets pushed around campus.

If the teacher finds that the student's name is not on the roster, she then says to the student, "I don't see your name on the list, but as I said, I'd love to have you in my class. If you'd like to stay, I'll fight for you to get in my class. Interested?" Her students sense an ally, and they *always decide to stay in her class.*

This teacher knows that many of her new students have never received a "Proficient" from any of their classes. Later in that first class, she promises every student that they will get a Proficient or *higher* in her class if they do only one thing: help another student do it, too. I have seen the grade contract that she uses. It's a real document that has the student's name with the agreement and conditions for meeting the deal. It gets signed by the teacher, the student, and the parent or guardian. The teacher knows that the last thing students need is to lose hope. Or to lose an ally who cares (and is good at her job). Remember the two student questions at the start of the chapter? This teacher knows them well.

Notice the power of equity in action. This high-equity teacher does *whatever it takes*. By the end of week one, here's what she has done. She has connected with and welcomed every student (using strategies like self-story, me-bag, and one-on-one intros). She has made the class a safe place to learn. (Students share personal stories and generate class norms.) She has assured every student that real success is achievable, and she has shown them a clear path. (Every student has a signed document showing that they can succeed in her class, and *how* to succeed.) She has *proven* that she is an ally, not an adversary. (She takes action in favor of a student at every turn.) Oh, by the way, 100 percent of her students reach proficiency every semester. Interested in having your own students do that? *Now you are starting to understand equity.*

Debrief Time

Let's pause to process the equity mindset. How did this (real) teacher answer her students' critical questions in just five days? Reflect on your reaction to her routine. Has your brain already marginalized this teacher as different, exceptional, creative, or courageous? Do you hear your brain start up the dismissive biases? Yes, it takes work to overcome these biases and become excellent. Debrief this teacher's class-opening behaviors in writing or in a discussion with a partner.

Connections to Poverty

There are strong connections between relationships and poverty. To achieve normal social and emotional development, all children need to attach to and develop a relationship with at least one primary caregiver (Ainsworth & Bowlby, 1991). Children from poverty are more likely than middle-income or high-income children to have attachment or relational disorders (Quevedo et al., 2017). The U.S. Census found that in 2018, 66.8 percent of poor children lived in single-parent families (Children's Defense Fund, 2020). Being the lone head of household may contribute to greater stress for single parents and reduce the quantity of unstressed time they can spend with their kids at home. That makes it extra hard on the child, who would love to have a fully present caregiver.

Of course, some kids have an emotionally available and supportive single parent who helps them understand, make sense of, and even compartmentalize any family trauma. These students may be able to behave well in school. But even more than other students, students who experience family instability need an immediate connection with a caring teacher (Wentzel, 2012). The most important mindset this chapter can convey to you is this: *Your students need to develop a relationship with at least one primary caregiver for normal social and emotional development.*

Manny is a good example of how childhood trauma can affect school performance. Manny seemed like a likeable student. Early on, most of his teachers said he seemed charismatic and had that "something extra." But that was usually followed with, "But he won't accept help. He wants to do things his way, and he gets in trouble a lot." The problem was, no one recognized Manny's behavior as a result of trauma. When Manny was 4, his father went to prison. To stop the pain, Manny's brain said, "Make adults irrelevant." Adults were not allies to him; *his best ally had been sent to prison.*

The brain systems that shape students' perceptions, their relationships, and the regulation of social-emotional information are modulated by individual differences from their life experiences (Vrtička & Vuilleumier, 2012). For some children, the trauma of a parent leaving is overwhelming. The trauma will constantly trigger toxic levels of stress because the child lacks control over their relevant needs (Rutter, Moffitt, & Caspi, 2006). Manny, for instance, had an experience where someone relevant, his parent, had left him. He didn't have control over that experience.

As a result, many students have learned not to trust adults. When there is a stressor that activates their trauma at school, these kids tend to act out in class, using aberrant social and emotional behaviors in an attempt to gain control. The uninformed teacher feels like their power is being challenged and lashes back by trying to impose more control and stricter discipline, the exact opposite of what should be done. This teacher gets irritated, and the student-teacher relationship is damaged.

Kids without a strong connection with an adult at home may be either withdrawn or needy at school. If these students frequently move schools, they may simply expect a loss, so they believe it is less painful to avoid connecting. If they stay at the same school, they may be more likely to latch onto their teachers and may seem needy (McKinnon, Friedman-Krauss, Roy, & Raver, 2018).

You might not know that good relationships are correlated with immune system strength, health, longevity, neurogenesis (the production of new brain cells), and, even better, cognition. Student-teacher relationships matter in more and different ways than you might imagine. For example, low-income students commonly miss a greater number of classes, with absenteeism rates of over 5 percent every year. Yet stronger relationships will keep a student healthier (Kiecolt-Glaser, Gouin, & Hantsoo, 2010).

Starting in the early grades, stronger student-teacher relationships enhance learning and produce benefits for years (Davis, 2013; McCormick, O'Connor, Cappella, & McClowry, 2013). Rudasill (2011) describes a wide range of studies that show that the quality of these relationships affects young children's language development, behavior, interactions with peers, and school adjustment. The benefits continue through the secondary level, where teachers can become valuable as mentors. In fact, students often work harder for teachers when there's mutual respect (Downer, Sabol, & Hamre, 2010).

Some may dismiss relationships as "fluff." But to some students, *they make all the difference* between liking school or not. From kindergarten to 12th grade, I had a good connection with just three teachers. Two were middle school English teachers (one male and one female), and as an adult, I became a middle school English teacher. Both were highly supportive of my early attempts to write. In their classes, I wished that I had a mom or dad *just like them*. I worked harder for them than for any other teacher. Years later, after I had authored several books, I went back to that school to thank them. That's the moment when a teacher feels affirmed and realizes that they can change lives. (So can you, if you know how and have the will to do it.)

You Go First: Check Your Biases

Having amazing relationships in your world makes so many other things go well. You give and you get, you laugh and you cry. When you become better at fostering relationships outside class, your relationships get better inside the classroom.

In contrast, when you're struggling in your own teaching, your biases and intentions are going to get exposed front and center. All of us are "damaged" in some way and have unconscious cognitive biases, says psychologist and Nobel laureate Daniel Kahneman (2011). No matter how smart, cool, or amazing you are, there's damage. I hid my own damage for years, mostly from myself. My poor relationships and equity biases were strong, but I could not see them at the time. It's time for you to notice some things about your own brain that may be keeping you from being amazing. Are you afraid this will take up more of your precious time (see Figure 2.1)? You *already* go home tired. Why not go home tired and celebrate another amazing day for your students?

You learned in Chapter 1 that your brain is designed to create biases. Many teachers demonstrate these biases by their actions all day and continue in their work as if nothing just happened. They may be unaware, or they just don't care.

As an example, a teacher may typically look for negative outliers in a classroom. Some students are noisier, can't (yet) sit still, or consistently

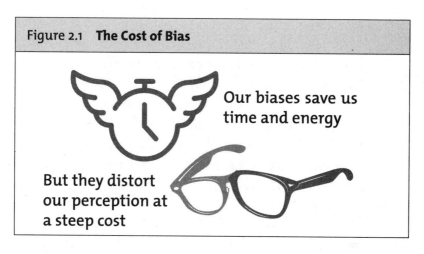

Figure 2.1   **The Cost of Bias**

Our biases save us time and energy

But they distort our perception at a steep cost

cross boundaries. Or a teacher may attend a conference, pick up a quirky, unproven idea, and go back and present it to peers since it is novel and easy to remember and use. (Most teachers need a mirror for reflection more than they need grab-and-go strategies.) Teachers commonly use their fast-acting System 1 brain, which takes cognitive shortcuts, rather than their System 2 brain, which can be painstakingly slow. There are risks and benefits with each of these brain systems.

For many, a common bias is rejecting the idea that the high-equity teachers you see could serve as models for your own growth. Let's say that you assume that the amazing teacher at the beginning of the chapter was an exception. Maybe you theorize that you can't possibly do what she did based on your age, skills, luck, ethnicity, or creative talents. That's the *self-handicapping bias*. That bias strategy is designed to *avoid effort in the hope of preventing your potential failure* in implementation (Thomas & Gadbois, 2007; Zuckerman & Tsai, 2005). "Well, that teacher can pull that off. She's creative."

Your System 1 brain often says, "Doing *less* saves time so I can live another day. It's just better *to do nothing*." Remember, you're wired to conserve resources such as metabolic energy and response time. The more information, complexity, and time constraints thrown your way and the sooner the decision is needed, *the quicker the bias forms*. Most schools never slow down, and teachers often feel like they're doing daily improv with no rehearsals. Your System 1 brain races to take the shortest, quickest reward route. It feels like a matter of survival.

And yes, speed *is* better if you're living thousands of years ago in the hills of Mesopotamia or the Okavango Delta, looking for food. Again, that's your System 1 brain, designed for surviving, not thriving. Biases are cognitive shortcuts that emerged as a survival tool. They are used to help you navigate and make sense in a fast-moving, complex world. (Figure 2.2 shows how these biases can be grouped according to the ways they meet our System 1 brain's needs.) It takes work to defuse biases. But you can do it. Your brain's System 2 insight is that *you will be working on yourself* as much as learning how to become a better teacher . . . for a lifetime!

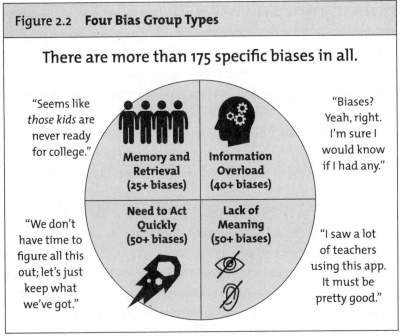

Figure 2.2   Four Bias Group Types

There are more than 175 specific biases in all.

"Seems like *those kids* are never ready for college."

Memory and Retrieval (25+ biases)

Information Overload (40+ biases)

"Biases? Yeah, right. I'm sure I would know if I had any."

"We don't have time to figure all this out; let's just keep what we've got."

Need to Act Quickly (50+ biases)

Lack of Meaning (50+ biases)

"I saw a lot of teachers using this app. It must be pretty good."

Note: Bias group types draw from Buster Benson's (2016) "Cognitive Bias Cheat Sheet": https://betterhumans.pub/cognitive-bias-cheat-sheet-55a472476b18.

Ethnic stereotyping is a type of bias that runs rampant in schools. When you have experience interacting with one or two members of a given ethnic group and make up generalizations about "them" as a group, that's a problem. Your brain is using the System 1 thinking that saves you from slowing down and examining the details, the individuals, and the real truths. You've been told *not* to stereotype, yet it's time-consuming to recheck each additional possible option, and biologically and socially, you may have already decided that it's a bit risky to trust those outside your own "tribe."

But is it true that all poor people "do this, but not that"? And that all rich people "do that, but not this"? Or is it true that "White people do not do this" and "All people of color do not do that"? You know the answer (Yeates et al., 2017). Keep in mind the risk of the *stereotype* bias: falsely judging others by a group they belong to. The worst part? Many teachers are completely unaware that their biases can and do ruin many students' lives.

Here's a quick example that may help illuminate the power of biases. Teachers are often surprised when they are told that they spend much more time with the girls in their class than with the boys (or vice versa). That bias rarely goes unnoticed by students, though, and it can impact their brains for years (Brown & Stone, 2016). Schools are one of the most significant sources of student stress. And because of the gene-environment interaction, genes may be impacted from traumatic events at school (Frías-Lasserre, Villagra, & Guerrero-Bosagna, 2018).

Any stereotyping is going to harm your relationships with your students. Ask yourself, how would you feel if others make those assumptions about you? We all stereotype, unless we have been taught otherwise. In Appendix C, there is a simple de-bias activity you can learn from and use to help you become the optimist who makes a difference with your students.

Biases can ruin a day of teaching if they go unnoticed, and your students suffer. But the answer is coming up.

Engaging Relationships on Three Levels

Some kids grow up with secure attachments; others have insecure childhood experiences and may feel safer avoiding adults and staying unattached. In supporting these kids, take small, careful steps. Build trust slowly and stairstep the relationship over months. Stay relaxed but keep moving forward, because this type of relationship may be just what helps the student become more physically and mentally healthy (Parker et al., 2020) and succeed with even the most challenging academic curriculum (Roorda, Koomen, Spilt, & Oort, 2011). Strong teacher-student relationships support a year and a half of growth for each school year (Cornelius-White, 2007). Kids are looking for role models—especially those of the same ethnicity (Goldhaber, Theobald, & Tien, 2019). Figure 2.3 shows how student-teacher relationships can move forward through three levels over time.

Even though students with trauma may not be very good at relationships, they need them. Be patient and never give up. They are looking

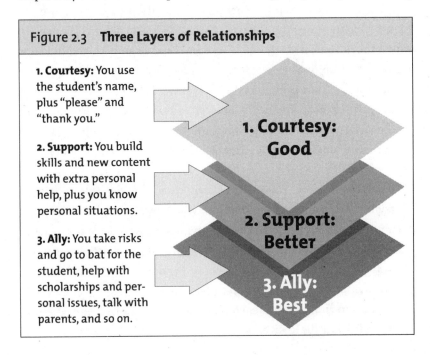

Figure 2.3   Three Layers of Relationships

1. Courtesy: You use the student's name, plus "please" and "thank you."

2. Support: You build skills and new content with extra personal help, plus you know personal situations.

3. Ally: You take risks and go to bat for the student, help with scholarships and personal issues, talk with parents, and so on.

1. Courtesy: Good

2. Support: Better

3. Ally: Best

for an adult they can believe in. *You be that teacher,* or you may lose the student's heart. How much do your actions matter? The next time you want to ignore a struggling student or one who acts out, remember this: Your actions are what matter *most* in the classroom.

Level 1: Be Courteous and Curious

Respect students' names. Do you make eye contact, smile, and greet your students at the door? Do you address your students by name? Using a student's name tells the student, "I see you." Because names come from various languages, it can be difficult to pronounce every sound correctly. Yet many students understand the joy of others getting their names right (often for the first time in school).

Teach Us Your Name by Huda Essa (2016) shares many ways to help students feel more noticed and included in your class. Here are some suggested questions you can ask students to get to know them through their name:

- **Family histories:** Have you or any of your past or present family members changed their names? How might this relate to other changes in your family history, such as minimizing or erasing cultural traditions?
- **Languages:** What language does your name come from? Is it the same language as the language of your national origin? Do you or any of your family members currently speak another language?
- **Social identities:** Does your name represent any of your social identities or influences, such as gender, religion, family, or ethnicity? Do any of those identities lead others to make assumptions about you?
- **Cultural norms:** Why were you given your name? Does it have to do with family or cultural traditions or values? How do names reflect different cultural norms?
- **Representation:** Which names have you been taught to view as "normal"? If you know your ancestors' names, would they all seem "normal" today?

Use any or all of these questions as a writing assignment, the starter for a team discussion, or an opening for a whole-class conversation. Ask students to teach you (and the rest of the class) how to say their names correctly; having the confidence to do this is quite validating. Ask students to write one page about their names—the history, spelling, meaning, and so on—and then share with other students. Use a memory game with student groups of four: One student says their name, plus one thing they love to eat or their favorite movie; the next student recalls the last student's name/movie, then adds their own; and so on. Having students present their name plus a trivia tidbit opens the door for more disclosures later. Soon, you realize you have a new "connecting point" with something about each student you recall.

Kindness matters. Are you polite with every student, every day? Using "please" and "thank you" tells students that you respect them, that you're not trying to use power to get what you want, and that you're being a conscious role model. Do you notice something about them that shows them you're paying attention? Always use personal courtesies, such as asking permission first: "May I ask you a personal question?" or "I want to respect your privacy. Would you feel OK telling me what you're dealing with at home?"

Take the time to physically and mentally be present when working with your students. Ask students whether they're feeling healthy, whether they have good energy, or what their favorite foods are. Simply spending time each day with each student can improve your perception of that student (Driscoll & Pianta, 2010) and cement their relationship with you.

Level 2: Support Students with Empathy

You have resources, skills, and strategies that can help your students succeed. For some students, their classroom community at school is where they feel safest and most accepted. When familial stability or connection is low, the teacher-student relationship is more critical and can mitigate the effects of a poor home environment (Benner & Mistry,

2007). In kindergarten, kids will sometimes call their teacher "Mommy" or "Daddy." Of course, you don't have to be their teacher *and* their parent—just offer the same safety and warmth that every child should feel at home. Make it common to give students a connecting handshake, fist bump, or hug every day. The following are some more ways you can offer every student that sense of safety and belonging at school.

Offer discovery time. The "me-bag" activity can be used at all grade levels. It takes under five minutes, in which a student (or the teacher) shares two to four items from a paper bag that are meaningful to them in their life. Items might include an object, a book, or a photo with special meaning. (The secondary teacher in this chapter uses the me-bag activity.) Make it a habit to discover three things about each of your students in the first 10 days of the school year. Start the first few days with disclosures to the class about your own life—the good, the bad, and the unusual.

Make empathy count. First, show your students that *you want them to succeed.* How? Do one favor or act of empathy so powerful that the student remembers it well. For example, when a student tells you of a bad experience from home, an empathetic response might be for you to touch your hand to your heart and say, "Oh, I am so sorry." Make soft eye contact, talk less, and listen more. Let the student talk. You might also offer the student a treat or some extra listening time a bit later. Remember, some students have a greater need for a caring adult than others, based on their home life. As you get to know each student personally, invest your time with the students who most need the supportive relationship you can offer.

Use a brief writing activity. Write-and-share activities can be powerful. Disclosures help many students care more about one another. Do a 10-minute writing assignment in which you, the teacher, write about "What I wish my class knew about me." Read it to your students. Then invite your students to take 10 minutes to write "What I wish my teacher knew about me." Of course, ask students to share these papers only if they volunteer to do so.

Give and share power. Every student's voice is important, but to make time for it, you'll need to use multiple "vehicles" for the voice: speaking, writing, and demonstrating with actions. Give students time to share with (1) a partner, (2) their teammates, and (3) the whole class.

Ensure that your students can engage both voice and choice when they need to feel heard. Let them lead in the moments when they're ready for it. Let students display talents by letting them be a class energy leader, DJ (with your approval), teller of the "joke of the day," or creator of the "underground news story" for the day.

Listen more than you talk. Finally, and most important, be a listener. Whether the student wants to talk about school or personal issues, when you listen without interrupting you show respect. Just ask if they could use a listener. Do this for at least five consecutive days, choosing a different student each day who needs a connection. Ask about, and know, their personal and academic challenges and dreams. Doing this will let the students know that they are worth your time.

Level 3: Be a Deep Ally

This level is the deepest healthy level of relationship. When you're an ally, you take risks and go to bat for the student. When a student acts out, you are the mediator. You might negotiate a student out of suspension through your relationship with that student. Be empathetic, and understand how your students think and feel about what is going on around them. Accept your students for who they are. Initiate extra care for them, just like a good parent cares for their child.

As an ally, you might contact the student's parent or caregiver weekly or even visit the home, if possible. You might buy a couple of books you think the student would like and bring them to the student's residence. Once there, ask the parent or caregiver how you might be able to support the student even more. The big message is, *show students that they are important to you.*

You and I know there are at least a dozen ways to measure student learning. Just one of them is called *effect size* (see Figure 2.4). It

Figure 2.4   **Know Your Effect Sizes**

Struggling students typically fall behind each year. Lock in and use tools and strategies with high effect sizes (0.50+).

0.00–0.20 = Mild, unclear effect

0.20–0.50 = Small to moderate effect

0.50 = Approximately one year's worth of gains

0.50–0.80 = Moderate to strong effect

0.80–2.00 = Robust effect

Note: Information about effect size draws from "Measures of Effect Size for Comparative Studies: Applications, Interpretations, and Limitations," by S. Olejnik and J. Algina, 2000, *Contemporary Educational Psychology, 25,* pp. 241–286.

measures the contribution to learning that is made by an intervention (versus a control group). The strength of the intervention is measured by a number (usually between 0.00 and 2.00). One year of gains (keeping up with grade level) is about 0.50. By taking all the talking and activities a teacher did, and measuring how many minutes per day they did each action and the effect size of each, researchers can measure that teacher's daily impact (Olejnik & Algina, 2000).

Top teachers have a greater effect on student learning because they do the right thing very well, for more minutes per semester or year. The impact of *relationships* is a 0.87 effect size for the upper-elementary level and middle school/junior high level, which is considered strong. That's well over a year and a half of gains (Marzano, Marzano, & Pickering, 2003).

Provide tools and support. Seek equity, not equality. Remember, equity is giving more to those who need it most. Introduce these students to study workarounds and "hacks" that will optimize their time studying. Give them memory tools and encouraging pep talks. Help them find an online video tutor that might explain a subject differently. Show emotional support by asking the students questions that can empower them to make a better decision and help them have a better day.

Show deep respect by giving students bold identities. Some teachers address each student as Mr. or Ms., plus the student's last name. Others start shifting their students' *identity in school* by addressing them differently. Some of the best identities you can apply to your students are *scholars, learners,* or *sages.* Imagine when another teacher asks you why you call your students scholars, and your students overhear you say, "They are amazing learners, my best students ever!"

Expose students to things outside their worldview. Take students to a garden, a museum, or an orchestral performance. Show secondary students life hacks, such as how to find cheap places to live or how to get an online degree inexpensively. Bring in guest speakers at the upper-elementary to secondary level to stretch students' brains. Focus on guests who share the ethnicity of your students, and those who can share their own voice and story.

Visit with students and their parents. You might visit your students' homes and meet their parents. Just connecting on their turf is a strong statement about being an ally. Keep in mind, though, that some parents live in extreme poverty; they may be homeless, live in a car, or have a small, crowded apartment. Also be aware that for some individuals living in poverty, their work can be grueling, and it rarely pays enough to make ends meet. Ask the parents to set the time, place, and day of the week that would work best for them to meet you. It might be best for some parents to meet you in a park or community center, for example.

When you arrive, announce yourself and connect with gratitude and a smile. Ask for the parent or guardian's advice or for insights that may be of value in meeting their child's academic and behavioral needs. In short, be a listener first, an ally second. Talk about *how you see strong potential in their child.* Share with parents how you can help them with the study process or the scholarship hoops.

Notice that each of the three levels of teacher-student relationships offers a different trade-off. You know time is the one constant that we cannot change. Realistically, you'll have to be strategic about which students you invest the most in. Not every student can get Level 3 time from you. Carefully choose the students who most need your extra help and time. That's the heart of equity: helping students who need support the most.

Emerging Equity Tool to Embrace

The way you introduce yourself to your students in the first days of school sets the tone for your high-equity practices throughout the year. Here's how the teacher in the story at the beginning of this chapter does it. The opening she uses answers many questions that students ask. "Welcome! I am SO glad to have you in my class this year. I'll do everything in my power to help you succeed. If that sounds good to you, say, 'I'm all in!'"

My common opening at the beginning of the year or semester was, "I struggled as a student. But a special teacher helped me succeed. I'll be that teacher for you. If you're up for it, say, 'Oh, yeah!'" Or "I promise you'll get an *A* or a *B* in my class if you help one other student get an *A* or a *B*. If you're all in, raise your hand and say, 'Yes!'"

Whatever your opening, you need to project warmth and empathy and establish yourself as an ally instead of a bystander or an adversary. You also need to provide answers to the questions students are likely asking themselves: *Is my teacher an ally or an adversary? Does my teacher believe in me (or not)? Will my competence grow with effort (is it worth it)? Will I be able to make friends (and be liked)? Can I succeed in this challenging academic class (keep up and do well)?*

At the secondary level, have students share a brief video of themselves responding to a few "get-to-know-you" questions and prompts (e.g., "How do you feel about school? This subject?" or "How do you feel about yourself?"). Some kids can do this at home using their own devices; others can do it at school. Watch students' video recordings while you eat lunch or decompress after class. Since time is always precious, find workarounds. For example, when using workstations in class, make *your own desk* one of the stations. This "social hack" gives you a few moments to connect personally with the students in that group.

Chapter in a Nutshell

This chapter focuses on just a few things: understanding the impact of relationships on students, challenging the bias mindset, and implementing the three layers of conscious connections. Each topic brings you a different way of thinking about your work. In each chapter, you'll be invited to do something different to support your growth. You're now the kind of professional who can notice your bias and overcome hurdles to achieving equity.

Revisit the Student Questions

➤ *"Is my teacher an ally or an adversary?"*

➤ *"Does my teacher see, hear, and respect me with empathy and show that they care about how I am doing?"*

Make a promise to yourself that you will orchestrate your thoughts, words, and actions so that your students would give you resounding responses: "Is my teacher an ally? Yes!" "Am I seen and heard? Yes!"

Before the Next Chapter

Chapter 1 invited you to explore clear and strong intentions. Intentions are far from a miracle pill. But they can nudge you toward your goals. How did that work? Do you do your daily repetitions? If not, it's time to start.

Here's your change tool to embrace in this chapter: debunking your biases. Becoming an amazing teacher means constantly challenging ourselves not just to be better, but also to admit we were wrong yesterday. Doing that, for most teachers, requires changing our biases, narratives, and identities.

Bias reduction is much harder than you might think. We all have the *bias blind spot*—we are unaware of our own biases or don't believe they are a big problem (West, Meserve, & Stanovich, 2012). De-biasing prepares you and accelerates your success in getting in touch with your System 2 brain. You can find a simple de-bias activity in Appendix C or download a more detailed version from www.jensenlearning.com/equity-resources. Follow the simple steps to walk through and alter your biases.

Maybe a fresh bias just jumped into your brain: "I am too busy to do this!" *Actually, you can make the time for it.* If your residence were burning down, would you find the time to rescue your family? If a loved one got in a car accident, would you visit them in the hospital? Of course you would.

The greatest producer of long-term results is simple: Learn to do the tiny things that others won't do. Learn to take action even when you don't feel like doing something. Remember those feelings, years ago, of self-discovery? One of the great sources of satisfaction in life is *learning how to run your own brain* for the better. Turn actions into the daily habits of becoming excellent. It takes many hours to become what's in your dreams. Those hours, days, or weeks never just appear in front of you, free for the taking. You must steal them fiercely from every stray moment. Start today and celebrate tonight.

3

Raise the Roof

Student Questions

➤ *"Does my teacher have high expectations and truly believe in me?"*

➤ *"Is my teacher willing to challenge me to get better?"*

➤ *"Do I belong in this challenging academic environment, and can I succeed at this subject/in this class?"*

This chapter is about more than what "raises the roof"; it's also about what might be keeping the struggle in your work. You will learn how to raise expectations with your students who come from poverty and how to do the same for yourself. We will focus on core changes you'll make to jump-start new possibilities. You'll get the solid *why* and *how* to become an amazing, high-energy change agent. This chapter's topics are:

- The Storyteller Who Changed a Life
- Connections to Poverty
- You Go First: Raise Your Own Expectations
- What Will High Expectations Be Like in Your Class?
- Emerging Equity Tools to Embrace

The Storyteller Who Changed a Life

Let's begin with a teacher who worked in a high-poverty elementary school. At a break during one of my multiday professional development events, this teacher came up to me and shared her story about a student in her class. The first day of each school year, she always put her students in a semicircle so they could see one another during introductions. Following each student's introduction and name, she typically asked the student, "And what do you want to be when you grow up?" Naturally, she knew that the answer was not carved in stone, but it always gave her an idea of each student's own self-expectations. Things got interesting when she asked one boy, "And what do you want to be when you grow up?"

He said, "I want to be like my daddy."

The teacher responded with, "And what does your daddy do?"

The boy said, "Nothing. He sits on a couch and gets a check every month."

The teacher took a breath and said, "Thank you" and moved on to the next student. She confided to me that in that moment, she knew her mission for the school year. After all, students' assessment of their own level of mastery is key to their success, with research showing an over-the-top effect size of 1.33 (Hattie, 2022). You and I know that you can solve problems many ways. One metaphor is that you can use either a hammer or a feather. A hammer would have been to have a direct one-on-one conversation with the student about dreaming big and having high expectations. That might work (or not). This teacher decided to use a feather.

She started up a weekly "Teacher Travels" segment in class. She'd share a three-minute story, including photos or other artifacts of somewhere she had been. It was told in a vivid, colorful way that made each trip seem like practically a National Geographic bucket list destination. In reality, her stories were just from life. She shared stories about taking trips to visit her parents, touring national parks, attending sporting events, exploring shopping malls, and going to local events like fairs and carnivals. For many of her low-income students, those "Teacher Travels" seemed as good as going to a foreign country. Every week all school year she shared another story, and they never got old.

So, did those "Teacher Travels" do any good? The teacher's measuring stick was the self-expectations that students expressed at the beginning and end of the school year. At the end of the year, the teacher put her kids back into a semicircle. She asked her students, "What were some of your favorite things from this year?" And the follow-up question was, "And what do you want to be when you grow up?" Only a few kids would remember what they said months ago, so the question was fresh.

She worked her way around the semicircle and came back to the same boy who "wanted" to sit on a couch. When asked what he wanted to do when he grew up, he sat up straight and spoke with resolve and confidence: "I want to be a teacher!"

This is what equity and great teaching are all about. The teacher *understood her students*. In this boy's case, she realized that his current world was the length of a couch. All she had to do was reveal an amazing world out there that was much bigger, better, and more thrilling than the couch. Once the boy got a taste of it, there was no going back.

Sometimes solutions are easy; many times, they are hard. Treat your students as if they represent your retirement account. Invest every week and be patient, and the dividends will come. This student simply needed a stronger *why*: a clear path and higher expectations. This teacher gets top marks in my book.

Debrief Time

Let's pause so you can embrace and process the equity mindset. As a short writing assignment or a discussion with a partner, debrief this teacher's strategy for raising expectations. Why did the strategy work? What were the elements needed to make that happen? What changed in the student?

Next, reflect on your response to this true story. Have you already marginalized this teacher as "exceptional," "creative," or "courageous"? Remember that our brains are quick to kick in with biases to protect us from failure. The *exceptionalism bias* is present when you assume that what another did was a rare exception and believe you couldn't do that yourself based on your talent level, age, skills, luck, ethnicity, or creative background. (Actually, her strategy was pretty simple: Tell weekly stories.) The *self-handicapping bias* is used to avoid effort in the hopes of preventing potential failure (Thomas & Gadbois, 2007; Zuckerman & Tsai, 2005).

Becoming excellent takes work instead of simply discounting possible options based on your identity. (Maybe you think, "I'm a teacher, not a story-teller.") Are you beginning to notice when your biases start up?

Connections to Poverty

For many teachers, high expectations are a big public charade. A large study by TNTP (2018) tells us that 80 percent of teachers outwardly supported high standards. It sounds great, but less than half of the teachers in the study *had the real-world expectations that their students could actually reach that standard.* In fact, only a miniscule 13 percent of the teachers believed that *all their students were motivated to succeed academically.* It seems, then, that teachers are not always confident that everyone in their classrooms can achieve academic success (Boser, Wilhelm, & Hanna, 2014). That tells us it's more about the teachers than the students. Let's unpack that.

Here, the *bandwagon* cognitive bias says, "Tell others about your high expectations. That's easy to say, and you'll now fit into the social club. But it might actually take hard work to make it happen." Maybe some believe that it's better to avoid big dreams because they might let you down. Recall that our System 1 brain says, "conserve energy." Sometimes your brain works against you.

Yes, you'll have to work hard as a teacher to notice your biases and then debunk them. Let your System 2 brain kick in and say, "Let's find out how much work it really is to have high expectations. If it is a lot, maybe we can chunk it down." And maybe other teachers have solved this same problem that you're taking on.

The source for this next data set is critical. The National Center for Education Statistics (NCES) ran an inquiry called the Education Longitudinal Study of 2002, or ELS (visit https://nces.ed.gov/surveys/ELS2002 for more information). This study followed the progress of a nationally representative sample of students for a decade. The study results allow researchers to link teacher expectations, student outcomes, school milestones, and demographics to individual student data collected over 10 years. What we are looking for in this study are high correlations.

At the high school level, evidence shows that teachers expected 58 percent of their White students and 37 percent of their Black students to obtain a four-year college degree. This disparity also foreshadowed a large difference in actual educational attainment: 49 percent of White students ultimately graduated from college, compared with 29 percent of Black students. When teachers held higher expectations about a student's future success, that student was *three times* more likely to complete college than a student for whom teachers had lower expectations. Students from poverty were 53 percent less likely to complete college when their teachers held lower expectations for them (Boser et al., 2014). Genuine, authentic *higher* expectations are essential.

Remember the little boy who said he just wanted to sit on a couch and collect a check every month? The 2015 National Teacher of the Year, Shanna Peeples, said, "You have to ignore it when a child says, 'I don't want to,' because what they're really saying is, 'I don't think I can, and I need you to believe in me until I can believe in myself'" (Gershenson & Papageorge, 2021). *Never let a hesitant student make your decisions* about whether that student will grow. Bring your A-game every day, and let your students know that nobody's going to fail on your watch.

You Go First: Raise Your Own Expectations

This chapter is about higher expectations. But it is also about the stories we tell ourselves. When I taught reading and study skills at the secondary level, my first-year mentor teacher was simply out of this world. Every year, he was getting some of the highest reading scores in the state. He said, "Whatever you think a student can do, think higher." That mentality stuck with me. I learned that students need a teacher who will push them and never give up on them. Few teachers are lucky enough to have a mentor like that. The message stayed with me *my whole career.*

There will be times when things go poorly in your class, and your students will be watching how you handle it. Avoid pointing fingers at your students or others. Start having higher expectations *for yourself.* If you fail to demonstrate high expectations, your students will see you as one who talks the talk but doesn't walk the walk. That costs you credibility with your students. Figure 3.1 explores ways you can raise your expectations.

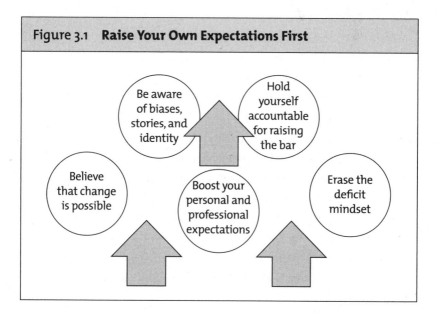

Figure 3.1   Raise Your Own Expectations First

You may have been told to simply "aim higher" or "expect more." Those are simplistic slogans. When we look at the national data, we realize *that path is failing*. The big five action items from Figure 3.1 would be on my "first things first" list. Read on for more about these.

1. Be aware of biases, stories, and identity. There are many biases that can smother the chances for higher expectations, both in you and in your students. The biases mentioned in this book so far include the following:

- Stereotype
- Confirmation
- Illusory truth
- Bandwagon
- Implicit
- Blind spot ("I have no biases")
- Exceptionalism (e.g., marginalizing the star teacher)
- Self-handicapping
- Familiarity
- Groupthink

These and other biases are key reasons for teachers' struggles in teaching students who live in poverty. For instance, the *illusory truth* bias is the tendency to believe that false information is correct simply after repeated exposure. A common example with teachers is hearing, "The apple doesn't fall far from the tree." The only reason these narratives get repeated is there's a grain of truth in them, even though they are broadly false. Simply recalling a slogan will strengthen its veracity with others (Ozubko & Fugelsang, 2011). Another one is the *stereotype* bias. That happens when we judge others by a group they belong to (males, females, LGBTQ+, Blacks, Latinos, Asians, Native Americans, and so on). The attitudes of teachers toward ethnic minorities are easily picked up by their students (Glock, Kovacs, & Pit-ten Cate, 2019). To begin the de-bias process, please use the tool in Appendix C or the longer, free version posted online at www.jensenlearning.com/equity-resources.

2. Hold yourself accountable for raising the bar. Avoid waiting for school leadership or your peers to keep the bar high; that's the *groupthink* bias at work. Doing what others who are struggling are doing is rarely the best option. Your teacher goals should start with one simple word: *growth!* How far can I grow in supporting my students every day in school? Top teachers set goals at or above grade-level proficiency, or even college-entrance-level proficiency, *for 100 percent of their students.* Any time you set class proficiency goals of less than 100 percent, ask yourself, "Which student am I expecting to fail, and why?" Cut the excuses and raise the bar.

One of the best ways to do that is with *dual* high expectations. Choose a high bar for both yourself and your students. This year, maybe you remove one sugary item from your diet every month. Maybe you allow yourself to complain only once a week. Maybe you share the joy in your class with 10 positive affirmations daily. Share your personal high expectations with your students, because they need to know that you walk the walk as much as you talk the talk. After all, if you have stopped growing, why should students see you as a role model?

3. Believe that change is possible. If you have just one molecule of doubt about students or their dreams, your students will sense it and you will become a dream killer. Have hope for every student. Dream big for them, even if they aren't dreaming big for themselves.

One of the more relevant qualities of the brain is neuroplasticity. This inherent property allows the human brain to make new connections, develop whole new networks, and even remap itself so that more or less physical brain space is used for a particular task. Neuroplasticity can be for the better (e.g., through learning), or for the worse (e.g., through trauma). It happens rapidly with relevance, repetition, and practice of new skills, thoughts, and actions. Skills are malleable, if we believe they are (see Figure 3.2). Brain changes happen with high-level

---

Figure 3.2   **Fixed Versus Growth Mindset**

Do you believe in and model a fixed or growth mindset?

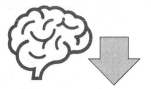 

FIXED	**GROWTH**
➢ IQ or skills are fixed; I am stuck.	➢ IQ and skills are malleable; they can be developed.
➢ Looking smart is important to me.	➢ Being a role model for my students is crucial for them to believe in their own growth.
➢ Effort is a negative. It might expose that I don't have what it takes. I am afraid to risk it.	➢ Taking action lowers my stress since it gives me control over my destiny.

---

cognitive skill building (Mackey, Singley, Wendelken, & Bunge, 2015). In fact, they can happen with just two hours of cognitive training (Hofstetter, Tavor, Moryosef, & Assaf, 2013). Music training changes the brain enough to counteract the adverse effects of poverty on literacy development (Slater et al., 2014). Our brain adds new gray matter with math practice (Draganski & May, 2008) and with learning a second language (Schlegel, Rudelson, & Tse, 2012). Can you intentionally and rapidly change the brains of your students? Engage these seven factors with your skill-building work this year:

- Relevance of learning (e.g., affiliation, fun, social status)
- Intensity of activity (block out distractions and lock in focus)
- Repetition of skills (10–14 minutes a day, 3–5 times a week, for 4–12 weeks depending on goals and student skill level)
- Actionable feedback with just one specific change at a time

- Challenge level (raise the challenge by 5 percent from previous high)
- Supportive context (cultural and social support)
- Rewards (e.g., social approval, fun, autonomy)

What you believe about your students comes across in both your verbal and your nonverbal messaging. If you think your students are stuck, there's a good chance that you are also stuck.

In short, effective teaching changes the brain for the better. Stop waiting for kids to "show potential." *They already have potential!* Struggling teachers undermine student hopes every day. But as you change, your kids will jump right in and follow behind.

4. Boost your personal and professional expectations. Students will rarely rise above the expectations of their teacher. Yes, it happens, but it's rare. I'm challenging you to raise the bar in your own life. How?

1. Start by deciding to become an in-house expert in a highly needed school area (e.g., within a specific subject matter, parental participation, discipline issues, energizers).
2. Ask for professional development opportunities from school leadership, and attend events at nearby schools or in the community.
3. Set your sights on a new role that may be a better fit for you at your school. Consider becoming a team leader, an instructional leader or coach, or a counselor.

The fact is, most teachers remain in their own comfort zone, especially after the first five years of teaching (Jacob & McGovern, 2015). Does every teacher at your school show year-to-year increases in student proficiency for every year they teach? No. There's no evidence that more years of experience make for a better teacher; most just get older. Some staff choose daily comfort over modeling the growth mindset *they ask of students.* Who are the ones with low expectations? *Your students think it's their teachers.*

5. Erase the deficit mindset. Let's say you're a White teacher at the secondary level who had a back-talking Black female student in your class. She grew up in poverty, became addicted to drugs, and eventually dropped out of high school. Your *confirmation bias* says, "I knew that would happen. She had a serious attitude problem." Your low expectations of her might have seemed realistic to you. All you paid attention to is what you *didn't like* about her, because it confirmed your bias!

So how did that mouthy high school dropout turn out? She went on to become one of only 14 people in history to have won the "Big Four" entertainment awards: the Oscar, the Emmy, the Grammy, and the Tony (plus three Golden Globes and 27 Emmy nominations). Let me guess; most of her teachers decided she "lacked potential." Otherwise they would have invested more time, intention, and empathy in her. Had her teachers avoided the *complacency* and *stereotype* biases, they could have enjoyed the results. Her name is Whoopi Goldberg. And the confirmation bias would have been, "I knew she was talented; I predicted she would be amazing one day!" *Please avoid deficit thinking.*

What Will High Expectations Be Like in Your Class?

High expectations are about believing that there is no ceiling for growth. For years, you've heard about the power of the *growth mindset.* Yet a curious anomaly surfaced when renowned researcher John Hattie dug down to find the effect size of having a growth mindset on school-age children. The effect on school achievement was a marginal 0.19, well below the 0.50 effect size of a year's growth (Hattie & Yates, 2013).

When Dr. Hattie was asked about the low impact on student learning, he said he likes the idea of growth mindset, but added that *unless the teacher is role-modeling the growth mindset, students don't believe it,* feel it, or even *want to* challenge their own mindsets. Hence, the low effect is real, but it does not have to be that way. Let's apply this new understanding: Teachers who are trying out new tools, routines, or habits *and* sharing the results with students are showing that they believe in the power of growth. Let's move on to the resources you can use to foster student growth that exceeds expectations.

1. Use Grade-Level or Higher Curriculum and Instruction

Deficit thinking is the pattern of assuming deficiencies among students, often based on race, socioeconomic status, family structure, or languages spoken. Most students—and especially students of color and those living in poverty—spent most of their school days with teachers who dumb down instruction. How do we know that?

Simple. Researchers surveyed 4,000 students in five diverse school systems to learn about their experiences. What they found was damning to the staff and painful to hear from the students. The students said they spent more than half their time (up to three hours a day) on assignments that were below grade level (TNTP, 2018). That's the equivalent of over *16 weeks of wasted class time* in each core subject.

Most students in Title I schools are bored out of their minds by dumbed-down content. If you think *they can't do it,* maybe you're really projecting your own expectations or insecurities. Reflect on your past expectations. Race and class bias are common for teachers with low expectations (Ferguson, 2003). Here are five simple, and often underused, tools to use in teaching grade-level or above curriculum:

1. Begin with prior knowledge.
2. Make your learning more culturally relevant than ever before.
3. Break new content into tiny chunks so every student can make sense of it.
4. Raise class engagement with deeper-dive questions.
5. Bring joy and encouragement, every day.

Avoid telling students to do their best. Many have no idea what their best is. If you ask them to set goals, be more specific—for instance, ask them to add another 25 percent over their last score.

Push them to keep getting better with encouragement daily. Start in small increments but stretch the gains upward. Push students to go further. Your goal is consistent growth. They may need 25 encouragements; how many have you given your own child in one semester or year?

Hold each student accountable for success or failure. Insist on their taking responsibility for their actions. Give them props for learning from failure, mistakes, and setbacks. Encourage them again and again.

2. Plug in Learn-to-Learn Skills

Some time ago, the dean of academic affairs at the university where I was teaching called me into his office. I sensed there was trouble. He began by reminding me of the university's academic standards and how hard it is for universities to maintain accreditation. Then he pointed out that nearly every student of mine had received an *A* or a *B*. "That's unacceptable," he said. "We don't just give away grades." Had I watered down the course syllabus? he asked.

"No, I didn't," I replied. I explained that when I started teaching, I had reflected on how lack of preparation had been an issue for *me* in college. So now, I invested the first two weeks of my courses in front-loading learn-to-learn skills. Ultimately, each of my courses required more reading and deeper class discussions than those of any of my colleagues.

At the end of my story, the dean said that I should not be using precious university class time on basic study skills. He said the students could get those skills on their own. I responded that I knew that, but once they were in my class, these students were my responsibility. He said, "The kids should show up prepared." My response? "I understand your point of view, and I'm sorry to hear that." I quit that day because I refused to compromise equity or lie to the dean just to keep my job. I never went back.

Avoid the "dumbed down" curriculum plague. If your students are struggling, build them up. At most struggling high-poverty high schools I have visited around the country, the leaders tell me that they're excited to be using a college prep program at their school. When I ask how many students are enrolled, I hear numbers like 20 percent, 10 percent, or even as low as 5 percent. Maybe the leadership and staff think that's how many students have "college potential." After all, their kids are "from poverty." But that's more than sad; I get angry when I hear it. That is a bias-driven policy.

Contrast those schools with a different school. It's a public school (combined middle and high school) I worked with in San Diego. One hundred percent of its students come from poverty, and *all students are automatically enrolled in college prep classes* through AVID (a college prep program). The school sends 95 percent or more of its graduates to college every year, and it is consistently ranked in the top 100 high schools in the United States. Do you still think offering *all* students a high level of challenge is a bad idea? Keep reading.

3. Offer Challenging, Brainy Options

What do students in pricey prep schools get? The same thing you could be offering at your school. In Chicago, when a fresh middle school math teacher arrived at his new job, only 35 percent of his students were passing math. What did he do to turn things around? First, he created a classroom climate of such strong emotional safety that kids were willing to contribute. Second, his instruction included a kind yet demanding rigor. He engaged every student with rigorous questions every day. Most of the student answers were met with his classic responses such as, "Why is that?" "How would you prove that?" "How does that tie in with. . . . ?" He engaged rigor with every single student. Today, he closes in on 100 percent proficiency and gets two years' worth of academic gains for his students every school year. So much for thinking that students who live in poverty can't do math. Maybe their teachers have something to do with it after all. *Can you be that teacher?*

Another middle school teacher saw that his students were bored and decided to offer an after-school club that taught kids how to write software code. The hook? He said to his students, "I'm guessing you all play video games. You can either keep paying money to those companies that sell the games to you, or you can write their code and have those companies *pay you*. What's it gonna be?" His afternoon coding club filled up fast. Starting pay for software developers with a high school degree is in the six figures.

It is possible that some of your students have been told to forget about college because of the cost. That's a problem; when teachers predict it is unlikely a student will go to college, many lower their expectations. If that sounds wrong to you, you're right—*but it happens every day*. Instead, be the bearer of good news to all parents: "Check out University of the People at www.uopeople.edu." Your students can now get an accredited associate or bachelor's degree for under $5,000 (scholarships are also available). This is a life-changer and offers hope to your students. It helps everyone in each student's life raise their expectations, too. Every one of your students can be "college-bound"! Now are you willing to raise *your* expectations?

4. Engage Cultural Relevance Daily

Is your "cultural stuff" saved for the *shortest month of the year,* Black History Month? Do all the culturally relevant materials go back in a closet on March 1? If so, your students might feel like it was just a "show and tell." Instead, celebrate the achievements of those who look like your students *all year round*.

Since 2000, more than half of all American Nobel laureates have been people of color or immigrants (S. Anderson, 2019). Your students have heard of Martin Luther King Jr. and Barack Obama, but are they familiar with the first African American to graduate from West Point (Henry O. Flipper), become an astronaut (Guion Bluford), have her own television show (Ethel Waters), become a billionaire (Robert L. Johnson), serve in Congress (Hiram Rhodes Revels), or be awarded the Pulitzer Prize (Gwendolyn Brooks)? We could take this same equity path and fill it with the names of Latino, Asian, and Native American figures who have also made significant contributions. But do your students know these names? Do they see them in the texts they read? *If not, why not?*

Let students look these up and share with your class the amazing history of those who came before them. Post pictures of people who look like your students. Give them reading materials with diverse characters they can relate to. Kids must know and believe that others like them have "made it."

5. Be Explicit: Tell Students You Believe in Them

Say to your students, "Some say my class is tough. That may be true, but you are tougher. Last year, kids just like you started the year wondering if they had it in them to succeed. Well, they did have it in them, and you do, too. How do I know that? Because I'll refuse to let you fail. In this class, we go full tilt ahead; it's your future we are building. Are you up for a challenge?" You can put this message in your own words, *but keep the tone of confidence.* Do not back off your promise to insist on the challenge and your support.

Students often need a strong reason *why* they should be their best, but they also need to know that *they can be amazing* and who is supporting them. Here are examples of what you can say:

- "I love that attitude and motivation. The sky's the limit for you!"
- "That's what I'm talking about! You were on your game today. That says a lot about your future!"
- "That was impressive! I see a big future for you."
- "You've got more than potential. You've got what it takes. You're growing your brain."

By the way, depending on grade level, peer-to-peer affirmations have as much or more impact than teacher-to-student affirmations. At the upper grade levels, use more of, "Turn to your neighbor and say, 'You've got what it takes!'" Repeat your belief in your students again and again and again in different ways.

6. Support Your Multilingual Learners (MLLs)

Most teachers in the United States are monolingual. Students from poverty have a dual challenge if they are learning a new language as a multilingual learner (MLL). There are more than 100 non-English languages spoken in schools in the United States, and the most common is Spanish. If MLLs are going to compete in a typical monolingual classroom, we must develop and use both of their languages. When MLLs learn their native language well, they can make an even better transfer to English. The growth mindset is imperative for MLLs who live in poverty because they have extra work to do. These students must learn class content, plus learn a new language, plus deal with their economic status.

Support your MLLs by teaching content that connects with their personal lives rather than impersonal printed materials. Ensure that your examples are culturally relevant for both MLLs and students who live in poverty. In class, use student-appropriate visuals, gestures, native-language songs, and colloquial expressions. Prep learners with pre-teaching and priming to get their brains ready to learn. As a teacher, if you're not learning a few of the core phrases of your students, there's far less of a connection.

Dr. Jim Ewing, author of *Math for ELLs: As Easy as Uno, Dos, Tres* (2020), recommends providing MLLs with multiple paths (listen, read, experiment, and demonstrate) to new content. He adds that it's important to keep high expectations and to embrace rigor, because MLLs are already overcoming the challenge of learning in another language. Your kind insistence on rigor as productive struggle is a critical tool for success. Many call that identity being a "warm demander." Never let a student's background lower your expectations for their potential.

7. Ask Students to Create Their Own Dreams

After students have a chance to hear and read about the dreams accomplished by others who were once kids like them, they are primed. Ask your students about their own dreams and visions for their future.

They can begin to share that in their writing. Help them fine-tune their voice, their path, and their strengths. Of course, you'll want to affirm their voice in class, digitally, and on paper. Then let them share their dreams with others and get peer approval and feedback. When students can create, draw out, and voice their dreams, those dreams begin to seem possible. Ask questions and help them develop a graphic organizer or a list of steps to take so that their dreams can start to get some initial footing and feel real.

8. Share Success Stories

Give students success stories from the real world. Countless books offer short success stories you can read to or share with your class.

When kids have teachers who look like them, they are more likely to do better in school. When a Black male student has a Black teacher in the 3rd, 4th, or 5th grade, it significantly reduces the chances that the student will drop out of high school. In addition, having a same-race teacher increases the likelihood that students of both sexes from poverty will aspire to and enroll in a four-year college (Gershenson et al., 2017). If there's a shortage of same-race role models at your school, bring in outside role models for students. Play clips from YouTube of living role models of the same ethnicity so that students can learn from them. Consider inviting a guest speaker of the same race or ethnicity as most of your students to talk to your class, and leave time for questions. Regardless of their jobs, the speakers can share with your students how they got their education and found a career. Many of the questions will be practical but highly necessary. Figure 3.3 summarizes your discovery list of how to raise your expectations.

Emerging Equity Tools to Embrace

Many teachers think of teaching as something they do with or to students. The truth is, teaching starts within, and so does equity. Fostering the higher-expectations mindset is more than a "to do" for your own

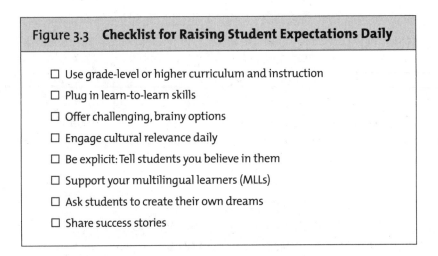

Figure 3.3   **Checklist for Raising Student Expectations Daily**

☐ Use grade-level or higher curriculum and instruction
☐ Plug in learn-to-learn skills
☐ Offer challenging, brainy options
☐ Engage cultural relevance daily
☐ Be explicit: Tell students you believe in them
☐ Support your multilingual learners (MLLs)
☐ Ask students to create their own dreams
☐ Share success stories

students. That message will never be genuine unless the person behind the mindset knows their own "ABCs." The *A-B-C* can stand for being *authentic, bursting* with energy, and *complimenting* your students every day.

This is what your students want to see and hear. When you are pushing high expectations, what are you working on in your own life? And are you sharing the process with your students? Seeing you work on yourself is more important to your students than you might think. They now see you as a role model, and your authenticity leads to credibility, which leads to them following you.

You're unlikely to raise your expectations for your students until you pause to de-bias your own expectations. Usually those who expect less of others also expect less of themselves. Your cognitive biases might have led to a long string of reasons for why you have or have not made choices that would raise your own expectations.

Your daily de-biasing will support your ease in shifting expectations higher. Read books that help give you the background to be more culturally responsive. Reflect on your biases, and bring an open mind. Some of the books that I would recommend are found in the Suggested Booklist in Appendix D.

Turn the slogan *growth mindset* into a reality. Unless the *growth mindset* is a *living mindset*, you'll fail. Consider a professional skill that you'd like to become very good at. How about choosing something in this chapter? Of course, you can also choose personal goals, which can also inspire your students. Take what you already do, and get better at it.

Chapter in a Nutshell

This chapter showed you how to raise expectations with your students from poverty and how to do the same for yourself. You read about some core changes you can engage to jump-start new possibilities. You got the solid *why* and the *how* to become an amazing, high-energy change agent.

Revisit the Student Questions

Many teachers simply assume that "kids are the way they are" and there's not much they can do about it. Actually, you *can* do a lot about it. As a starting point, recall these student questions from the beginning of the chapter:

➢ *"Does my teacher have high expectations and truly believe in me?"*

➢ *"Is my teacher willing to challenge me to get better?"*

➢ *"Do I belong in this challenging academic environment, and can I succeed at this subject/in this class?"*

The first student question invites you to consider whether you have high expectations. Start showing your students that you do, using what you've learned in this chapter. This is a *living mindset.*

Before the Next Chapter

Let's say you chose the goal of working to keep cultural relevance on display. Maybe you could plan to read from an impactful article or book for just three minutes a day and then have a discussion with your students. Over time, you'll learn from them, and they'll like what you're doing, too. Work with your team at school so that all of you have reading partners. That can help you to get feedback along the way. Plus, you'll stay more psyched up. Start this right away.

Here's how to get this expectations party started. It's time to believe in yourself and engage your growth mindset. Pick one area where you already perform moderately well, but where you'd like to improve to an *expert* level. For example, maybe you want to improve your eating habits, and you identify three factors that affect your performance: what you eat, how much you eat, and when you eat. To create a scale of competency, begin by rating yourself from 1 to 10. Then create five milestones (spread out over five months) to excellence, making it a goal to reach each milestone within 50 days. Adopt tiny habits—or, as I call them, "micro-strategies"—that take just 30 seconds to three minutes to put in place. For example, one micro-strategy might be switching out one sugary snack for one healthy snack each month. This will lower the hesitancy threshold. Now get started before you begin reading the next chapter.

4

Equitable Environments

Student Questions

➢ *"Am I in the in-group or not? Is my culture respected?"*

➢ *"Will my voice be heard?"*

➢ *"Are my classroom and my school safe places to be myself and be free from harm?"*

This chapter is about the question that many teachers struggle with: "How do I create an amazing classroom climate for learning?" Here we focus on the one thing that matters most: making sure that your students feel comfortable and safe being in, and taking risks in, your class. In this chapter, you'll get the solid *why* and *how* to foster a great classroom of equity. Our topics this chapter are:

- Singing His Way into the "In" Crowd
- Connections to Poverty
- You Go First: Start Small and Keep Moving
- How to Engage In-Group Equity
- Cultural and Equitable Responsiveness
- Emerging Equity Tools to Embrace

Singing His Way into the "In" Crowd

Born into a family of sharecroppers in Simonton, Texas, Laurence Brown knew exactly what it was like to live on the "wrong side of town." He lived in poverty, and what kept him going was music. By the mid-1960s, mainstream pop culture was waking up to the jazz, soul, and gospel contributions of African Americans. He had his goals, and at just 17, he packed his bag and moved to California to make his mark in music. In Los Angeles, Laurence met Sonny Bono, who suggested that he record under the name Dobie Gray.

Back then, every up-and-coming musician wanted to be on the biggest national television stage of its time, Dick Clark's *American Bandstand*. After all, the songs that resonated with teens on the show usually went on to become big hits. On January 23, 1965, Dobie Gray got his chance. The song he performed, "The 'In' Crowd," resonated with what he knew about personally. He hit a home run with the song, which reminds listeners that in high school, the clique mentality—the "in" crowd—is everywhere. The singer boasts that he knows the latest dances and the hottest clubs, and he gets respect just walking down the street. The song was a hit, and decades later it remains on countless oldies playlists along with his other, even bigger, hit "Drift Away." If you've never heard "The 'In' Crowd," check out the lyrics now on YouTube.

But the takeaway here is not about Dobie Gray's fame or fortune. It's all about the universal message of in-groups and out-groups. In your classroom, all kids want to belong to the in-group. The out-group is the group of students whose culture is different from, or not acknowledged by, the teacher. The defining feature of students in the out-group is a lack of belonging to the larger community. Because humans are social creatures, feeling isolated often contributes to a stressful experience at school. In classroom environments that are successful, every student feels like they are in the in-group, even if it's just for the duration of the class (Knowles, Lucas, Molden, Gardner, & Dean, 2010).

In our next segment, you'll find out why in-groups are so important and how to foster the right kind. Then you'll explore how to foster greater cultural responsiveness. And finally, you'll get tools to build safety and nurture student voice.

Debrief Time

Let's pause for reflection time. Did you read the student questions at the start of the chapter? One of the very few things that is a must for students is a sense of belonging with the in-group. *Is your class an "in" crowd for every student?* Take three to five minutes and process this as a brief writing assignment or a discussion with a partner.

Connections to Poverty

You may have had a teacher who exemplified an *exclusive* classroom: "This is *my classroom*. I make the rules, and you follow them." From the start, many students feel like they have to earn their way into the teacher's in-group. Maybe some teachers forget: Students are required by law to be in school. And then they must *earn* their way into their teachers' good graces? That's ridiculous. Add that to the fact that many students are already discriminated against because of their socioeconomic status or skin color. Let's change the game.

Students of color commonly perceive that their White teachers discriminate against them. Although teachers might not think they are discriminatory, *it is the student's perception that matters most.* And because of this perception, minority students commonly report feeling that their academic efforts are pointless (D'Hondt, Eccles, Houtte, & Stevens, 2016). As a result, you'll see less effort and energy. But there are even more serious risks: Students may generalize their school experiences into the bigger perception that effort in life is not meaningful (Stillman et al., 2009). Take a second to absorb this. When students feel discriminated against, they often feel as if the game is fixed. With that mindset, *why should they try?*

It is painful to be excluded—literally. Exclusion increases pain sensitivity, and the brain feels social pain just like physical pain (Bernstein & Claypool, 2012). When socially excluded by White participants, distressed Black participants showed greater social pain-related neural activity and reduced emotion regulatory neural activity (Masten, Telzer, & Eisenberger, 2011).

The departure of underrepresented students participating in STEM majors is confirmation of the power of out-group feelings. Evidence shows the departures result from reduced feelings of social belonging more than any alleged lack of academic preparedness (Wilson et al., 2015). *Stereotype bias* was initially keeping many kids of color and girls out of the program, and then *the culture within the programs* was keeping them from feeling that they belonged.

Chronic stress associated with being part of the out-group impacts several areas of the brain, including the emotional systems, attentional systems, memory systems, and more. Unfortunately, chronic stress degrades cognition. When this plays out day after day, students who don't feel part of the in-group may have lower levels of academic achievement (Frazier, Gabriel, Merians, & Lust, 2019). The constant worries ("Do I fit in here?" "Am I seen here?" "Will I be harassed today?") consume the emotional systems of the brain, led by the amygdala. That leads to increased emotional responses and decreased class focus.

Since social survival is of greater importance to the brain than dividing fractions, worry about inclusion is constantly diverting attention away from the lessons. This, in turn, significantly decreases the likelihood of accurate memory formation (Quaedflieg & Schwabe, 2018). And when the ostracism does happen, it's far more painful for students (Jones, Carter-Sowell, Kelly, & Williams, 2009).

A sense of belonging is critical; it helps shape students' biases about themselves, their potential, and the learning situation. Top teachers consistently create more fairness, greater inclusion, and deeper engagement with a more equitable and positive student experience. When these elements work together, it changes brain chemicals and fosters a "herd" identity (Stallen, De Dreu, Shalvi, Smidts, & Sanfey, 2012).

Take the time to learn about your own students. Otherwise, your out-group students are likely to feel the discrimination and to struggle in school. This can lead to students in the out-group being mislabeled and placed in special education classes. Without support or intervention, these patterns can be perpetuated and confirmed by teacher biases.

You Go First: Start Small and Keep Moving

Creating a whole-class, inclusive in-group is tough but doable. This process may invite you to ask for help among colleagues. I have been terrible at asking for help most of my life. Working well with colleagues and groups meant a lot to me; but asking for help meant I was "needy" or "not up to speed." I have since learned that life is full of a lot of "asks" and "gives." Ask for help.

Initiating an in-group takes identities and qualities that may include those of a counselor, a physical education instructor, a social director, and a security officer. If it sounds a bit overwhelming, it is. These are personal skills as much as professional skills. Start with one small step. Then, move on to the next one. It can be a hard, piece-by-piece process. But you can do it. Supporting your students is priceless. The takeaway for you is simple: Start small and keep moving.

How to Engage In-Group Equity

Let's unpack how to foster in-group equity in class. Part of this process will be exposing biases. Check your biases daily on your growth path. Here's how to take notice and pivot for improved classroom equity and a robust in-group. Figure 4.1 shows the path.

Not long after they begin class, nearly every student knows whether they belong to the in-group or the out-group. Both favoring and disfavoring certain students can contribute to an inequitable climate.

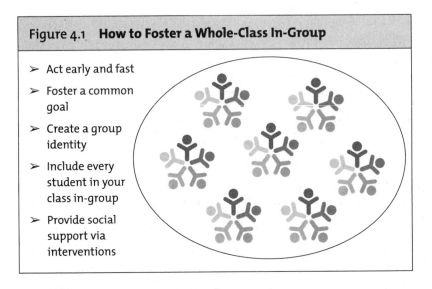

Figure 4.1   **How to Foster a Whole-Class In-Group**

➤ Act early and fast

➤ Foster a common goal

➤ Create a group identity

➤ Include every student in your class in-group

➤ Provide social support via interventions

But teachers who know why they should include all students in the in-group, and how to do it, can reap huge benefits for both the students and themselves. When you give your students a solid sense of belonging every day, life changes for them. They feel connected, respected, and supported. Their level of trust goes up both with peers and with you as the teacher. Most important, they feel valued as a person who belongs and can learn with the best of them. Here are a few of my own favorite tools for forming an in-group.

1. Act Early and Fast

This applies the most in secondary schools, where the clock seems to move faster. Avoid the *time-discounting bias*—the false assumption that the further into the future you go, the less the time matters. Secondary school teachers who wait more than two days to form their whole-class in-group often lose out; secondary students will choose a *student-led in-group* over having nothing else to belong to because they feel it's better to be in any group than be in none at all. At the elementary level, you have about a week to establish your class in-group. So fast action is the first tool.

How you do this: Start on day one. Talk about how being on "our class team" is a huge benefit. Drop hints right from the start about what it is like on the class team. Be inclusive in how you build the in-group. The inclusive group path embraces *all* students *immediately* and the class moves forward.

2. Foster a Common Goal

It is amazing how just one thing can turn a potentially random crowd into the in-group. In sports, fans of the home team instantly identify themselves as the in-group at any home game. They view the other team and its fans as the out-group. For a short time, while cheering on their team, members of this in-group display cooperation, good will, and a sense of solidarity and kinship. They are even willing to embarrass themselves by wearing flashy hats, T-shirts, masks, and face paint in support of the group (Masuda & Fu, 2015). Now you have the second tool for creating an in-group: a common goal or purpose.

How you do this: In the secondary grades, your common goal is what the whole class fights hard for all semester. It's that "one big thing." Maybe you challenge your class to write to politicians to advocate for issues that are important to them, or to beat the test scores of a highly ranked neighboring school. Orchestrate your in-group to mobilize *for something.* Build equity simultaneously by encouraging your in-group to fight together to expose and reduce discrimination. Some teachers foster a whole-class team in which all are discovering their heritage, helping hurt or sheltered animals, or supporting wounded veterans. Doing something together as a class, where teamwork is required from each class member, builds a sense of in-group affiliation (Efferson, Lalive, & Fehr, 2008). The whole class works hard when you encourage it, sell the value of it, and reward effort. (Corny celebrations do work.)

In the elementary grades, consider working for a local food bank, growing a school-based garden, helping at a senior center, or conducting a classwide reading drive. Or find a global cause and build support. Get all your students cheering for the same local sports team or supporting a community nonprofit organization. This can inspire students. In 2020, Katie Stagliano was named a National Geographic Education Young Explorer along with a handful of other young adults from six countries who had improved conditions in their communities. It all started when she was in 6th grade. Today, her charitable organization, Katie's Krops, organizes young people to grow food and distribute it to those in need (www.katieskrops.org).

3. Create a Group Identity

Use the language of a family—words such as *we, us,* and *ours.* Avoid words like *you* and *I.* Call your class "one big family." Do family things like sharing stories, jokes, and, when possible, food. To maintain the strength in your family in-group, task students with the job of building community. Encourage them to work with partners, use kind words, and list three positive qualities of another student. Now you have the third tool for building a great in-group: helping your students co-create and reinforce in-group values.

Maybe the identity you want to reinforce in your students is empowerment. How would you feel if you were a 4th grade teacher, and a student of color in your class founded an international youth empowerment organization with 24,000 full-time volunteers from 41 countries? Would you have expected his success? Let's be honest; we all typically underestimate our students' potential. Are you still looking for "potential" in students? Stop it; you don't have that superpower. You're not a fortune teller; you're an equitable, energetic educator with high expectations for your students.

By the way, the student mentioned above—Dylan Mahalingam—spoke at the United Nations at age 9, was named a Top 20 Teen in the USA by *People Magazine,* and met with three presidents and the Dalai Lama. His nonprofit, Lil' MDGs, has raised millions for disaster relief and eradication of poverty.

How you do this: When you address students, call them Mr. or Ms. plus their surnames. When you respond to a raised hand or a shout, focus on the "Big Three" every single time: Make eye contact, smile, and appreciate the student's contribution. A simple "thank you" will work at the start.

Once the initial level of safety is established, start asking more of your students. After a student shares a thought or an answer, it might be appropriate to ask follow-up questions, such as "Can you say a bit more?" "How is that different from _____?" "Where could we find out more about that?" Questions like this promote rigor and still let the student's voice be heard and valued. And be consistent doing that; each of your students will remember all the times you were responsive to others, so you had better be responsive to that student, too.

Be sure to exude the joy and other advantages of being in "our group." Here is where you share with your class your own top five team values statements. Your students get to create and vote on the other five. Once each cooperative group or smaller class team has contributed to the 10 class values statements, they feel more ownership. The class reads these statements aloud *every day of school*. Reading these statements in unison reinforces not only the values within the document, but also the sense of in-group camaraderie and solidarity. Figure 4.2 shows an example (credit for the idea of the Daily Class Read goes to Dr. Lionel Allen). Take the ideas from it, customize it for your class, and do this daily to start your class.

4. Include Every Student in Your Class In-Group

Savvy teachers continually embrace others and expand the circle to include every one of their students as part of the in-group. Your in-group must be authentic and worth being a part of. Otherwise, students who sense injustice, bias, or unfairness from a teacher may feel that the class in-group is a waste of time. When you explicitly support students of all ethnicities and backgrounds in class and use overt expressions of help, encouragement, and celebration, students see that the teacher's in-group is a safe place to be.

A simple way to foster an inclusive in-group is to eliminate any permanent ability groupings. The evidence suggests they are detrimental

Figure 4.2   **Daily Class Read: Class Values Statements**

We believe.

We are the growing scholars of [school name].

We will face and defeat any obstacle before us.

We are exceptional because we work hard, learn from our mistakes, and keep getting better.

We seize the moment; our future is boundless and unlimited.

We are dedicated, committed, and focused.

We succeed because we persist and avoid excuses.

We foster empathy, problem solving, and kindness.

We respect ourselves and, in doing so, respect all others.

We take care of our physical, emotional, and mental health.

We embrace our responsibility to family and community.

We believe in our capacity to make the world better.

We believe.

to students' belief in themselves and their achievement (Dumont, Protsch, Jansen, & Becker, 2017). Consider temporary, needs-based small-group instruction. Evidence for it is strong, with an effect size of 1.07, and it taps into the Response-to-Intervention (RTI) model of instruction (Hattie, 2012). In contrast, permanent ability grouping and tracking may have a negative impact on learning, students' sense of self, and their willingness to engage in class (Dumont et al., 2017). Now you have the fourth tool for a great in-group: pulling every single student (along with the help of their peers) into the in-group with a goal of 100 percent inclusion.

How you do this: Make contact with those "not yets" in your class. Learn about their lives. Ask questions. Listen, then ask more. Do this in a small group or individually. Remember, your goal is to have 100 percent of your students in your in-group. Even for teachers who believe they have no student biases and treat students wonderfully, just the thought of having or expressing a bias influences their behavior (De Houwer, 2019). Many students have never felt that they are truly heard, and that's a gift you're giving them. Second, make weekly promises you can keep. "I promise to hear your concerns this week, to check in with you and respect your safety." Then keep your promises. That will start the trust process, one step at a time.

5. Provide Social Support via Interventions

Traditionally marginalized students who feel awkward in new social or academic groups often need reassurance that they can make it. There is evidence that several programs are highly effective in providing this reassurance. In one intervention, college students were shown findings from a survey of more-senior students of the same ethnicity at the same school, saying that everyone questions their belonging during academic transitions but that the concerns often decrease over time. This small intervention improved the students' resilience as well as their grade point averages throughout their college years (Walton & Cohen, 2011; Yeager & Walton, 2011).

It can be reassuring to hear that it's normal to be a bit cautious and that success is still possible. In another study, the teachers emphasized both high standards and the sincere belief that their students could meet the high bar. This feedback nudged the students enough to resubmit an essay and improve its quality (Yeager et al., 2014).

How you do this: As a teacher, be mindful about whether trust is eroding. If you think it might be, assume it already has. Ask the student. "Are we doing well together, or have I dropped the ball lately?" Rebuilding trust is crucial. One study (Yeager, Purdie-Vaughns, Hooper, & Cohen, 2017) found that when staff members in middle school followed up any grading event with a personal note that built trust, students were more likely to enroll in a four-year college immediately after graduating from high school compared with those who did not receive the follow-up notes. The takeaway here is simple: Many minority students are used to uncertainty, lack of support, and fuzzy paths ahead. Be the teacher who opens the door, shows a clear path, and confirms fullest support.

Cultural and Equitable Responsiveness

Culturally responsive teaching is the intentional use of students' knowledge and experiences to make learning more appropriate and effective. It uses what students bring with them to form bridges to rigorous student learning. Culturally responsive teaching goes beyond putting up posters that reflect diversity; it reflects the respect you have for students' cultures, customs, languages, and traditions. It is a student-centered approach to education, reminding us that every student brings unique cultural strengths to the classroom (S. King, personal communication, Jan. 27, 2021).

Cultural responsiveness is a broad field. It includes such topics as equity, language, culture, approach to learning, pedagogy, racism, identities, policies, and class culture. There are many superb books on cultural responsiveness. Check out those by Zaretta Hammond, Yvette Jackson, Baruti K. Kafele, Randall B. Lindsey, and Pedro Noguera.

When I encounter educators who are still a bit skeptical of the recent movement to infuse cultural responsiveness into their classrooms and their school at large, I am empathetic. Why? I've been there. Many White teachers believe that the kids in their class are like them except that they have *deviations* away from the White culture. That's a huge bias against the students' culture. Bad idea.

Each culture affects how the brain develops (Kitayama & Uskul, 2011). Maybe the most salient recent finding is the extent and breadth of the influence of culture on the brain. Culture influences nearly every area of the brain, both cortical and subcortical. The brain responds to even the daily routines and regularities in the cultural stream of one's life (Domínguez, Lewis, Turner, & Egan, 2009). Culture is not an *add-on*; it is *essence*.

Having said that, let's broaden our learning about culture. Research suggests that the differences in both social habits and cognition that have been shown to exist *between* cultures or social classes do not correlate with individual differences *within* those groups. A student's culture tells you only part of the story. But it's an important part, so learn it. In short, still get to know your students, one by one. But it takes more than that; it's time to hold up a mirror. That's why it's so critical to understand two "isms": *sexism* and *racism*.

Gender Biases Hurt Your Students

Females' and males' experiences in life are quite different. Males often get hired first, promoted faster, and paid more for the same work as women. Males who are rude or lewd rarely get called out for it in public. Males are less likely to be interrupted, and others are more likely to assume they know what they're talking about. Men can usually buy a car without salespeople assuming they can be taken advantage of (so men are often offered a better price than women, too). There is simply a different universe of experiences between males and females. The differences between the sexes are (of course) spread widely on a bell-shaped curve. Commit to ensuring you consciously take *both* girls and boys seriously without any added bias from you.

I would argue, depending on the teacher, that *both* boys and girls experience gender bias. The studies back that up. Girls are consistently held to lower expectations by teachers in math and science but are subjected to higher expectations for reading and going to college (Robinson-Cimpian, Lubienski, Ganley, & Copur-Gencturk, 2014). Boys get the reverse: They are held to higher expectations in STEM classes, but lower expectations for graduating from college (Gibbs, 2010).

Action Steps. Be a role model for the optimal behaviors. Call yourself out first, as you make tiny mistakes. Let students write down any time they hear you express a bias. Notice when students show a serious bias in their speaking or writing. Ensure that you point it out in a kind way. Read short stories to students about the effects of gender bias

(Brown & Stone, 2016). For a broader perspective, I suggest two books, each asserting that the other gender is getting cheated: *Failing at Fairness: How America's Schools Cheat Girls*, by Myra and David Sadker; and *The War Against Boys: How Misguided Policies Are Harming Our Young Men*, by Christina Hoff Sommers. These resources are great for raising awareness and reducing bias.

Do You Have White Privilege?

In addition to female and male privilege gaps, there are also gaps between people of color and those with *White privilege*. I never even heard the phrase until 20 years ago. The first time I discussed the topic in my monthly newsletter, I got emails that asserted there is no White privilege. Oh, how I wish that were true. White privilege is a dependable, everyday collection of invisible, *unearned* assets. White people can depend on cashing in these assets any time without requesting them or apologizing for them (Dewar, 2020). Yet most White people are oblivious to them. So, what are those assets?

As a White person, if I need to move, I can rent or buy in almost any area I want. Upon moving, I can be pretty sure that my neighbors in such a location will be neutral or pleasant to me. I can go to stores alone and feel safe and confident that I will be free from harassment or accusations of shoplifting. I can check out any media source and see people of my race widely represented in everyday life, and rarely as criminals. When I am told about our U.S. heritage, I am shown that people of my origins helped make my country what it is. I can go into a supermarket and find the staple foods that fit with my cultural traditions, and I can go into a hairdresser's shop and find someone who knows how to cut my hair.

Whether I use checks, credit cards, or cash, I am certain my skin color is a nonissue for what I can afford. If a police officer pulls me over, it's typically for something legitimate as opposed to harassment, racism, or bullying. White parents educate their children to be aware and to look both ways before crossing the street. However, we don't have to teach our children how to respond when getting pulled over for DWB (Driving While Black). I am never asked to speak for all the people of my racial group. I can choose any hotel, motel, or bed and breakfast without fearing discrimination or mistreatment. When I need legal or medical help, my ethnicity never works against me. I can travel alone or with my spouse and children without expecting embarrassment or hostility in those who deal with us. My children's textbooks have pictures that explicitly support my culture, skin color, and history (McIntosh, 1989).

When hearing of White privilege for the first time, many White people deny receiving any type of conferred invisible assets. "I worked my butt off for what I have," they say. I can understand that response. *I used to feel that way.* But today I know better. Yes, I do work hard, but actually, luck played a big role in my life. Did I choose my DNA, my neighborhood, or my school? No, I chose none of those. So how can I take credit for a safe neighborhood, nearby stores that charged fair prices for healthful food, or decent schools? I can't. And that's just the start of the list.

When I was caught shoplifting as a kid, the police could have taken me to the station; instead, I got off with a verbal warning. When I apply for a loan, I am taken seriously. When I am stopped for a traffic violation, my license is returned quickly, and my car has never been violated with illegal searches. These responses would have been much less likely to happen to a person of color.

Systemic racism is like that: so embedded, so implicit, that it presents a relentless, tiring fight. That's partly because racism is always a moving target. It is generated less by hate and ignorance than by policies that serve the current self-interests of people and institutions in power. It is perpetuated by biases that are never examined and dismantled. Worst of all, it becomes invisible when others refuse to acknowledge its existence. In short, there are racism "generators" in high places, often with wide reaches, where access, power, and money are all at stake.

African Americans, Latinos, Asians, and Native Americans were far more responsible for the development of America than history has given any of these groups credit for. Any sense of belonging to the broad human circle of life should be an unearned entitlement of every human being. All people living in our country should feel like they belong here. That means you embrace every student in your class; they belong.

Most teachers would assert that they are not racist. That may sound good, but in today's world, you're likely complicit *in allowing racism to occur* in your classroom (McCoy, 2020). For you, I suggest Ibram X. Kendi's (2019) book *How to Be an Antiracist*, or Vernita Mayfield's (2020) book *Cultural Competence.* Read, digest, and engage fully and ethically in your life. Embracing antiracism has been a bumpy path for me. Even (or especially) from one of my good friends, it's hard to hear. Over dinner recently, he was recounting the daily biases he faced, such as being harassed by police and getting pulled over for DWB. I said, "Wow, this is real $#!%." His experiences *personalized the pain for me.*

Emerging Equity Tools to Embrace

Social tools involve engaging others at each step of the way. The value of this pathway is the capacity to enlist others for support, planning, foolproofing, feedback, guidance, accountability, and celebration. Where can you start? Engage your students in class as well as colleagues outside your classroom. Consider enlisting the help of a like-minded colleague, a home partner, or school leadership. Invite them to join you in the path of growing.

When you find a colleague who wants to go forward with you on your journey, they might be a perfect addition to your "growth mini-team." The best number of members for this team is three to five. Too many on your team, and each may feel like they are fighting for time. Too few, and your team may break down when just one is out sick. A great place to start is by asking questions like, "Who on this team has ever successfully created their class as an in-group?" Follow up with questions from this chapter to build a step-by-step road map.

For group-driven social tools, enlist the help of students in your class or use school teams. Invite your students to grow together and change with you. Ask them to start small and dream big. Ensure high expectations and use a simple accountability tool where you check in daily. Meet weekly to review the indicators of improved results.

The following are some of the simple actions you can share with your growth mini-team and work on together.

Start now. Remember, you can take almost any small step forward toward equity. Students of color are often asking, "Who am I?" and searching for anything that is relevant to their culture, identities, and experiences. For some culture-parched kids, seeing a YouTube clip of the *Hamilton* cast performing at the White House is like finding an oasis in the desert. Show more of those types of clips and you may start finding your students to be more inspired.

Strive for equity, not equality. Some students have a greater need for a caring adult than others do, based on their home life. As you get to know each student personally, invest your time with students who most need the supportive relationship you can offer. Remember, equity is giving what is needed to those who need it most. As an example, it turns out that Black and Latino youth who feel peer-based discrimination are the most likely to suffer serious depression (Stein, Supple, Huq, Dunbar, & Prinstein, 2016). Those who are already in the in-group, with a better-paved pathway to success, are less likely to need your extra support.

Bring in role models of ethnicities that match those of students. Yes, we could use far more teachers of color. But if you're a White teacher, you can start to make the difference in students' lives today by inviting people from the community who can bring a role model to life for your class. Find the influencers, writers, actors, artists, chefs, mathematicians, doctors, scientists, musicians, coders, builders, nurses, and engineers who can be the positive role models that exist and whom students desperately need to see. A 45-minute talk in person or by Zoom, with time for questions and answers, can change lives.

Invest a few minutes a day. Spend time with students who might be considered in the out-group in your classroom or school. Learn about their lives. Listen. Ask questions. Then, listen some more. There is evidence that spending just a few minutes a day with an individual underserved student can improve the teacher's view of that student (Driscoll & Pianta, 2010).

Review and revise what students read. Children of color need books that have same-ethnicity characters. A national assessment of children's literature revealed mostly books with a White main character. In one study, fewer than 10 percent had a Black protagonist, and fewer than 3 percent featured main characters of Latino, Native American, or Asian and Pacific Islander origins (Cooperative Children's Book Center, 2020). How about using books that celebrate the amazing successes of people of color for their achievements (instead of stereotypes)?

Be empathetic, not sympathetic. The well-established *empathy gap* between teachers and students of different cultures creates a barrier to learning worthy of attention. Recognizing and respecting all cultures in your classroom will yield high results both relationally and academically (Bottiani, Bradshaw, & Mendelson, 2016).

Be explicit. Kids may be able to get a sense of you. But they often wait all year to directly ask you the questions posted at the start of this chapter. Stop the mystery. Be direct, clear, and explicit about how you feel about them. Say, "I love having you in our class." With this one statement, notice that you shared affection, you were direct and personal, and you said, "This is *our* in-group."

You can create your own list of affirming statements like the following:

- "You make our class better."
- "Always good to see you. I miss you when you're absent."
- "Your contributions help our class grow."

Stop waiting for the perfect moment to say these things to your students. Every moment you wait makes the moment less and less "perfect" as the student begins to disconnect from school.

Use culturally relevant instruction. As you prepare for each upcoming unit, evaluate your curriculum to ensure that it represents all the students you teach. Your reading materials, the characters you study, the music you play in your classroom—it all sends a message to your students. Draw students out about their culture. That's what will motivate them. Make adjustments to ensure that all students can find a way to connect to the characters, stories, and themes of your curriculum.

Engage culturally specific events all year long. Speak with your students and ask what is relevant, important, or missing for them. Some students may want an opportunity to teach the rest of the class about one of their own cultural traditions. Knowledge and awareness are the seeds from which tolerance and compassion grow. Feeling excluded, isolated, or rejected increases the levels of cortisol in the brain. Simply put, feeling that you're in the out-group is stressful. The chronic stress experienced by minority cultures often has a devastating impact on a student's body and brain (Stanley & Adolphs, 2013).

Become an antiracist. Remaining silent about racism *is giving tacit approval to it.* Speak up. There will be times when you hear another make a racist comment. You have an obligation to speak up and be part of the solution, even if it's simply saying, "Can we back up a moment? I'm not sure you meant what I think I heard." You want your students' respect? Be an ally, not an adversary.

Provide relevant avenues to content by incorporating visuals, gestures, native-language songs, food, and colloquial expressions from students' cultures. Continually remind your students, "Brains can change and grow; so can you!" Stay connected with Level 2 and 3 relationships from Chapter 2. That means you're both a supporter and an ally.

Chapter in a Nutshell

To reach students living in poverty, make your class an inclusive in-group where all students feel safe and included. Exclusion is painful. Everyone needs an in-group; if you don't provide one for your students, they may seek one out on their own. That's why you need to act fast to create your class in-group, enlist students in a common goal and group identity, and intervene when students are in danger of feeling left out. This chapter gave you a collection of tools—including ways to challenge your own biases and use culturally responsive teaching—to create an equitable classroom.

Revisit the Student Questions

Let's review the student questions from the beginning of the chapter:

> ➤ *"Am I in the in-group or not? Is my culture respected?"*

> ➤ *"Will my voice be heard?"*

> ➤ *"Are my classroom and my school safe places to be myself and be free from harm?"*

How can you show your students that you respect them and their culture? Try sharing narratives and stories that highlight and foster strengths in your students, or any of the other suggestions provided in this chapter.

Before the Next Chapter

Here's how you can mobilize yourself to take one action to grow yourself and to move your life and career forward. What new habit from this chapter will you choose to grow? With whom will you start the process? What is your plan? Get started today. Why? Remember the time-discounting bias: We typically think we'll have more time in the future to do this. But we know that isn't true. Let's try this out: If someone could only see your actions and hear none of your words, what would they say are your priorities in life right now? Once you have your right priorities, take action.

5

Rousing Relevance

Student Questions

➤ *"Does this work have real value (relevance), and does my teacher share the why with me every day?"*

➤ *"Will my teacher keep me connected, captivated, and engaged?"*

➤ *"Will I be bored and tired or energized and celebrated each day in class?"*

This chapter is about using intentional relevance to uplift your students. Not that long ago, teachers expected students to do what they were told in class, ignoring relevance. A typical response to the "Why are we doing this?" question was, "Because I said so, and I'm the teacher." The result was a bumpy stream of compliance behaviors.

That might have been commonplace 50 years ago for instilling a factory-worker mindset. But in today's world, we ask for much more than compliance from workers and citizens. We often want collaboration, leadership, creativity, and responsibility. It's the same in our classrooms. Teaching for compliance is outdated. It's time for you to empower willing learners. Our topics in this chapter are:

- The Teacher Who Told Students, "I Was Just Like You"
- Connections to Poverty
- You Go First: Make the Relevance Connection at Home
- A Starting Point for Motivation
- Seven Ways to Rouse Relevance in Your Class
- The Framework for Relevance: Culturally Responsive Teaching
- Emerging Equity Tool to Embrace
- A Note About Stories

This chapter will illuminate how to end compliance behaviors once and for all and replace them with collaboration. In addition, you'll learn which tools can optimize energy and engagement as well as how your stories can change lives.

The Teacher Who Told Students, "I Was Just Like You"

Twenty-eight kids were in my class, and all eyeballs were on me. It was day one of a six-week after-school program. The middle school students had been registered by their parents for my study skills class. Each class went from 2:15 to 3:45 p.m. in a stuffy room with no air conditioning. Outside air temps were in the 80s every day.

All the kids were failing in school. The kids grew up experiencing racism and low expectations. The typical family thought their son was a hero if he just graduated from high school. Minimum wages were expected for their likely future jobs as cooks or housekeepers. My job? Help students stay in school to graduate by teaching them learn-to-learn skills and mindsets. It could have been a recipe for disaster.

But it wasn't.

All I could remember in that opening moment was saying, "Eric, remember *E-R-I-C*." That's my personal acronym for *Engagement, Relevance, Identity,* and *Connection.* I opened with a brief personal story about how I had also been bored out of my mind in middle school (true) and how I struggled in most of my classes (true). I told them

my grades were not good (true; I graduated from high school with a
C+ average). By now, my students were leaning in and listening (and
maybe connecting with their teacher).

I told them my grades only allowed me to get into a local state college.
I continued to struggle in college, but I noticed that my friends studied
much differently than I did. They knew what to do, how to do it, and
for how long. I finally could see what was missing: I had no idea *how
to learn!* So, I went after it. The summer between my sophomore and
junior year, I took acceleration classes to retool my brain, and I finally
learned how to learn. By the end of the summer, I had gotten really
good at studying, taking notes, reading, and learning *like a scholar*. My
identity was changed, and I was a hungry, confident learner!

How did my school year turn out? I began my collegiate junior year
buzzing with confidence. I registered for double the usual number of
classes (eight versus four in the previous year). I kept my job at the
grocery store and was still working 20–25 hours a week, just like the
previous year. But I made the dean's list for the first time in my life. And
for the rest of my academic career, I never earned below a 3.5 GPA.
Study skills kept me in school and helped my confidence, big-time. I
even managed to have fun on the side.

But the biggest takeaway? I learned that an average student could
learn and apply key skills in ways that could *change their life.* As my
students were wondering how we would start, I jumped right in and
said, "You want to do more gaming, racing, hanging with friends, or
surfing? You can learn how to learn like those smart kids, *and you don't
have to act like them.* I'll show you how you can do it." During that six-
week class, I took photos of the kids. You can see them at 3:00 on hot
afternoons, absolutely locked in, learning how to be better students.

I answered the common questions before students even asked
them. "Why do we have to do this? What's in it for me? What if I'm
not smart?" I gave them hope for their future, explained how I would
upgrade their toolkit, and promised I'd make it fun. I used engagement,
relevance, identity, and connections. The students stayed in school and

graduated. This chapter focuses on a critical ingredient in the recipe for equity: rousing relevance.

> ### *Debrief Time*
>
> Let's pause for critical reflection. Do this as a brief writing assignment or a discussion with a partner. Reflect on your response to my classroom story. Did you hear any biases pop up in your brain? "Yeah, but I don't have the life story that you had." That would be the *exceptionalism* bias. To you, I was an outlier that you can't learn from. In my after-school study skills class, I focused on engagement, relevance, students' identities, and connection. These tools are the *how* of getting the job done. Are you buying into this strategy? Finish up your brief writing assignment or your discussion with a partner, and we'll dig in.

Connections to Poverty

Relevance in instruction and materials is typically scarce in low-income schools. When asked why they left school, most dropouts in one study suggested that they would have had a better chance of completing school if their schools had been more relevant, engaging, and realistic through real-world, experiential learning (Azzam, 2007). Yes, students want to see the connection between school, work, and the real world. But they rarely get it. Do culturally relevant instruction and curricula matter in high-poverty schools? Yes. Is there evidence that ethnic studies courses, multicultural literature, and culturally relevant pedagogy make a difference? There is.

Several schools identified hundreds of students who had low 8th grade GPAs and assigned them to an intervention course. The course used instructional practices and content aligned with minority students' real-world experiences. Simply attending this course boosted their next year's 9th grade attendance by 21 percent and their average GPA by a whopping 1.4 grade points (Dee & Penner, 2017). Students do care about relevance. Cultural relevance fuels and infuses your students' brains with high energy and engagement.

You Go First: Make the Relevance Connection at Home

Where to start? You guessed it—it's with you! Again, we begin with your at-home behaviors. Do you roll your eyes when your partner asks you to do tasks at home? If so, why? The rolled-eyes display often says, "Give me one good reason why I should do this task, because I don't feel like doing it."

If you have children, and don't give them a *why* for the tasks you ask them to do, this is a good place to start. When you're having a heart-to-heart talk with your children, try this out: "I am so sorry. Many times, I assumed you should just do a job around the house because I said so. But I have never told you why your job is important, why it needs to be done for our family and yourself. How about I fill in those blanks?"

When your personal life is better, it supports a better "you" at work. As an example, when you become better at regulating your own stress, you are calmer and more poised at work. Your students will feel more at ease; they'll like you more and you'll have fewer discipline issues. You will enjoy your job more and have good days more often. Relevance is critical to all of us. Start at home, and then with your students.

A Starting Point for Motivation

For many staff members in your school, attempts at motivation are about not-so-subtle coercion and, ultimately, settling for compliance. Compliance begins when students are bored and they decide to go through the motions because it is often hard to sleep in class. It keeps them out of trouble. Sometimes peer pressure to "go along" works.

You've often heard that the antidote to compliance is choice. Well, yes and no. Choice can support better learning and memory (Voss,

Gonsalves, Federmeier, Tranel, & Cohen, 2011). The choices must be at least slightly attractive but not *heavy*. There are constraints on offering choice, and yet it is still worth it. In a large meta-study, researchers discovered what works with choice, and it may surprise you. The impact of choice on intrinsic motivation (Patall, Cooper, & Robinson, 2008) was stronger when the teacher

- Gave simple instructional choices (versus complex ones),
- Provided multiple successive choices over small things (creating a cascade effect), and
- Avoided giving rewards after the choice offering (the choice itself was the reward).

Now we know . . . be mindful and thoughtful about how you use choice. Most teachers find benefits in using choice (Flowerday & Schraw, 2000). So, it can be a valuable tool, but it's rarely a miracle worker. That's where relevance can come and do the heavy lifting.

Start building in relevance by making sure the learning experience meets one or more of students' basic, underlying needs, like autonomy, fun, and a sense of belonging. These approaches will work when used with variety; every student has their own core "drivers" that work at some time. A teacher who struggles says, "You can lead a horse to water, but you can't make it drink." Consider a different approach: "How do I *induce* thirst in my students?"

There are multiple theories about what generates motivation (Cook & Artino, 2016). Following are the tools found in common with the most cited studies. Your classroom actions may be more effective when you strive to

- **Foster competence** (go for mastery instead of a dumbed-down curriculum). Show students your excitement. Sell the value of pride and confidence; let them know they can more easily meet future demands by putting in the work today.
- **Foster value** (show the relevance to students' lives, such as family, health, and identity). Frame the activities in ways that show

students how these activities benefit their values. You can do that by sharing personal examples or using the next tool, attribution.

- **Employ attribution** (spell out the causal effects of engagement). Ensure that students know *what* they did that got them that result. Be explicit in the message. "You tried a new strategy on that last problem, and it worked. That's going to help you do well in getting into college next year" (or "help you be a star next year in 3rd grade").
- **Create engaging interactions between individuals** (a sense of affiliation or belonging). Formation of in-groups, partners, teams, or clubs with a strong identity does the trick.
- **Enhance learning context** (give students autonomy and challenge, and foster meaning-making). Support students in developing agency and self-regulation skills to make the magic happen.

These effective elements from the motivation research provide a good backdrop, but what do you do to get started? You can use the seven tools outlined in Figure 5.1 to initiate engagement.

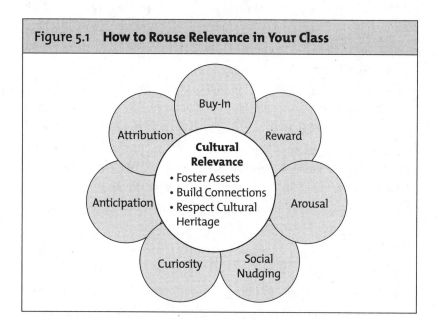

Figure 5.1   How to Rouse Relevance in Your Class

Buy-In

Reward

Attribution

Cultural Relevance
- Foster Assets
- Build Connections
- Respect Cultural Heritage

Anticipation

Arousal

Curiosity

Social Nudging

Seven Ways to Rouse Relevance in Your Class

How do you foster all the good things that rouse relevance for your students? The simple answer is, one step at a time. Notice your response in class when a student rolls their eyes or asks, "Why do we have to do this?" Avoid judging, because that's actually a brilliant student question.

What the student is really saying is, "Tell me why I should invest in this. The relevance is missing." In this case, the student is telling the teacher there's a gap. It is likely that

- The teacher didn't know the student well enough to share the *why*.
- The teacher didn't care enough to do it (low priority).
- The teacher ran out of time (which happens often).
- The teacher simply did not know any better (that's common, too).

The need for relevance (the *why* for doing this task) *runs* your students' brains, beginning very early in their education. You may know of teachers who have been fighting this battle and blaming students for their entire career. The students are the ones who are right. Why *should* they do 25 geometry problems? Unfortunately, many teachers feel like they are in survival mode. The truth is, it helps to understand how your kids' brains really work.

Here's a bias check before we start. The *endowment bias* is when you use an idea, a skill, or an item over time, so you feel ownership of it and value it more than others might (Kahneman, Knetsch, & Thaler, 1991). The thinking is, "I've used my strategy or program for a long time; it must be good. I should stick with it." If you notice this bias, pause and ask yourself, *How often is this strategy or program truly effective*? If you're ready for an upgrade, consider the tools about to be offered. Let's unlock our seven-step "start it up" toolbox.

1. Arousal (Waking Up the Brain)

This is a short-term, physical approach used to influence a student's metabolic state. Rapid, fun movement can bump up dopamine, noradrenaline, and cortisol, all "uppers" and genuine activators for the brain (Meeusen, 2005). You can shift students from lethargy or apathy to excitement with a simple 90-second energizer. Imagine your students running in place, or touching four corners of the room, or circling five tables. Remember, when you put students in charge (each team has an energy leader), other students will usually follow. This can be a priceless setup for the next step. When we are aroused and excited, we are more likely to buy into an idea and say, "Yes!"

2. Buy-In (Getting an Immediate "Hook")

Once students' brains are buzzing after an energizer, jump in with buy-in. This is a short-term tool, like putting bait on a fishhook to "reel in" a student to your next step. A buy-in question to ask your students would be, "How many of you would like to do an experiment with me?" Hook students with curiosity and anticipation; done well, both will become go-to tools. Your buy-in might come from a great, short, effective story that resonates. You'd be surprised at the motivational stories from well-known cultural icons you can find in five minutes of searching online. Get ideas for buy-in at www.jensenlearning.com/equity-resources.

3. Reward (from the Prediction, the Process, or the Completion)

Initially, your brain loves the surprise of the reward. But the cues are remembered, and the next time, the brain gets excited simply over the *anticipation* of the action or treat. You can use this to help your students' brains conjure up an implied or future reward. When the reward is appealing enough, the brain will exert extra resources in pursuit of it (B. Anderson, 2019). Music teachers reward a student's hard work in class with the chance to play in the band or orchestra. Sports coaches reward a student's effort to learn the plays during practice with more playing time in the next game. In martial arts programs, the reward is earning your next belt. What are your rewards?

There are nuances to this. Sometimes a student will experience a reward through the joy and love of learning during the process itself. And intermittent and random rewards are more powerful than constant rewards. But here's a secret: Many times, simply noticing that something was done can reward the brain. Post monthly paper calendars, and have teams put a big *X* on each day they complete *XYZ*. Within a week or two, the urge to keep the string of *X*s going becomes stronger. Motivation becomes filling out the calendar. Fancy that.

4. Attribution (the Reason *Why* Things Turned Out a Certain Way)

Attribution is a reason given to explain the performance of a person on a task (Korn, Rosenblau, Rodriguez Buritica, & Heekeren, 2016). We typically attribute positive outcomes to our own actions but attribute negative outcomes to external factors. Sometimes the attribution bias is simply self-serving (Mezulis, Abramson, Hyde, & Hankin, 2004)— for example, when a teacher says to a student, "Now, what I did for you that got you a better grade was . . ."

Let's alter that. What if, when a teacher notices that a student did well on a test, she instead says, "Hey, your strong effort seems to have helped you get that *A* this time." Or, conversely, "Sorry about that lower grade. Let's make a plan to change things. I know it's been hard for you to concentrate, hasn't it?" or, "Your extra effort was amazing. That hard work may get you into the college you wanted." The core understanding is that rarely does any student link up cause and effect in a good way; every student could use a healthy dose of positive attribution. The effect on student learning is strong enough to use it often.

5. Curiosity (Never Smother It; Foster and Fuel It Daily)

We are naturally curious—our brains are wired to learn and discover the meaning of things (Kidd & Hayden, 2015). Maintaining and encouraging this level of curiosity can be challenging in an educational environment that is purely driven by standards and assessments, but it can be done. It is often as simple as framing a "standard" through questions or experiments that spark students' natural curiosity.

Just asking a question differently can invite curiosity. Curiosity may be used in hundreds of ways in class. There's something about an unopened mental "package" that invites our brains to unwrap it, dive in, and explore.

6. Anticipation (Predicting Outcomes)

Being able to predict and anticipate possible outcomes provides a tremendous survival advantage to any species. The anticipation of malice or threat creates immediate motivation to act (Nelson & Hajcak, 2017). Even better, the anticipation of a reward or pleasure can be a sweet hook for the brain (Dubol et al., 2018).

Some teachers use a calendar, the class clock, or a timer. The secret to using anticipation is timing. Use expressions such as "Coming up next . . ." "In just a few seconds . . ." and "First thing when you're back tomorrow . . ." Remember to follow up on your anticipated promises, or you may lose the hook.

7. Social Nudging (Giving Students Power to Lead Their Peers)

When I started teaching, I got things done in my class by doing most of the work myself. That gave me more control of the situation. It was also a huge mistake. It was exhausting. Over time, I learned to trust my students. I gave them roles such as team leaders or energy organizers. Those roles allowed students to feel some control, build responsibility, and gain social status, too. The student teams were in groups of five, and they became the "starter motor" for most of my transition shifts. Here was the sequence I used for revving up class energy.

For an energizer moment, I simply said to my class, "Oops; we are running late" (or "Time to ramp up our brains," "Let's kick it into high gear," or "Time for a quick energy boost!"). "Turn to your team's energy leader and say, 'You're up!'" Guess what? Once I started the music, the leaders got their teams up and moving! Then I said, "Whatever your team leader does, you do, too." Then I'd play upbeat music like "Follow the Leader" by the Soca Boys.

You can find an easy-to-use list of energizers and a list of buy-in questions and statements at www.jensenlearning.com/equity-resources.

The Framework for Relevance: Culturally Responsive Teaching

The seven tools described here can light a fire, but you need fuel for the journey. These tools can give students much of what they are most hungry for, but their value is primarily for the short term. Add a framework of culturally responsive teaching and give your students greater fuel and acceleration for the long haul. It's what has been missing and what students have been hoping for *all their school years*. This is as blunt as I can be: Give your students a strong *why*, or you may as well stop teaching that content.

Start with understanding your students better, one by one. Without an understanding of your students, you may be perceived as inauthentic, despite your good intentions. What might be most critical to your students for connecting behavioral relevance? Your best relevance connectors are the ABCs. The acronym helps you recall and use strategies that foster **A**ssets, **B**uild connections, and respect **C**ultural heritage.

Foster Assets

Begin finding your students' strengths and tying them into the learning. Deficit thinking is actually your mirror for your own inadequacies. Some teachers spread the blame around when things go wrong. That's the *superiority* bias, when we fail to see our own faults and irrationalities, only those of others (Ames & Kammrath, 2004).

The truth is, we all have assets and liabilities. You got your job based on your strengths, not your faults. Your students will succeed based on their strengths. Discover those strengths and help them flourish.

Build Connections

Your personal connection is crucial. Share your struggles, failures, biases, restarts, and personal favorites (e.g., TV shows, sports teams, food). Students need to know you are real. And, crucially, students do need your support. A large study showed the importance of connectedness (students' perceptions of school support and the number of adults with whom they had positive relationships) when students from poverty made the transition to middle school (Niehaus, Rudasill, & Rakes, 2012). The students did better academically in the transition year when they perceived higher levels of teacher and school support.

Just as important, bring in monthly role models with the same ethnicity as your students as guests. Why? For many students, such an experience is priceless, allowing them to meet a successful, likeable adult of their own ethnicity who is "making it" out in the world and who has the confidence, the skills, and the generosity to share their story. These role models may be found all over the town or city you live in. They can help demonstrate the relevance of school and maybe the subjects you teach. If it's a hassle for one of them to come to the school, offer a Zoom interview.

Respect Cultural Heritage

Share the significant contributions of African American, Latino, Asian, Pacific Islander, and Native American cultures to fields such as literature, music, architecture, politics, biology, physics, history, technology, art, and the law. Some teachers think, "I don't have time for this!" Did you know that many students of color rarely see those who look like them portrayed as leaders, as innovators, as brilliant individuals with powerful voices? It's important to make the time.

There are connections you can make between your students' backgrounds and your class content that will draw them in *like a magnet*. Simply find and respect the "hidden" or stolen past to make the connections. Did you know that there were six Latino MacArthur

Foundation "Genius Grant" winners in 2021 alone (Martinez, 2021), and that African Americans have won more than 70 of these grants (Kaba, 2020)? More important, do your students know? Did you know that African Americans were among the driving forces behind the economic engines in America's history? That includes the building of key structures from the U.S. Capitol to Wall Street. You may know of the Black female mathematicians who played a vital role in NASA during the early years of the U.S. space program, featured in the 2016 movie *Hidden Figures*. Students may never have had a teacher connect these dots for them. Be that teacher. Be curious, and you can find cultural connections in every subject area.

What's the payoff? Students lock in! When pursuing something that is culturally meaningful, the student's brain naturally suppresses distractions and gives laser focus to the relevant task (Stemmann & Freiwald, 2019). When the brain sees a task as engaging, it can lock in for minutes or even hours. Students will spend hours deeply engaged in music, dance, sports, a favorite book, or theater training. This is a fairly long-game approach to learning, and it needs reactivation often. Use it well, and the students who were avoiding learning can become voracious scholars.

Emerging Equity Tool to Embrace

Let's revisit the practice of *de-biasing*. A thousand strategies are useless unless you have begun to clear out the damaging biases that hurt your workplace performance. Remember, you'll want to learn how to run your own brain better every day of your life. That means learning how to manage your stress, regulate your emotions, and outsmart your brain's "box of biases."

Several biases apply to teachers' struggles with implementing culturally responsive teaching. The *authority* bias is giving greater weight to the opinion of an authority figure and assuming that what they say is obviously accurate (Juárez Ramos, 2019). For example, if an administrator, a mentor, or a staff developer told you, "We don't teach culture" or "We don't cater to any ethnicity," would you follow that lead? Could that be a reason why you might be avoiding cultural relevance? A person in a position of power with a high-level title can be wrong just as often as a fresh new face on the staff. Many struggle with these common daily workplace decisions.

The *stereotype* bias says, "*Those* kids shouldn't be getting college prep classes; they're just not ready for such challenging material." During my visits to school campuses around the country, I often see college prep courses offered only to students who have already achieved a high GPA or passed an advanced test (i.e., 5–20 percent of students). What if the kids who have not been offered the college prep classes are bored out of their minds, are being taught a misleading curriculum, or think they don't "deserve" college or their family can't afford it? All are false assumptions.

Finally, the *exceptionalism* bias means that when you hear about another teacher doing something well, you marginalize that teacher and decide there's nothing you can learn from them. Big mistake. Refer to the de-biasing steps in Appendix C to tackle biases that might stand in the way of your culturally responsive teaching.

A Note About Stories

Powerful stories can change your students' lives, as shown in Figure 5.2. Be the person who shares emotional, riveting stories that inspire your kids. Stories do not "take away" from your lesson planning or curriculum. They are a critical and essential part of it. When you value your students' cultures, their lives, and their stories, they will lean in, feel it, and be ready to make changes. That's just part of the power of stories.

A story has a beginning, middle, and end. It may or may not be factual. It could be short or long. A *narrative* is different. It consists of your choice of which events to share, which order to tell them in, and the "spin" you put on them. A narrative might be, "Look at the company she keeps; *you know* . . . birds of a feather." Narratives can

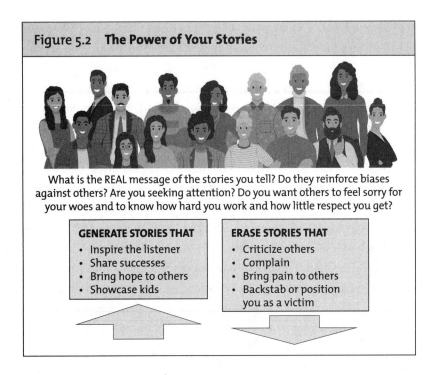

Figure 5.2   **The Power of Your Stories**

What is the REAL message of the stories you tell? Do they reinforce biases against others? Are you seeking attention? Do you want others to feel sorry for your woes and to know how hard you work and how little respect you get?

GENERATE STORIES THAT
- Inspire the listener
- Share successes
- Bring hope to others
- Showcase kids

ERASE STORIES THAT
- Criticize others
- Complain
- Bring pain to others
- Backstab or position you as a victim

extract from the story details, proverbs, descriptions, and accounts. A narrative could be a couple of one-liners. "This school's going nowhere. Haven't you seen what happened when our local plant shut down?" Stories and the narratives that are extracted from them can be used to inspire and engage—or to diminish and erode.

Humans love stories. Our brains seek coherence and meaning through these convenient "thought packages" (Hagoort, 2020). They get remembered and told enough to feel true. But many are a lie. A closed coal mine in rural Appalachia does not erase hope. It is the stories adults tell each other about the scarcity of jobs and the illusion of our diminished human capacity that erase hope. It is not the darkness that ends our options. It is the lack of faith and hope that diminishes our spirit and our will to choose new and better options.

We have stories we share with colleagues. Most stories help us feel better and maintain our identity. They allow us to present ourselves to others in our social group in a culture-confirming way. In addition, we construct stories to demystify any deviations in our behaviors by positioning them to others in a more comprehensible way (Bruner, 2001). You might say to your school grade-level team, "Listen, I know I didn't start that new lesson plan last week like we talked about. But you know me; I'm dependable. I had some emergencies at home. I'll be on it this week, for sure." This allows you to fit right in with your school culture with an intact identity of *dependability*.

One reason many teachers struggle is that they create and share damaging stories and narratives. For instance, maybe a teacher tells the story of a student who was failing and eventually dropped out. Commonly, teachers who struggle with kids from poverty are likely the very same ones who point fingers at the system, the kids, and their school. These struggling teachers can tell you all the reasons why kids can't or won't succeed. But who are they really talking about? Commonly, their opinion is about themselves. And it can become a self-fulfilling prophecy.

Shift away from negative expressions. Instead of saying, "I can't," say "I won't." Instead of "I have to," say "I'm going to." Pay attention to the language you use and get rid of any phrases that imply that you are helpless ("I gotta do this, or else . . ."), or that there is only one possible option. Kids listen to you when you least expect it. When you lack confidence in yourself, your kids stop believing in themselves.

I refer to stories as the living *virtual partners* in a person's mental dialogue or in a school's evolving history. Notice the stories that you and others tell. Learn to foster stories that highlight and foster your students' strengths and increase their ability to succeed. Remember, we all tell stories and construct narratives to make meaning, gain acceptance, and bias our listeners. All I am asking for is awareness.

Chapter in a Nutshell

This chapter told you how you can become more intentional in uplifting your students' success by building relevance into your curriculum and instruction. It described the importance of being aware of your own need for relevance, and the ways relevance can increase student engagement and buy-in. You read about energy tools, motivational strategies, and relevance options. You learned that cultural responsiveness is critical, but there's more.

Finally, this chapter introduced you to the power of your narratives and stories. For many, this is the single most important tool. Begin noticing the types of stories others share and the feeling you're left with. Are they inspirational or demeaning? What about your own stories? Is it time to rewrite them? Check out how to create your own stories at www.jensenlearning.com/equity-resources.

Revisit the Student Questions

Review the student questions from the start of the chapter:

> *"Does this work have real value (relevance), and does my teacher share the why with me every day?"*

> *"Will my teacher keep me connected, captivated, and engaged?"*

> *"Will I be bored and tired or energized and celebrated each day in class?"*

Your students really care about these questions. Do you? If you do care, have you read about enough tools in this chapter to at least begin addressing those questions? If so, just start with one thing. Begin it your next school day. A small step forward is far better than a big step untaken.

Before the Next Chapter

This chapter is about many things, but it ends by discussing the stories we tell. Your next step is to make your stories a source of energy and inspiration. Here's an affirmation to get started: "I share narratives and stories that highlight and foster the strengths that will help my students succeed. I am committed to sharing school and personal narratives that create agency, enthusiasm, and results."

Remind yourself of the power you grow when you tell positive stories about the daily successes that you have with your students, instead of damaging stories (Spilt & Koomen, 2009). Ask yourself, "If the story I am telling were about me as a kid, would I like hearing it?" Finally, your identity might be bolstered: "I'm a champion for equity who connects with the kids who need me most."

Get started with those better stories. Write out three one-paragraph stories, one for each of three narratives you want to reinforce in your brain. One might be about a student who moved from failure to success. Another might be about you—maybe a low-energy to high-energy or low-impact to high-impact story. The third? How about a story that supports the school narrative of "how our school is getting better"? This is the brain practice you need to ensure it becomes automatic. After you create some stories, go tell them! Get ideas for writing out your personal narrative at www.jensenlearning.com/equity-resources.

In your workplace, hearing and repeating stories about "the way things are" becomes the dominant, reinforcing narrative in your own head. For some, the stories in their heads are full of failing, indifferent students who will never change. But brains can change, and people can change. We call uplifting change stories *regenerative,* and they can be life-changing, fueling a positive future (McAdams & Guo, 2015). It's time to make your life a different, and much better, story.

6

....

Scaffold the Scorekeeping

Student Questions
➤ *"Where am I right now?"*
➤ *"Where am I going?"*
➤ *"How do I get there?"*

This chapter is about your process of improving feedback. All of us have both received and given feedback many times in our lives. You'd think we'd be pretty good at it. Yet most students, especially those who are struggling in school, don't receive effective feedback. Despite its well-advertised effect on student learning, quality feedback is in short supply.

Students tell me that their desired end product is rarely described in advance by their teachers. Feedback commonly comes too late, it's rarely actionable, and the students usually don't know what they are supposed to do next. For teachers, this daily moment in which students need quality feedback is often hard to find. On top of those issues, students continually feel dependent, rather than active, in the process. To foster robust learners, you want to empower them to become learning partners with you—partners who can evaluate their own learning. Ultimately you want to foster the agency they need to illuminate, diagnose, decide on, implement, and direct their own learning.

The phrase *scaffold the scorekeeping* reminds you to build layers slowly, as if you are constructing scaffolding. Our topics in this chapter are:

- The Kid Who Understood Dreams, and the Teacher Who Didn't
- Connections to Poverty
- You Go First: Assess Your Progress Daily
- Feedback Is a Culturally Responsive Partnership
- Fostering a Cultural Identity
- Feedback Has Just Three Parts
- Building Equity into the Three Parts of Feedback
- Emerging Equity Tool to Embrace

The Kid Who Understood Dreams, and the Teacher Who Didn't

Fewer than 10 miles inland from the Pacific Ocean sits the city of Salinas, California. It's known as the "Salad Bowl of the World" for its large, vibrant agricultural industry. Monty was born here into an itinerant family. His father trained horses, and, to help his dad, Monty would go from stable to stable, farm to farm, and ranch to ranch, working with horses. As one might guess, his grades in school suffered.

In his high school senior English class, Monty's teacher gave the class the assignment of writing about what they wanted to do after they graduated. Monty decided that he wanted to own a large horse ranch with a beautiful, sprawling home and raise and train thoroughbreds. In his seven-page paper, he even drew a diagram of his 200-acre dream ranch in great detail, showing the location of all the buildings, the stables, and the track. This was his vision, and he put his heart and soul into the paper. Monty was pretty sure he did well; beaming, he turned his paper in. Two days later, he got his paper back with a big *F* on it, with a note telling him to see the teacher after class. Monty was shocked. The boy with the big dream stayed after class and asked the teacher, "Why the *F*?"

His teacher explained to Monty that the costs of developing the career he wanted were huge. The dream he wrote about was "impossible for a boy living in a camper" on the back of a pickup truck. Ultimately, the teacher said, his paper was totally unrealistic—that was why the *F*. The teacher added, "If you'd like to rewrite this paper with a more realistic goal, I will reconsider your grade." Saddened, Monty went home and thought about it long and hard. He also consulted his dad on what to do. His father said he should make up his own mind. Finally, Monty went back to school and turned in the exact same paper. With deep resolve, he said to his teacher, "You can keep the *F*. I'm keeping my dream."

In case you're wondering, Monty Roberts turned out just fine. He was the original horse whisperer. He wrote multiple best-sellers, and a Hollywood movie was made about his life. And today, he enjoys his 200-acre ranch, with a beautiful, sprawling home. He trains horses and their trainers from around the world. Years later, that same teacher who tried to kill his dreams was invited to visit Monty's ranch. He brought his class of 30 kids to camp out on the ranch for a week. When that teacher was leaving, he said tearfully, "Look, Monty, I can tell you this now. During those years I stole a lot of kids' dreams. Fortunately, you had enough gumption not to give up on yours."

By the way, Monty still has that *F* school paper. It is framed, hanging over his fireplace. This story illustrates plenty of biases, but we're going to apply it to feedback. Studies have shown that too much negative feedback can discourage student effort and achievement (Hattie & Timperley, 2007). True, even if you are terrible at giving feedback, a student here or there may have enough identity, resolve, or support to do what Monty did. *But don't count on it.* The odds are seriously against the student.

Debrief Time

This story was about possibly the harshest and worst feedback a student could get. Why the story? It's real, and it's happened to students living in poverty thousands or maybe even millions of times over the years, in different ways. The teacher in the story clearly knew that his students were from low-income families. The low expectations he held for these students shaped the feedback he gave them.

By this stage in the book, you're starting to see how things fit together. Prejudices, expectations, biases, narratives, and identity all play a part in how well students do. Millions of those who came from poverty have, over the years, had to deal with teachers like Monty's. Monty had a strong identity, and he resolved to ignore the biases of the teacher. He was, of course, an exception.

Process this story in writing or with a colleague. Here are your leading questions:

- Did it appear that the teacher clearly presented the parameters and guidelines for the assignment?
- Did the teacher take what he knew about his students into consideration?
- Could you give the teacher a better alternative to the choices he gave Monty?
- Would you guess that teacher has some biases? If so, what were they?

Take a few minutes to write out your responses to the questions or discuss them with a partner.

Connections to Poverty

Some students in Monty's situation would have lashed out, angry at the teacher. But because of solid home support, Monty had the resiliency (Kong, Ma, You, & Xiang, 2018) he needed to persist in school. He did it with even greater resolve for his dream. For low-income students, their self-assigned identity (influenced by parents, peers, and media) is a driving force in decision making. Monty's identity was "I am already a very good horse trainer." There was no way on earth a teacher was going to erase that identity. For Monty, it was about building and growing his existing identity so that he could enjoy the fruits of his developing expertise (horse training).

Schools and teachers are crucial in supporting and enhancing poor immigrant students' cultural identity. School culture, policies, and teaching staff are predictive of children's perceptions of discrimination and their sense of ethnic identity. One study found that successful Mexican immigrant children in a predominantly White school district felt that when the community held positive and important ethnic identities for them, they perceived low overall rates of discrimination. The students' attitudes about school and their academic performance were related to *the characteristics of their schools and teachers* (Brown & Chu, 2012).

Many students growing up in poverty have a tough time seeing themselves becoming highly capable adults with technical or rarified college degrees and well-paying jobs. There are too few role models, and schools have rarely offered a clear path. The solutions? In one program, students first built pathways to college and strong career identities (e.g., "I am a successful and influential Mexican American") even while experiencing money issues and cultural alienation. Second, these mentored students were taught to embrace "giving back" to families, peers, schools, and communities. Ultimately, students grew to become cultural brokers and, later, transformed their institutional cultures (Cooper, Domínguez, Cooper, Higgins, & Lipka, 2018).

For students from poverty going into the medical profession, the secrets to building and maintaining the identity of becoming a doctor were simple. Open discussion time and safe, inclusive pedagogical opportunities to discuss socioeconomic status were key (Conway-Hicks & de Groot, 2019). There were two additional core traits that supported professional identity development: empathy and responsiveness to health inequities.

The key to building lasting success is focusing on creating a new identity first. Students' current behaviors are a reflection of their current identity. What they do now is a mirror image of the type of person they believe they are (either consciously or subconsciously). We need to help students build identity-based habits. Monty had built those in his work with his father. That's why he stayed with his dream.

You Go First: Assess Your Progress Daily

Assessment is as much about the teacher's growth as it is about the student's. Remember, your students want to see you as a role model. When you embrace that role, they get what they wanted—a person who is authentic and a true ally for them.

Even today, I gather feedback daily on both my personal and my professional life. I have created an "identity and narrative story" that I read every day as soon as I open my laptop. Then I pause and ask myself, "How am I doing?" When I miss a day, the narrative helps me foster the resolve to come roaring back, so I avoid missing two days in a row.

My daily story is what reminds me who I am and what I want to become. It has statements about health, emotions, career, relationships, habits, and more. I used to hold grudges for years. My daily reminder of kindness and forgiveness pushed me to grow and release. When I finally decided to let them go, my relationships improved. You can learn how to create your own daily identity and affirmation story at www.jensenlearning.com/equity-resources.

My question for you is, how do you assess yourself daily? What markers do you use in your own life? Many people use a fitness tracker, and others may use a food tracker. It appears that self-tracking the food you eat is one of the best (and cheapest) ways to trigger weight loss (Hollis et al., 2008). Don't want to track? Go ahead, answer that question honestly. Often those who need the change the most refuse to track the food they eat. That's the *ostrich (head in the sand)* bias (Karlsson, Loewenstein, & Seppi, 2009). That's a shame, because the habit of awareness will begin to trigger the eating changes you want. It's your System 1 brain's shortcut biases that are getting in your way.

The bottom line is, unless you self-track your own progress and show your students how it benefits you, you may struggle with supportive student scorekeeping.

Feedback Is a Culturally Responsive Partnership

Students have heard plenty of feedback over the years. What's going to get their ears to perk up, jaws to drop, and hearts to sing? It can happen when a student feels that the teacher "gets" them. That's one small part of providing culturally proficient feedback.

Cultural proficiency begins with you being grounded in your own cultural identity. It's about being an effective thinker and educator in cross-cultural situations. Cultural proficiency is a reflective process for examining your own mindset, assumptions, practices, and relationships. It includes the values and behaviors that enable educators to engage effectively with students, families, and groups that are different from them. This invites you to integrate what you know about yourself personally with your students' cultures to help find the strongest points of connection. Then you're primed to create assessments that include the students' backgrounds and cultures within a relationship of mutual trust. Figure 6.1 identifies ways to implement culturally responsive assessments.

Cultural proficiency also drives your adaptive teaching process based on respecting, understanding, and supporting students culturally and fostering student agency. Once an educator commits to cultural proficiency, the result is cultural responsiveness (S. King, personal communication, Jan. 27, 2021). When your students feel they are supported in ways that include their culture, they feel empowered to become more autonomous, and their motivation rises.

Figure 6.1	**Culturally Responsive Assessments**	

Become a Learner	**Well-Used Examples**
• Begin discussions with your colleagues about what might work better.	• Some write in a conversational format (then it can be edited later).
• Review traditional assessments. Find ways to engage students' cultural knowledge.	• Others talk through topics with a Q&A format.
	• Some may draw.
• Scaffold new learning with what students already know.	• Media mavens find and sequence video clips to show their learning.

As an educator, remember that your long-term goal is to foster student ownership of the assessment process. This takes time, but the rewards are immense, because when there's a way for students to take charge of part of their schooling, it is usually embraced. There are other benefits; eventually you'll have less work for yourself. For students, the sense of control over their destiny contributes to lowered stress levels.

Fostering a Cultural Identity

Because labels play an important part in our thinking, as a first step in empowering students to take charge of their own assessment, you might want to help them become more aware of the identities they claim. What are the identities of your students? What are the labels you hear? The long list of pejoratives includes descriptors such as *minority kids, project kids, urban kids, trailer-park kids, disadvantaged kids, at-risk kids, socioeconomically disadvantaged kids,* and *marginalized kids.* What are the images or associations you have with those terms? Personally, I am tired of the labels. Can you create something more uplifting and inspirational?

I have conducted surveys in high-poverty, high-performing schools and found that staff members have typically been purposeful about shifting the identity of their students. Some refer to their kids as *leaders*, or *students of promise*, or *scholars*. Others use phrases like *learners*, *sages*, or *academics*. The identity you use reflects the level of your hope for your students. I struggle with the ideal way to label our students. Whatever phrase you want to use, run it by your colleagues or students and get some reaction to it. You might come up with an even better way for us to identify our students as the inspiration for the next generation.

Another part of your work in class is helping your students understand how their own narrow identities can keep them from being a roaring success in school. May I suggest you also give them a strong *why* for the goal of having a stronger class identity (e.g., respect, better grades, less trouble)? The word *identity* can be a bit heavy, like a winter coat. That can lead students to feel stuck about having a new identity, but here's a strategy you can use.

Start by asking students to write down the many "hats" they wear in school and at home. Remind students that this will not be graded, and it will be kept anonymous. Give them some starter ideas, all statements that start with the phrase "I am." You might post three to five of your own "hats you wear" and share some "identity hats" other students have come up with:

- "I am *an athlete* who gets better every year."
- "I am *a big brother* who helps my siblings."
- "I am *a student* who is trying to do well in school."

Once the students have written down some "hats" as identities, give them some prompts they can use to add a few more:

- Who am I to others in the neighborhood?
- To a really good friend, who am I?
- In class, what temporary identity would help me succeed?

Once students start to realize that identities can shift depending on context or situation, it becomes safer to have a stronger classroom "label." Suggest to them ideas such as *leaders, academics,* or *champions.* In specific subject areas, use labels that match up. The student becomes, for a short time each day, *a mathematician, geographer, historian,* or *writer.* One of the names might stick, or you might find that your students invent one they like more. One of the most amazing English teachers I know of asked every student, in the first week of the semester, to pick an author that they would like to emulate. All semester, the teacher would ask that student, "Well, what would your author role model do in this situation?"

My question is about *your* identity. Are you just a teacher, or are you *an equity builder, a change agent, a high-energy community builder,* or *an engaging, equitable teacher and learner?* The answer is, "What are you trying to do *at the moment?*" Again, you'll need multiple "hats" to wear as you move through your workweek. For the moment, maybe your identity is, "I am *a highly engaging and equitable teacher."* Then you can incrementally foster newer identities that both you and the students want. You can foster your students' identity of, "I am *an engaged student* who loves to do active, relevant learning." How? Use three or more micro-steps.

First, invite students to share their identities (then give them a standing ovation). Second, have students put their identities into the team statement that each learning team reads out loud every day. Third, after a small learning success, ask students to turn to their neighbor and say, "Yes, you *are* a [identity]!" Then repeat that in various forms—have students write it, affirm it within a team, and repeat it as a whole class. Inside a month, it will start to take hold. Identities take time, but once established, they can be powerful drivers of behavior.

Remember that as you and your students claim your identities, culture is never an add-on. Culture is an essential property of your being. You can become proficient in assessing students who are different from you through relationships. Only then is quality feedback possible. Without mutual respect and cultural understanding, all you're doing is imposing your own culture on another. That's unlikely to turn out well. When you're ready to get to a high level of culturally responsive feedback, take the time to learn about your students. Watch, listen, and ask. There's no embarrassment in being curious. Zaretta Hammond's work has been transformative for me in this process; for a deeper dive, you may enjoy her book *Culturally Responsive Teaching and the Brain* (2015).

Feedback Has Just Three Parts

Ultimately, the student questions at the beginning of this chapter (*"Where am I right now?" "Where am I going?" "How do I get there?"*) come down to just three things: awareness (both yours and the students'), expectations, and growth. High-quality educational assessments help students answer these questions.

Dylan Wiliam is a world leader in classroom assessment and has done the heavy lifting of research for many of us. His research and resource books have changed lives for countless teachers. We're going to weave his work into our solutions and reveal why it is so appropriate for students from poverty (Wiliam & Thompson, 2008). Wiliam's work has helped teachers shift from assessment *of* learning to assessment *for* learning. This suggests two things: (1) the teacher becomes more of a partner with students in the learning, and (2) each student becomes more of a partner in assessing themselves for better learning.

Before we jump into the three parts of feedback and their relationship with equity, let's review what we already know about assessment. The effect size is the impact on student learning over a year's time; that's one of many ways to measure student gains. There's a strong effect from feedback in general, but the effect is greater on the three questions students care about (Hattie & Timperley, 2007). Also, when using specificity (focus on the strategy taken, effort given, or an attitude), the effects are robust (Wisniewski, Zierer, & Hattie, 2020).

Building Equity into the Three Parts of Feedback

You could guess that taking on assessment as three parts is a bit audacious. Yes and no; each part is simple. Implement small steps, one at a time, and within a few weeks you'll see a remarkable difference in classroom behaviors. Figure 6.2 gives an overview of the three parts.

1. Awareness

Your mindset should focus on being aware of your students' thoughts. More, fresh, and less-biased eyes will reveal the truth. Students are wondering, "Where am I right now? Does my teacher take me seriously?" Your students wonder how they will be assessed, so ensure that you spell out the feedback process and let them know that assessments will be fair and equitable. Enable your students to gather much of this information for themselves. That can happen with a journal, a tablet, or work the student team posts online. Consider the following equitable assessment tools to foster awareness:

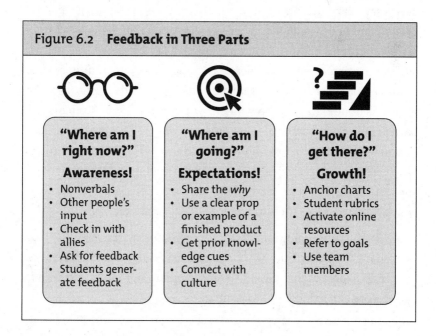

Figure 6.2   **Feedback in Three Parts**

"Where am I right now?"	"Where am I going?"	"How do I get there?"
Awareness!	**Expectations!**	**Growth!**
• Nonverbals • Other people's input • Check in with allies • Ask for feedback • Students generate feedback	• Share the *why* • Use a clear prop or example of a finished product • Get prior knowledge cues • Connect with culture	• Anchor charts • Student rubrics • Activate online resources • Refer to goals • Use team members

- Pay close attention to nonverbals (eyes, facial expressions, body language). These cues give you nearly instant feedback on student buy-in to the learning.
- Use input from others. By looking for input from several sources each day, over a week's time you may get 10–15 bits of valuable information. An example? Do a gallery walk to see the posted work of each of the class's learning teams.
- Every day, do a check-in at the door when students arrive. "Hi, I see you look a bit low on energy, what's going on?" Also consider formatting your own version of an Individualized Education Program (IEP) for each student.
- Ask students to give you their own feedback—verbally, with a note, in an exit pass, or any other way to keep you in the loop.

2. Expectations

Your mindset should be to set higher expectations for every student, every day, with joy and support for their life. Is the student's culture part of, and being included in, this conversation? Students ask, "Does my teacher hold high expectations for me? Do I have a clear picture and description of what excellence is?" Show students multiple, clear examples of finished work. Explain what is considered proficiency, what was done right, and how much "wiggle room" your students will have to do it their way. Give them different ways to be amazing in addition to taking a typical test; allow them to show their learning through other assessment methods, such as giving a demonstration, writing and delivering a speech, or making a mural. Consider the following equitable assessment tools to foster high expectations:

- Clarify your intentions with the assignment. Ensure that you share the *why* of the work and the assessments and share your high expectations. Give students tangible relevance and buy-in before expecting them to jump in.

- Be sure to do a prior learning discovery to check out what they already know. This can happen in many ways. For instance, you could have students do a quick-write or take a brief quiz on the topic, provide a partially completed graphic organizer and have them complete it, or just call on students randomly to assess their prior knowledge.
- Break the learning and assessment into stages. Start at the beginning and chunk it down so students can see that it is doable. In some cases, you'll want to give a clear description and show and tell for just the first stage of the learning assignment. Then add the descriptors as the students are ready for them. Communicate early information to students using metaphors, perhaps from music or movies that tie into student culture.
- Ensure that you have and use culturally relevant learning materials. Sometimes if the "perfect text" is unavailable, you can find one for a lower grade level and use that as a review to prep for the start of the subject.
- Share evidence of past students. Show your scholars how past students have gone on to lead amazing lives. One 5th grade teacher in a high-poverty school in South Los Angeles did just that. He put up college banners around his room. But that was just a part of the inspiration. The best part was that he wrote, underneath each banner, the names of the students *from his class* who had gone to that college or university.

3. Growth

Your mindset should focus on what students need for growth: the *why*, a clear path, and support. Are you including the culture of the student in this conversation? Different cultures may have different signals for growth. "Does my teacher know *how* I can get better? Can I grow enough so that I'm at or above grade level?" Enable your students to gather much of this key data for themselves. Consider the following equitable assessment tools to foster growth:

- Empower students to become increasingly autonomous in self-assessments by posting an anchor chart of seven prime ways to self-assess (available at www.jensenlearning.com/equity-resources). Your students may be able to contribute to the chart early on.
- Provide methods and tools for students to receive actionable feedback immediately. Students can get feedback from a rubric, a self-quiz, or a partner, or you can provide display tools for both individuals and their teams. Have students create the quiz and a grading guide for it. Or have students grade one another to give weekly feedback.
- Activate students to notice, explain, encourage, and be an instructional resource for a partner so that the two of them can grow together. Collaboration will help students see and hear where they are.
- Student team leaders can use the deep-dive questions that you or your students create and practice asking them with the members of their learning team.

Emerging Equity Tool to Embrace

Seventy-five years ago, many female teachers had two identities at the same time: "I am a mother" and "I am a teacher." Mothers never quit being mothers, and teachers would teach until they retired. But in large societies, the signals of integration into each new culture require different identities (Smaldino, 2019). Why are identities so critical?

Identities are critical because they define the boundaries of not just who you are, but *what you believe* and *what you will do*. Someone who identifies as an *empathetic teacher* will listen to a student who has problems at home and needs to talk. A teacher whose identity is "I create a *student-centered classroom*" will need to embrace student decision making. Unless you purposefully choose the specific change or area in which to broaden your identity, change will be difficult (Lewis, 2014). In my own professional development sessions, I embed and broaden my audience members' identities because it makes it easier for them to choose to make changes to expand their roles (Steinert, O'Sullivan, & Irby, 2019).

I struggled when I started teaching. Why? My identity was, "I am an excellent, engaging teacher." That might sound good, but it left gaping holes in my teaching. Although I did many things right, I also ignored many critical issues. For example, I was blind to the whole domain of relationship building. I failed to learn about and discover a more culturally responsive mindset and skill set. It took several kind and bold individuals to catch my attention and talk candidly with me. I had just never realized how ignorant I was (and still am). Today, I think I wear 8 to 10 identity "hats" on a weekly basis. As a professional developer, I am still working on better identities.

Maybe you've been considering a slightly different identity at school. Your new identity choice just for this chapter might be one of the following: "I focus on high expectations for my students. I am a *cultural collaborator* with students about their learning." Or "I track growth steps and help my class make progress to better design the next steps."

Chapter in a Nutshell

The title *Scaffold the Scorekeeping* reminds you to layer things slowly, as if you are building a scaffold. Regardless of how you spin it, the data are clear. Based on my own visits to schools, most students and staff in Title I schools struggle. You can be different. By focusing on students' awareness, growth, and expectations for their own assessment, you can be a *big* part of the solution at your school.

Revisit the Student Questions

Let's begin with reviewing the student questions from the start of the chapter:

> ➢ *"Where am I right now?"*

> ➢ *"Where am I going?"*

> ➢ *"How do I get there?"*

This chapter suggested equitable assessment tools to answer each of these questions. Which might be valuable for you?

Before the Next Chapter

What is your identity? The truth is, you already wear many hats. Start the process of asking yourself, "Which hats would I like to wear, and when?" For example, when I become aware of a bias of mine, my hat might be, "I am a change agent who continuously reflects on biases and is committed to debunking them." After all, are you someone who is committed to debunking harmful biases? Or are you going to stick with your existing identity and simply go through the motions of de-biasing? For a big list of possible equity identities, check out www.jensen learning.com/equity-resources.

In this book, there are many ways you can choose to grow. They include strong intention, growth, antibias and antifragility mindsets, positive stories, diverse identities, brain-building skill sets, social support, and self-care. Maybe you've put off changes so far. Maybe you've already tried to negotiate with yourself: "Is there an easier way to do this?" Different, yes; easier, no.

Would you make changes with just a habit app? Maybe—there are actually hundreds of them, and I have tried many. Several with strong published evidence supporting their efficacy are Noom.com, Woopmylife.org, and Beeminder.com. If you're a constant tech user, check out each, pick one, and start today to form new habits and track your behaviors.

For this chapter, let's expand the types of "hats" (identities) you wear daily. You'll want to consider at least three different new identities. Choose the three new ones and list them like this:

1. Identity #1: _____
2. Identity #2: _____
3. Identity #3: _____

Once you have them ready to go, your assignment is to read them daily for a week. You're just trying on some new mental "clothes," so be gentle with your observations. Repetition is the key. No judgment. Get this done, and I'll see you in the next chapter.

7

From Discipline to Coaching

Student Questions

➢ *"Does my teacher understand where I'm coming from? Will my teacher keep class culturally responsive, fair, and just?"*

➢ *"Can my teacher use whole-class student awareness to create a positive climate?"*

This chapter is about more learning and less friction. It's about doing your work with empathy and using coaching to help your class flow smoothly. Doing that may require fostering novel attitudes and new skills. I'm simply inviting you to switch your perspective from doing the "dirty work" of fixing and punishing kids to coaching them with empathy and empowerment. The topics explored are:

- Five Headwinds: What Were the Chances for Success?
- Connections to Poverty
- You Go First: Self-Regulate Your Stress
- Moving from Blame to Empathy
- Foster Better Classroom Environments with Three Steps
- Emerging Equity Tools to Embrace

In this chapter, you'll read about the importance of being receptive to learning more about yourself and others, especially others who are different from you. This chapter also reminds you that if you want to be an amazing teacher, you'll need to manage your own stress better. Lower stress and a better class go hand in hand. You can start to love your class every day. Before we jump into the details, let's check into a teacher's challenge in a Colorado classroom.

Five Headwinds: What Were the Chances for Success?

As a child, Alonzo faced five headwinds: racism, having a disability, having no father at home, growing up poor, and attending systemically ineffective schools. Alonzo is a Black male who experienced severe brain damage from a fall as a child. His IQ was estimated to be 40–50. In school, he could not read, write, or do math, and he was unable to tie his shoes or eat on his own. There was a massive gap between the special services that Alonzo needed and what he received.

How would you treat Alonzo if he were your student? Would you be hopeful about his future? Go ahead and make a guess about how Alonzo turned out as an adult:

   a. He later learned to read exceptionally well.
   b. He overcame racism, but not his disabilities.
   c. He can now feed and dress himself.
   d. He became a world-famous math savant.
   e. Other

You have likely seen many students with disabilities, so the natural cognitive bias would be to expect very little from Alonzo. Maybe you'd think it would be painful for you to expect more. Most teachers would outwardly say, "I'll never give up on him," but would inwardly feel that the odds were against him. You and I have learned in this book that outward statements often fail to match up with actions.

Alonzo's mom said that after his fall and the resulting head trauma at age 3, he started to work with his hands. In school, he would sit silently in the back of the classroom, molding bits of wax or clay into tiny animals. His teachers perceived this as mind-wandering defiance, and they felt disrespected. They would take the clay away from him, hoping he would pay attention more. Instead, he began scraping bits of pliable tar from the pavement around his school. He used the tar and wax to work on molding sculptures at home.

The correct answer among the multiple choices above is "Other." Today, in his 60s, Alonzo Clemons is still learning delayed. He doesn't read, write, or do math. But over time, his work with animal shapes evolved from amateurish to spectacular. He trained his brain to develop an uncanny ability to visualize and sculpt animals in exquisite, lifelike detail. He has been a world-renowned sculptor for decades whose works have sold for upwards of $50,000. He has competed and medaled in the Special Olympics, and he appeared on *60 Minutes* and Discovery Channel's World of Wonder. He currently works with both kids and adults at the YMCA of Northern Colorado, and his work is available at www.alonzoclemons.com. So much for the bias of low expectations for a severely disabled, academically disengaged boy of color who grew up in poverty.

Debrief Time

Let's pause so you can process your response to this story with an equity mindset. Debrief Alonzo's classroom behaviors and the challenges his teachers faced. What would you have done, in the moment, if he had walked into your class? How would you have reacted to his "misbehavior" of "playing" with clay in class? How could you have treated him to maximize equity? Has your brain already marginalized this student as *different, exceptional, creative,* or *courageous*?

Maybe you already said to yourself, "Oh, I would have seen the potential in his obsession with creating clay figures; I would have believed in him." Seriously? Believed in him to do what? That's a *hindsight* bias ("I knew it all along"), the tendency to see past events as predictable after you hear the real outcome (Pohl, 2004). It takes work to notice our biases, doesn't it? Go ahead and formulate your responses in writing or in discussion with a partner.

Connections to Poverty

For people living in poverty, life is often full of threat and deprivation. If there's been exposure to acute stress or chronic stress, the brain adapts as it learns from experience. Many low-income people have had incidents triggering acute or chronic stressors, which can lead to behavioral changes. Some common changes are states of anger, hyper-vigilance, and reactive decision making (Sripada, Swain, Evans, Welsh, & Liberzon, 2014). Evidence suggests that elevated stress levels play a big role in impulsivity (Roos et al., 2017). That student will get in a teacher's face and never give an inch in a heated moment. Teachers who are ignorant will do a power play to show who's boss. That's a terrible idea; the kid has a stress disorder and is unlikely to stand down. You'll learn what to do instead later in this chapter.

You may also have students from poverty in your class who appear lazy. This *learned helplessness* is a stress disorder first identified as "giving up" (Maier & Seligman, 2016). With exposure to either trauma or chronic stress, the brain changes (Evans et al., 2016; White et al., 2019). Bad things have happened in the past, and the brain gives you a simple way to avoid pain: Just quit caring. This apathy begins with an original event where the ability to affect the circumstances are overwhelmingly low. This is what school feels like for many students. The student gives up, believing that any effort will be unlikely to end well (Buzzai, Sorrenti, Tripiciano, Orecchio, & Filippello, 2020). You'll learn what changes to make to overcome learned helplessness later in this chapter.

Additionally, when students arrive at school with stress disorders (which can lead to behaviors perceived as violent tendencies), some unknowing leaders decide that bringing more police on campus is the solution. Statistically, the presence of school police leads to disproportionate harm to students of color and students with disabilities:

- During the 2015–2016 school year, Black students represented 15 percent of overall student enrollment—but 31 percent of students who were referred to law enforcement or arrested.

- During the 2015–16 school year, students with disabilities represented 12 percent of overall student enrollment—but 28 percent of students referred to law enforcement or arrested. (U.S. Department of Education Office for Civil Rights, 2018)

When I see these numbers, something seems way off. And when we home in on suspension rates, things don't get better:

- Students with disabilities represented 12 percent of overall student enrollment—but 26 percent of students who received an out-of-school suspension.
- Black male students represented 8 percent of overall student enrollment—but 25 percent of students who received an out-of-school suspension.
- Black female students represented 8 percent of overall student enrollment—but 14 percent of students who received an out-of-school suspension. (U.S. Department of Education Office for Civil Rights, 2018)

These suspension data suggest that many youths from poverty are bringing stress disorders to your classroom (Evans, Gonnella, Marcynyszyn, Gentile, & Salpekar, 2005). The disorders can show up as impulsivity, back talk, defiance, and disrespect. In fact, most complaints about kids *are a result of teachers misreading genuine stress disorders.* I also see *stereotype* biases with little sense of responsibility ("It's their fault!"). Yet the evidence tells us that we as educators have something to do with those behaviors (Losen & Martinez, 2013). When there is implicit racial bias, people feel less empathetic to the situations of others, and teachers are less likely to take positive coaching action (Forgiarini, Gallucci, & Maravita, 2011).

Commonly, the largest discipline gaps between Black and White students occur for reasons that teachers describe as "defiance," "disrespect," and "uncooperative behavior" (Fabelo et al., 2011; Losen & Martinez, 2013). It is not a coincidence that White teachers often report less warmth in their relationships with Black students compared with White students (Hughes, 2011).

Many White teachers assign the emotions of defiance and anger to Black people and perpetuate the stereotype that Black people are "angry all the time." Here's a different understanding. The teacher lacks an intention to form a relationship; the teacher's biases are triggered; the instruction is unresponsive to the student's culture; the teacher mismanages the student's stress responses; the student feels judged, disrespected, and excluded. Friction flares up, and the teacher wonders, "Where did all that anger come from?"

A common source of justifiable anger is *moral anger*. Moral anger is an aroused emotional state emerging from an appraisal of a violation of moral standards—a wrong that affects not just oneself, but also others. It reflects the need for addressing injustice and stems from a belief in values and rules associated with a civil society (Lindebaum & Geddes, 2016). The angered person demands the corrective behavior needed to improve the social condition, often at a significant personal risk. You'll often see feelings of moral anger expressed at demonstrations. Like protesters on the street, students at school are often acting out with their bodies, their emotions, and their voices: "Pay attention to who we are and respect our culture!"

You Go First: Self-Regulate Your Stress

The evidence suggests that elevated stress levels, in both teachers and students, play an interactive role in student behaviors. When you're faced in real time with a student misbehaving, *your stress* exacerbates the situation. As long as you ignore your own stress, you will likely be miserable. But breaking the interactive stress cycle gets tricky.

Students who grow up in poverty are more likely to have chronic stress, too (Evans & Kim, 2012; Evans, Li, & Whipple, 2013). So, what do many Title I teachers do? They often show up at work stressed themselves. *Stress plus stress is a recipe for a mess!* Your impact on your students is now toxic. Stress is contagious and can move in both directions, from students to you and vice versa (Dimitroff et al., 2017). Your stress hurts you, and their stress hurts them, and together it's like throwing gasoline on a fire (as seen in Figure 7.1).

You can start managing your stress better. Stress is generated by the perception of loss of control from an aversive person or situation that you deem relevant. That's a mouthful; but here are tools that can lower your stress. Simply select one of these:

- Write your stressor down for later; offload it from your brain to a list on paper or a tablet/laptop to reduce its relevance to you.
- Use the one-week rule; if this stressor won't matter a week from now, make it less relevant and stop stressing over it.
- Redirect your attention elsewhere and move on to something different.
- Reframe the experience by turning it into a positive or at least a lesson.
- Refocus; go burn off energy with play, a walk, or a workout.
- Practice mindfulness or meditation.
- Go talk it over with a friend; get or give hugs.

Figure 7.1   Stress + Stress = A Mess

Ownership

- Stress is the mismatch between what is needed for the situation and the strength of your coping tools.
- Stressed teachers and stressed students often make for a mess.
- No one else stresses you out; *you* stress you out.
- Your stress is your own responsibility; take charge.

And reduce the stress level in your classroom by starting with one of these:

- Give greater control to students; it's very empowering for them and it lowers their stress.
- Provide more small choices daily (and often) within each class.
- Give students roles in class (leaders, energizers, summarizers, etc.).
- Hold a weekly open mic for voices to be heard.

To get one of these habits started, set up a time, trigger, behavior, and reward. Chapter 9 provides a template you can use. For greater guidance on stress management, go to www.jensenlearning.com/equity-resources and download "15 Ways to De-Stress."

Let's start to tie all this together. Teachers bring stress to school. Students bring stress to school. Kids may experience frustrations, especially in an unresponsive class. Sparks fly. Moral anger is expressed. Teachers misinterpret it as defiant and disrespectful. A teacher decides she's had enough and takes the shortcut—suspension. But every suspension increases the likelihood of a kid dropping out.

Until you and hopefully your whole school's staff see the need for social justice that de-escalates conflict, problems will persist. Your long game is to coach students into becoming a healthier part of the school community. That's another opportunity for equity and cultural responsiveness. If your whole school is not yet ready, at least you can start in your own classroom today.

Moving from Blame to Empathy

For many teachers, the "behavior problem" is all about *those kids*. First of all, remember that they are *our kids*. The kids in your class are the ones who will one day be drawing your blood at a hospital, making decisions in public office, or writing the code you'll be using in a software update. Second, maybe the "behavior problem" label is all wrong. If you've ever had an aquarium or even a fishbowl, you know how sensitive fish are to their environment. It's the same way for students in class. Things you are comfortable with *may be toxic to certain kids.* Focus on the student *behind* and *underneath* the behaviors. Remember, the behaviors are the surface issues.

The dynamics of the student, the teacher, and the culture are inseparable. Please, stop the finger pointing. I am now asking you to go down a new path. It is hard, but it's doable and worthwhile. First, build the relationships. Marzano, Marzano, and Pickering (2003) found that teachers who had strong, quality relationships with their students had almost one-third fewer discipline problems and rule violations over a year's time compared with teachers who had weaker relationships with their students. Second, remember that the starting point is doing your work *with empathy.* Stop paying attention to the behaviors; focus on understanding the student's personal challenges. Partner with the student to figure out solutions together. Finally, get your own stress under control with healthy self-management.

Foster Better Classroom Environments with Three Steps

Let's examine a three-step process for reducing classroom discipline issues (shown in Figure 7.2). Over the long haul, if you follow these steps, your students will gain respect for you and for themselves, self-regulation skills, and a sense of agency. The subtitles seem simple enough: *prevention, intervention,* and *follow-up.* But of course, each requires a bit of unpacking.

1. Prevention

Prevention begins with your taking ownership of what goes on in your classroom. You have more to do with your student behavior disruptions than you think you do. Many teachers simply lack the know-how to deal with a student who struggles with behavior in class. More important, they don't recognize how their own stress levels, situational

Figure 7.2   **Three Steps for Better Behaviors**

Prevention	Intervention	Follow-Up
Learn the 7 Action Steps	Learn the 7 Action Steps	Learn the 7 Action Steps

blindness, and lack of training are all linked to student behaviors. That's the starting point. Be a learner. Be proactive. Learn about yourself and your students.

Let's piece together the impact of prior stress in a classroom. *Allostasis* (versus *homeostasis*) is the brain's survival response to chronic or acute stress. It is an altered set point that creates a new normal for students. In class, stressed students will likely be hypervigilant (assertive, in your face) or hyporesponsive (disengaged). Students with either of these two stress disorders have had traumatic events or chronic uncertainty in their past. They have experienced loss.

The hypervigilant student's brain may be saying, "Next time you feel challenged, fight for your rights and you may prevent a loss." *The student who talks back to you is fighting for their life.* It's essential that you give that student control and ensure that they feel heard. For the other type of stress disorder, the hyporesponsive student, the strategy is different. This student's brain may be saying, "You cared before, and it resulted in a loss. Just quit caring, and you won't get hurt." This condition requires greater empathy and relationship building. First, take on the student's perspective and refrain from judgment. Tell the student you can feel that "something's not right," but never try to guess the student's emotion. If you're wrong, you create a disconnect.

Remember the filters of stress, bias, racism, classism, and sexism. Keep your ears and eyes open for a deeper daily discovery. Remind yourself—you can be better than before. Figure 7.3 shows that a great starting place is giving students more control, which can help lower stress. In fact, the student's (and your) perception of actionable control is the single biggest factor in reducing stress (Maier & Watkins, 2010).

To build a class where students feel ownership, use these culture-building strategies:

- Create an inclusive classroom culture that includes instead of excludes.
- Ensure that students have their voices heard so those voices are never bottled up for an explosive episode. Encourage students to express their voices in open discussion; in a monthly letter to the teacher; on Post-It Thursday; and via team projects, video displays, or writing projects.

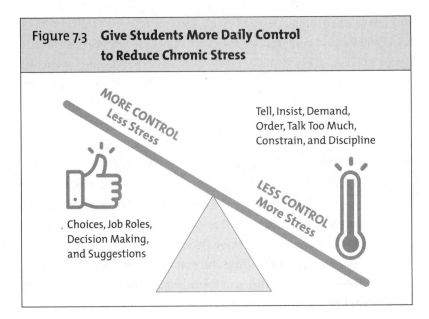

Figure 7.3   Give Students More Daily Control to Reduce Chronic Stress

MORE CONTROL
Less Stress

Tell, Insist, Demand, Order, Talk Too Much, Constrain, and Discipline

LESS CONTROL
More Stress

Choices, Job Roles, Decision Making, and Suggestions

- Teach students the critical social and emotional skills so they know how to respond to adverse situations. Then role-play to ensure the skills are in place. Build partnership with a class pact or class creed that everyone can get behind.

Once both you and your students have accepted ownership of your behaviors, you can get started on prevention by looking at mindset and evidence. Then you'll be ready to take the seven action steps.

Mindset. "I love my class and prepare well. My misbehavior incidents will be few and far between. When they happen, they'll be a learning experience for me. I create the weather in the class, so if it's raining, I will own it, listen, and bring out the sunshine. I am a cultural partner in the classroom behaviors process. I am here to foster assets via communication, a class pact, and mutual respect."

Evidence. De-bias yourself. *Attribution bias* is a predisposition to a point of view. For example, a teacher or an administrator could assume that the reason a student is tardy is because she does not care. That's an assumption, not evidence. Maybe the student had to stay at home to babysit until her aunt showed up . . . late. Or maybe the student has PTSD and a small incident triggered a reaction, and the student was taking enough time to calm down before coming to class (Malle, 2011). Can you see how your own biases can cloud perception?

Keep in mind the effectiveness of de-stressing tools, such as slower movements, stretching, purposeful breathing, and tense-and-release movements. These are highly valuable and very powerful. Stress can also be reduced before a cognitive activity with faster movements, such as walking, mimicking others' movements, dancing, running in place, or circling tables. The positive effect size of intermittent movement is sky-high at 1.51; that shows it is solid gold (Erwin, Fedewa, Beighle, & Ahn, 2012). Make these energizing movements a habit by modeling the options for a week, and then empowering students to do them. Student energizer leaders make your job easier, and students enjoy the leadership.

In older students, higher-intensity activities improve health and cognitive functioning (Jeon & Ha, 2017). A large study was done with nearly 1,500 students from three low-income schools. Through scientific monitoring systems, students' on-task behavior was tracked prior to initiating a long-term physical activity program. After 6 weeks of regular physical activity, the chance of a classroom reaching 80 percent of on-task behavior was *7 times greater than prior to the exercise program.* After 12 weeks, the likelihood of on-task behavior had jumped to *28 times greater than before the exercise program* (Burns, Brusseau, Fu, Myrer, & Hannon, 2016). Teachers who complain that they don't have time for energizers are not just "missing the boat"; they're missing a whole ocean of opportunity.

Be trauma-informed. Attend to the practices, policies, and aspects of the culture that often traumatize children at school. Intervention efforts with students should target not only attachment security but also emotional competence skills (Kidwell et al., 2010). Many students have their day filled with microaggressions, bullying, insults, and trauma. Then, at the end of the day, they go home and get more (Nadal, 2018).

Teach students how to respond in class. Many students, when "called out" over something, will respond in ways that teachers perceive as disrespectful. But these students may have no idea what the teacher *wants them to do.* The reality is, there can be a *lot* going on, and one of the issues might be a lack of life skills. Post and practice some ways to be respectful of others in class.

You will never get your students to respond the way you think they should respond unless *you teach them the preferred emotional responses.* These responses include empathy, forgiveness, gratitude, and fairness. Teach one a month. Be a role model for a great attitude. Read and discuss short stories with great-attitude characters. Ask students to perform skits showing how they would act before and after learning the attitudes. Over time, your class will begin to work better. You must earn your students' respect by meeting them where they are and teaching them what they need. That's equity.

Action Steps

1. Foster relationships within your class as a cultural community (see Chapter 4). When every student is in the in-group, the group will often manage the behaviors. Always start with quick (two- to three-minute) team-building routines.

2. Cultivate a sense of safety in your class in-group and maintain a strong awareness of your students' emotional states. Check in often during class.

3. Establish simple norms that every student knows. Create a class pact or set of approved norms with the class.

4. Appreciate, state, and reinforce the norms daily. Your in-group will do much of the heavy lifting for you.

5. Teach students how to behave. Many students don't know your expectations. Make it a daily process to foster kindness, gratitude, hope, empathy, and forgiveness.

6. Engage often, shift how you do things, and redirect attention to keep focus. Be on top of the energy levels; use energizers every 10–20 minutes.

7. Give more control in choices, jobs, and small habits. Also teach students how to manage stress and anger with self-control.

2. Intervention

Intervention that works requires making choices, planning, and taking action. Effective intervention is about *your choices up front.*

Engage students culturally with the point of view that respects their culture as spoken by the student. Students recognize when a teacher is aware of their culture and behavior. When asked, students describe this teacher as "aware of what's going on" or "having eyes in the back of their head." This is the situational awareness it takes to be good at your job. Any time you get blindsided by a student behavior, use it as feedback to pay broad, sweeping attention to all your students, every day. Let's look at three intervention responses *to avoid:*

- *Punishment model.* Stop trying to get even or get revenge for how you believe you have been insulted, put down, or hurt. Always ask, "How do I help this student develop the behaviors they will need to succeed?"
- *Power model.* Stop trying to show who's the boss. Your need for power is about *your* control insecurities. Your students *hate* being controlled. Be an ally, not a dictator. Help students gain more control, not less.
- *"Taking it personally" model.* Stop making it all about you! Can you see the world from the student's point of view? Focus on helping students figure out how to survive in a healthier way.

Mindset. "My students are partners with me in the pact, the process, and the community. I respect each and every student and hold high expectations for all."

You know that behavior events can hurt everyone, so you ensure that students have a way to communicate without being disruptive. Use time for open questions, read from your suggestion box, and do a "Teach Me Friday" where you ask for verbal feedback on your teaching, once a week. Your class is always a partnership with you, the students, the class pact or creed, and the context each day. Live daily with empathy.

Evidence. Many school leaders must make choices along the lines of "We can afford this, but not that." The data on school suspensions (Balfanz, Byrnes, & Fox, 2015; Wallace, Goodkind, Wallace, & Bachman, 2008) suggest that some school leaders think suspending kids is cheaper than providing professional development on cultural responsiveness or stress reduction. Let's examine the numbers in light of our cultural responsiveness mindsets:

- 1.7 million students were in schools with cops but no counselors.
- 3 million students were in schools with cops but no nurses.
- 6 million students were in schools with cops but no school psychologists.
- 10 million students were in schools with cops but no social workers. (U.S. Department of Education Office for Civil Rights, 2018)

Although some school leaders believe that putting police on campus will make their school "work better," maybe that's a euphemism for "having more control over our students." Remember, stress is about our need for control over a potentially aversive situation or person. Your students of color experience countless microaggressions daily, which includes being judged by skin color, spoken language, parental income, or neighborhood. When kids feel the stereotype threat bias (Gershenson, Holt, & Papageorge, 2016; Powers et al., 2016), their stress goes up. Now you have a can of gasoline, a match, and fumes in the air.

Staff often want more control over kids to reduce the perceived risk. But students often feel manipulated, unheard, and *overcontrolled*. What we see in successful high-poverty schools is a partnership. The students know that the leadership and staff are running the school, but they feel heard, seen, included, and respected. They know that they matter (Carey, 2019). As a result, they see the school as a vehicle to get where they want to go in life. In your classroom, the greatest predictor of student behavior is not the student, but you, the teacher (Yoon, 2002).

Action Steps

1. Head off disruption. Small disruptions may grow, so show your leadership by using energizers. Why? Many times, students get restless and bored and just need a release. Instead of reacting with criticism, say, "I just thought of something good for our brain. Please stand up." Catching micro-misbehaviors early and redirecting the energy is far better than putting on a "police" or "regulator" hat. Of course, always know your resources available for backup (e.g., a whole-class signal for change of activity).

2. Boost variety for greater engagement. Switch students from solo work to groupwork, from passivity to activity, from sitting to standing, from one table to another, from listening to talking. Have students create a quiz and test a partner. The more variety within the same topic, the less boredom. The less boredom, the more engagement you'll get.

3. Elicit student thoughts and voices. Ask students to vote on your next move. Vote on something coming up soon. Ask students to talk over a topic within a team and report the results. Ask all students to take a survey. Just ask a thought-provoking question and hear 5–15 voices. Have student team leaders summarize a team discussion.

4. Be prepared to de-escalate. Some students will get in your face, raise their voices, and use profanity. That's how some have learned to communicate. Stop judging and instead use clarifying, paraphrasing, and open-ended questions to ensure that the student is aware you have understood them. Before you begin, *take a deep breath.*

You will de-escalate only when you stop trying to control students. Start listening, and let the student know you respect them. Use the student's name. *Never* tell students how they feel or how they *should* feel. You have no idea how they feel, because if you did, you would never have provoked this situation.

Your empathy needs to be palpable during conflict situations. Even if you do not agree with the student's position, expressing your empathy and trying to understand why that person feels a particular way will help resolve the conflict. *Your first rule of intervention is to connect.*

Use any of these four phrases:

- "I **respect** your right to . . . (have your voice heard)."
- "I **agree** that . . . (this was probably a terrible idea)."
- "I **appreciate** that you . . . (let me know how you feel)."
- "I **love** your . . . (take-charge leadership)."

Any other response may show you are full of yourself and uninterested in what the student has to say. Remember, the student will keep being a "problem" *until they feel respected, heard, and valued.* Put on your "be an ally, not an adversary" cap, and listen.

5. Avoid using controlling language. Yelling *"Calm down!"* is an easily read, manipulative expression of labeling and control. Instead of shouting out an order, ask, "How can I assist you?" or "Are you feeling safe? If not, let me help out." The student deserves the same level of respect, courtesy, and patience as your best friend would. Once the student feels heard, you might say, "We can finish up our talk privately after class." For additional support, get the free download "Top Ten De-Escalation Strategies" at www.jensenlearning.com/equity-resources.

6. Use the model that fits your style *and* works with the students you have. Following are descriptions of the reinforcement, relationship, and redirect models. One of them will work for you.

- *Reinforcement model:* Affirm what is good, instead of pointing out what you dislike. Affirm that you like what is happening. Affirm student identity: "I love that you stand up for yourself. If you don't do that, life is hard." Or affirm the content *and* student identity: "I love that you stand up for yourself. That shows leadership, and that you are a caring person."

- *Relationship model:* Be an ally, not a dictator. "Now, some adults might not like *how* you stand up for yourself. But I will always be on your side. You're a good kid. After class, I'll show you how to be a stronger leader in ways that will keep you out of trouble and help you graduate." Or choose the privacy strategy: Lower your voice, make eye contact, pull up a chair, and talk softly when it is possible.

- *Redirect model:* Give students tools. "What you want is important to me. Let me show you two ways to do that *without getting in trouble.*" "At our school, and especially in our class, I'll show you how you can get what you want. You're a leader, not a bully. Can I show you right after class? Are we good?"

7. Remember that nonverbals matter! Notice your body language. *Avoid*

- Turning away from the student during the incident for any reason.
- Using piercing or demanding eye contact.
- Touching the student during an altercation.
- Pointing or shaking your finger at the student.

Instead,

- Stay at the same eye level. Stand up if the student stands up; sit down if the student does.
- Allow extra physical space between the two of you—about three big steps. Let any anger and agitation fill that extra space. Use spacing to foster safety, set the pace, and move to where you want the two of you to be.
- Allow the student to break their gaze and look away (never demand eye contact). Ensure your eyes are soft and empathetic. Keep your hands out front where they can be seen.

3. Follow-Up

The old saying "Hot heads and cold hearts never solved anything" is particularly true of conflict resolution. As education professionals, we need to show compassion and empathy and give the conflict our full attention through resolution. Avoid the police officer role; that's not what students need to grow and behave better. Make sure to always follow up after the conflict feels resolved.

Mindset. "I want any harm done to be acknowledged, apologized for, and healed. How can we do this better next time?" Ensure that all parties feel heard and respected. With a well-done closure, there are no grudges, and the class can move forward with a healthy ease. Ensure that everyone feels like things were handled well.

Evidence. Once the current conflict has been resolved, consider taking a proactive, evidence-supported follow-up step to help prevent future conflict: Make time for recess! The common rationale for dropping physical education or recess is lack of time. For most teachers, reducing recess time has made things worse—as the evidence could have predicted. Ensure that students get recess and P.E. Among elementary children, having a *daily recess period of more than 15 minutes in length was associated with better class behavior scores* (Shaffer, 2019). Yet uninformed teachers still use eliminating recess as a punishment for alleged misbehavior. Never, *ever* take away activity as a punishment. There's zero evidence that recess deprivation works as a causal factor in better behavior or improved academic performance (Barros, Silver, & Stein, 2009).

Action Steps

Set appointments to check in, and hold weekly meetings with your troubled students. Use a simple, student-run tracking system to follow up. Set up classroom climate teams that use restorative justice. More participation, by more students, predicts success. Your simple follow-up script goes like this:

1. Reaffirm the relationship. "Listen, I like having you in class. I'm on your side and I want you to succeed. Thank you for staying after. You're a good kid. Now, a lot of adults don't know you like I do. Maybe some would have suspended you for what you did today. I know you're going to go places in life. But you can't go anywhere unless you stay in school and you graduate."

2. Meet them where they are. "I am going to guess you've had a few adults give you a hard time before. Am I right?"

3. Form a shared goal. "My goal is to help you stay out of trouble, keep you from getting suspended, and ensure that you graduate. Will you work with me on this?"

4. Generate a strategy. "Earlier, right before you got upset, something set you off. What was it, and how might you respond differently next time so you stay out of trouble?" Ideally, get the student to propose a solution: It is very hard for someone to stay angry at you if they are proposing a solution to the problem. If the student's idea seems unrealistic, ask, "How can we achieve this?" If the student has no suggestions at all, offer a choice of two options.

5. Check for understanding. "Just to make sure I got it right, tell me what you heard me say." If you like it, say, "Sounds like you nailed it. Now, I want to be 100 percent sure what you meant. For a moment, I'll be that other student who bugged you. Show me what you'll do differently." If you don't like the clarification, help fill in the blanks.

6. Confirm the plan. "Sounds like we have a plan. Let's plug it in next time there's an issue and see how that goes. Thanks for staying after; see you tomorrow."

7. Write it out. At the end of the activity, participants summarize and endorse messages through a "saying is believing" writing exercise, in which they attempt to persuade future students to hold to an incremental theory of behavior change. They just need to pick one habit and follow it, and growth will follow (Walton & Cohen, 2011).

Emerging Equity Tools to Embrace

There are many programs that deal with classroom disruptions via teacher-student empowerment. One of my favorites is Ross Greene's evidence-based approach, Collaborative & Proactive Solutions (CPS). This is valuable because it is centered on solving the problems that cause the behavior, not the surface issues. When you understand why and when your student struggles, you can help them see this as a personal challenge—that you and the student can solve together in a collaborative and proactive way.

Dr. Greene shares two critical tools to reduce challenging episodes. First, he says, identify both the skills the student needs and the specific unmet expectations (unsolved problems). Second, he asks you to collaboratively solve the underlying problems leading to the misbehavior. To learn more, check out his 2016 book *Lost and Found: Helping Behaviorally Challenging Students.*

Another one of my favorite tools is *restorative justice,* an ongoing process that focuses on fostering community, empathy, and perspective-taking. When students can understand what happened from another's point of view and feel empathy, there's hope. Restorative Circles often provide healing for those involved in conflict, enabling them to repair harm through a facilitated dialogue. First, all those gathered share their perspective. For example, the teacher may express remorse for overreacting to the student's outburst. Maybe another student reflects on her own struggles with anger management.

During a Restorative Circle after one disruptive event, the young man whose words sparked the episode apologized. He added that his own stress from a tough morning had boiled over in class. The student then agreed to help his teacher set up her presentation and distribute books at the beginning of each class as a way of acknowledging that his classmates had lost instructional time. Restorative Circles show how everyone, in a safe place to share, can get what they want so that harmony prevails (Ortega, Lyubansky, Nettles, & Espelage, 2016).

Check your intentions. Can you say that, as you finish this chapter, you are more convinced than ever that your intention is crucial? Is your intention to foster a culturally relevant class where 100 percent of your kids feel heard and respected? Remember that with stress as the primary instigator in your class disruptions, you want to be on your A-game every day, managing your own stress. In any dispute, assume that the student's gripe is legitimate and begin with empathy. Only when your student feels heard do you have a chance to de-escalate. Even if the incident is minor, always follow up.

Say to yourself, "I will share narratives and stories that highlight and foster strengths in my students to succeed. My story in this chapter is a set of affirmations. I will read these daily for the next 30 days. If I see results, I will read these until they are a part of me."

Chapter in a Nutshell

This chapter described the "Big Three" steps to better classroom behaviors: *prevention, intervention,* and *follow-up.* For *prevention,* prepare each of your options and engage more energizers. For *intervention,* rehearse with colleagues or in front of a mirror. Remember what to avoid and what to say. Once you've practiced a few times, your confidence will go up. The third step, *follow-up,* is often ignored or lost in the shuffle, but it's actually the very best step for strengthening relationship bonds.

Revisit the Student Questions

We started with two student questions:

> ➤ *"Does my teacher understand where I'm coming from? Will my teacher keep class culturally responsive, fair, and just?"*

> ➤ *"Can my teacher use whole-class student awareness to create a positive climate?"*

You are now likely to have new beliefs, strong evidence, and a pretty strong set of skills to help answer these questions.

Before the Next Chapter

Revisit and debunk your biases. Two that need revision are *stereotype* bias and *hostile attribution* bias (the tendency to believe there is a hostile intent, even when the behavior is ambiguous or benign) (Anderson & Graham, 2007). Apply the de-bias activity in Appendix C and make progress.

The superpower from this chapter is gained through multiple pathways. First, manage your stress better. When your stress is high, nothing good happens in the classroom. Second, practice empathy every day. Persist at these two; they are amazing traits that most struggling teachers lack. The three steps to reduce behavior problems will be easier for you once you tackle stress regulation and empathy. Remember, *the great chef's first meal was as bad as anyone else's first meal.* The great teacher's first experiment went like yours. Keep the faith. Continue the de-biasing.

8

....

Cognitive Climbers

Student Questions

➤ "If I struggle, is my teacher culturally and cognitively competent enough to help me succeed?"

➤ "If I make mistakes, will my teacher still believe in me?"

➤ "Can my teacher make changes for the better, and help me and my fellow students improve as well?"

This chapter is about building better brains and fostering capacity. In this chapter you'll learn serious, evidence-based ways to ensure that your students grow quickly. I hope that's what you want. You'll learn how to build better brains in students and in yourself. Knowing how brains grow is a must for successful teachers.

Students' brains grow through inclusive, enriched environments. But most of all, brain growth requires relationships, relevance, and rigor. This is hard work, but you can do it. I have faith in you. Brains *can* change, and if your students' brains are staying the same (below grade level or low growth), this chapter is for you. Always remember who you work for. You don't work for the county, the state, a school, or an organization. You work for your students, and your goal is to make a positive difference in students' lives. Let me repeat that: You work *for your students*, not against them. Our topics for this chapter are:

- The Disappearing Talent Act
- Connections to Poverty
- You Go First: Understand How to Build Your Brain
- Can Teachers Boost Intelligence in Students from Poverty?
- Seven Ways High-Poverty Schools Can Build Stronger Brains
- Emerging Equity Tools to Embrace

One of the first places to start is to shake off any dusty, stagnant biases. Let's begin with a true story about biases that were setting obstacles in the way of some great brains, and what it took to get exceptional results.

The Disappearing Talent Act

College usually sounds like a good idea, but some time ago, a strange problem kept happening. Year after year, some of the best and brightest Black students in high school were falling apart in their first year at UC Berkeley. These students had high math scores on the SAT and top marks on college-level calculus classes in high school. But at Berkeley, the average freshman grade for these students in calculus was $D+$.

Dr. Uri Treisman and his Berkeley faculty mentor Leon Henkin were determined to find out why. They sent a note to all 400 Berkeley professors, along with the calculus student pass-rate data, and asked them to comment. The responses they got back shared multiple strands of opinion about the reasons for the students' underperformance:

- The students came from poverty.
- The students attended weaker, lower-level high schools.
- The parents of the students were poor role models.
- The students were unmotivated.

After collecting the responses, Treisman followed up and investigated each of these possible faculty-submitted reasons. After a thorough search, he found that *every one of the four reasons was clearly false.* The professors, who had doctorates and experience with thousands of students, turned out to be terrible at understanding their own students.

Treisman then asked his assistants to explore which students were *already doing well* in calculus. The most successful group was Chinese students. For more than a year, Treisman shadowed both cohorts of students with video and a notepad. He discovered multiple nearly invisible factors that were shaping the students' grades. None of the reasons for the lower grades were among the professors' guesses.

The Chinese students studied, shared success tools, and supported one another in small groups for an average of 14 hours a week. The Black students, who had often been the exceptions at their high schools (and often ostracized for their high achievement), generally studied individually. They had few, if any, academic friends. These students dutifully studied alone for eight hours a week. They had earned their way into Berkeley alone, and they were determined to make it alone. Their real downfall was low expectations by their professors and a lack of faculty support—two reasons that were notably absent from the faculty's list.

Treisman then developed a plan to help students overcome the stumbling blocks he observed. He gathered faculty support for the formation of an Emerging Scholars club. The club meetings were quite different from those of remedial programs, which often have high failure rates. They were afternoon collaborative sessions—sponsored and supported by faculty—in which students worked on advanced-level calculus problems with deliberate practice.

Many visitors to the program thought the secret to its success was group learning. But at the core were the deeply challenging problem sets that drove the group interaction. The side benefits were also immense. Students developed academic friends and social support in their new "in-group." They formed a new identity: "I do tough college calculus; I am a scholar." And they shared other college and life success tips they would not have gotten elsewhere. Another identity formed: "I am making it in college now." How did these calculus clubs turn out? Black students in the Emerging Scholars programs did so well that more than 70 percent got As and Bs in calculus (Fullilove & Treisman, 1990).

What can you learn from this? First, the "esteemed" faculty in the original survey had pointed fingers at the students' parents, their "weak" high school curriculum, their lack of motivation, and, of course, poverty. The faculty members' biases had blinded them to the factors that really mattered. Notice the biases *and how much they mattered.*

Treisman, a MacArthur Grant winner, recommends starting with faculty sponsorship. Then, foster collaboration; engage strong, new, successful identities; and keep expectations sky-high with deliberate practice on challenging problem solving. His program was a perfect example of how to create equity. So much for the faculty biases that claimed, "Black students from poverty can't do it because . . . "

Debrief Time

Let's pause so you can look at the problem, the process, and Treisman's strategy for raising student grades with an equity mindset. Reflect on your response to this story. Have you started to notice the biases among the UC Berkeley faculty? How about the biases at your own school? "Oh, we couldn't do that at our school." How about your own personal biases? "But those college kids already showed promise; they were exceptional." So now we're back to square one. Teachers want to *wait until the kids succeed* and then say, "I knew they could do it!" That's the confirmation bias again. Sometimes when I hear teachers express these biases, I almost laugh at them—except I don't. Why? I have had many of the same biases myself, and I'm still working on the rest. *Every* student has potential. Never wait for it; go out and embrace every student's possible future. Every time you do your very best, the student's future just got better.

It takes work (as opposed to not seeing the biases or ignoring them) to become excellent. The funny thing is, when you put in the work initially, the rewards come back for a lifetime. Maybe this time, you *did* notice the biases coming into play. Next, can you predict the kinds of narratives and stories that must have emerged? How might those biases and stories have affected the Black college students? Why did the Emerging Scholars strategy work? What were the elements needed to make that happen? What was changed in the students? Do this as a brief writing assignment or in discussion with a partner.

Connections to Poverty

The first thing you saw in the story about Black college calculus students was that *circumstances matter.* Being in the Emerging Scholars Club (the "in-group") and engaging in the activities within the club (doing difficult, interactive cognitive work; forming new identities; and socializing) all turned out to be equally important. The strategies and activities are as critical as the context. But how do we connect the story about the calculus scholars with equity and poverty?

Evidence suggests that children from families with higher socioeconomic status (SES) tend to perform well above children from lower-SES families regardless of whether those children had high or low cognitive abilities at age 2 (Noble, Houston, Kan, & Sowell, 2012). In 2019, the average reading score for 4th graders in high-poverty schools was 34 points lower than the average score for 4th graders in low-poverty schools (206 versus 240). The pattern is the same at the secondary level: The average reading score for 8th graders in high-poverty schools that same year was 30 points lower than the average score for their counterparts in low-poverty schools, and in 2015, the average reading score for 12th graders in high-poverty schools was 32 points lower than the average score of 12th grades in low-poverty schools.

In fact, students from low-income families have made little progress in national reading proficiency levels for more than 30 years (Hussar et al., 2020). The issues in schools remain present everywhere. So, can we help kids living in poverty to become successful readers? There is some research evidence that preschool, done well, can get students up to speed (Tucker-Drob, 2012).

We know that lower socioeconomic status is correlated with structural brain changes in the early years (Hanson, Chandra, Wolfe, & Pollak, 2011; Jednoróg et al., 2012; Tomalski et al., 2013). So, are the students doomed because of their genes and early environment?

Studies using identical twins shed light on the relative importance of each of these factors. Identical twins have the same genes, so studying them can help us determine whether adversity from poverty can be reversed. In one such study, reading achievement test data were collected on elementary school children in Florida by school staff. The student samples were identical and fraternal twins. The amount of variance in the oral reading fluency of twins with identical genes increased as the quality of their teachers increased. When teacher quality was high, genetic variance rose and reading scores bloomed. In contrast, poor teaching impeded the ability of the students to reach their potential. In other words, the strong teachers mattered *more* than the students' genes (Taylor et al., 2010). This is good news. It shows that the brain can change if teachers and school leaders commit to effective instruction and know how to do it.

An early reading project was initiated in four kindergarten classes in a low-SES bilingual school. Statistical analyses of the pre- and posttests showed that in only nine weeks, the kindergarten students were able to learn phonological skills critical to the reading process. By contrast, a significant number of students in the control group (a traditional kindergarten class) showed serious reading lags on the same reading test. Every student can be reading at grade level by 3rd grade (Hus, 2001). What would it take for you to believe you can do this at your school?

You Go First: Understand How to Build Your Brain

How do you lead by example? Each day, the typical teacher asks students to work hard, behave, and learn well. But who is the students' role model for this illusive promise of brain growth? How about you? Start every school year or semester by sharing *your own personal goals* with your students. They need to see you working toward your goals. In addition, add one cognitive goal, like reading a book a month. When you share those goals and track them, your students see an authentic, real person making changes. They want to be as good as you, and they just may follow your modeling.

Brain-Building Requires Rigor

For your brain, boredom is the enemy of change. Stop pitching to your students, "This will be easy." Your class motto is now *Harder makes us smarter.* Because brains need challenge and rigor to make cognitive improvement, your instruction and curriculum must be rigorous, with high expectations every single day! And do make the connections to the real world that students live in, but drop the assumptions. Being Latino, Native American, or Black never automatically means the student is living in poverty or will struggle to keep up. If you'd like an easy-to-use graphic on the "Seven Top Learning Factors" you can use right away, check out www.jensenlearning.com/equity-resources.

Learn about your students' situations one at a time. Yes, most students of color have experienced systemic racism to a significant degree. You can grow their brains by fostering stress-regulation tools in your students (or yourself) to mitigate chronic or acute stressors. You can grow them more quickly by using the specific rules of neuroplasticity (which most educators are spotty on). But your keys to success start with debunking your own biases and building relationships of honesty and trust. Your biases may be around gender, socioeconomic status, race, sexuality, or ethnicity. Only by working on yourself can you have an equitable classroom.

Genes or Environment?

What is the greatest factor in student brain growth: genes or environment? The answer is, both! The role of epigenetics (how the environment affects genes) suggests that there is no simple "either/or" answer to this question (Kanherkar, Bhatia-Dey, & Csoka, 2014). We now know that many of our genes may either be *expressed* or *suppressed*. There are at least five ways in which environmental forces can modify, alter, or damage genes. And this process seems to be universal among all mammals (Schwanhäusser et al., 2011).

The magnitude of gene heritability on intelligence is inversely proportional to the socioeconomic status of your students. The lower the SES, the lower the heritability of students' IQ from their parents. In short, a baseline of lower IQ *increases the opportunity for amazing teaching to make a difference.* This means you never want to hear another teacher say, "Well, of course she's struggling. I taught her dad 20 years ago, and he was no Einstein." The bigger problem is that apparently that teacher hasn't learned much in 20 years or is using the same lesson plans. That's why holding high expectations and providing relevant rigor every day are so crucial. Never give up on your students, or yourself.

Can Teachers Boost Intelligence in Students from Poverty?

There has been an abundance of emerging evidence about human brain malleability in the last generation. Today, we know the heritability of intelligence increases from about 20 percent in infancy to perhaps 80 percent in late adulthood (Plomin & Deary, 2015). This means that the younger the subjects, the less "set in" the intelligence. Can education help raise intelligence? A large meta-analysis (42 data sets from more than 600,000 participants) demonstrated an increase in intelligence test scores of between 1 and 5 IQ points (3.4 points on average) *for each additional year of schooling* (Ritchie & Tucker-Drob, 2018). This study was the first to show more than a correlation. The results show that education has a *causal effect* on intelligence test scores, and this finding was replicated in another large-scale study (Hegelund et al., 2020).

We now know that it's possible for human brains to increase intelligence. The next questions are just as critical. Has this theory ever been tested in an experimental study (control versus experimental group)? There are two common measures of intelligence. The first is *fluid intelligence*—your adaptable, quick thinking based on the immediate situation you're in. It's your ability to process, learn, and find novel solutions to an immediate problem or question. The second measure is called *crystallized intelligence*—content and problem solving based on what you have acquired in the past from experiences, schooling, and culture. We measure it with tests, quizzes, general knowledge of trivia, languages, and vocabulary (e.g., a Stanford-Binet IQ test). Now, let's check out an experiment that measured both kinds of intelligence.

Two high schools were recruited for this study. One school was treated as the control (with 147 randomly selected students with an average age of 15, about 50 percent of the school). The other was designated as the experimental group (with 149 randomly selected students in the same age group, 50 percent of the school). Both groups were given a battery of 28 tests measuring both *fluid* and *crystallized* intelligence. In the initial stage of the experiment, the control group had a slightly higher average score (0.2 standard deviation higher) than the experimental group. But after three years, the experimental group showed a stunning increase of 10–15 IQ points *more than the control group*. And their scores went up even further for two more years (Stankov & Lee, 2020).

What "brain training" did the experimental student group get? They got one class per week on creative and rigorous problem solving, while the students in the control group stayed with their same routines. The duration was critical; the intervention lasted for three years. Creative and rigorous problem solving has a strong effect size of 0.93 (Hsen-Hsing, 2009). Researchers identified the component of *defining a problem,* which included restating the problem in as many different ways as possible before beginning to solve it, as most critical. This was *cognitive rigor at its best;* hard, nearly unsolvable problems every week. Yes, intelligence can be raised.

So, can we increase the intelligence of children from poverty, and if so, how? Developmental theory predicts that the influence of genes (parent IQ) on a student's intelligence and academic achievement are suppressed in poverty (versus more fully realized in higher-socioeconomic-status students). This theory has been validated in the United States, where school variance is high, but not in countries where social policies ensure more uniform access to high-quality education (Tucker-Drob & Bates, 2016). This suggests that schools can act as powerful agents of change.

A large study (Bates, Lewis, & Weiss, 2013) using 1,702 adult twins (ages 24–84) with intelligence assessment data available looked at interactions among childhood socioeconomic status, genetic effects, and environmental effects. What the researchers discovered was that students from lower-income families *have a higher upside in intelligence* than those of higher socioeconomic status.

Let's unpack the meaning of *upside* here. If the mean IQ in a culture is 100, then getting to an IQ of 120 to 140 might be great, but difficult. Why? The existing IQ suggests that many of the common IQ driver "cards" (environment, enrichment, parenting, etc.) have already been played. But if the IQ is 80, there are many simple changes (enrichment, better teaching, supportive environment, challenging classes, etc.) that can raise the IQ to 100 or more. The study results suggest that rather than setting lower and upper bounds on intelligence, genes *multiply environmental inputs* that support intellectual growth.

Most kids you have in your class are tired of boring repetition of dull content. In fact, the brains of kids from poverty are thirsty for challenging rigor. That's why accelerated programs work well and advanced placement courses are so critical. Start putting kids into every challenging opportunity you have (and more)—with support.

Start with the raw materials that ignite a rapid brain-building process. Your brain is a dynamic organ that's designed to rapidly respond to environmental input. You have multiple intervention pathways that influence brain structures, leading to behavior change. The process is called *neuroplasticity.* This feature is an inherent property of the brain and can change any brain for the better (through learning a language, learning how to play an instrument, etc.) or for the worse (through trauma, violence, chronic stress, drug addiction, etc.). For an overview of how to activate this core property of neuroplasticity in the growth of your students, review Figure 8.1.

The relevance, intensity, and repetition of simulation or mental activation matter the most. Those triggers engage the intermediate response genes to operate as a class of signals to activate the release of chemicals like acetylcholine to trigger learning and memory (Miasnikov, Chen, Gross, Poytress, & Weinberger, 2008). This is the core of neuroplasticity; *brains change fast in response to only certain types of stimuli.* (Yes, trauma can change the brain fast, but obviously that would be a terrible teaching strategy.)

We know that teachers must grapple with multiple constraints during each fast-moving school day. With that in mind, do your best every day. Avoid criticizing yourself over a "lost" day; simply make it better the next day. Just stay on the growth path. Here are five conditions that will maximize rapid, positive brain changes.

Figure 8.1   How to Grow Smarter Students

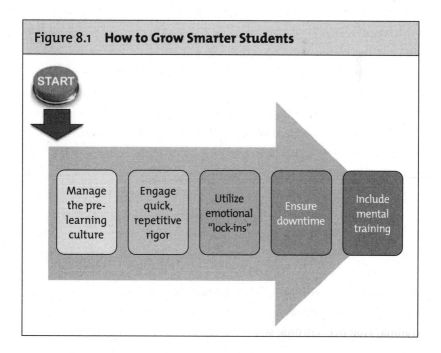

1. Remember to use priming. Foster culture with high-quality social, physical, cultural, and emotional states. The learning environment must trigger just the right mixture of neurochemicals to make the magic happen (Gupta, 2019). This opening establishes the neural receptivity for learning. Greet students with a smile and an affirmation. Use physical activity to foster the optimal brain chemicals (noradrenaline, dopamine, etc.). Optimize safety (no embarrassment or harm), challenge (just above comfort level), hope (the feeling that success is likely), and intention (relevance and urgency to learn). As usual, relevance keeps students locked in (Wei & Kang, 2014).

2. Engage quick, repetitive rigor. Make the work challenging as you employ specific, actionable feedback. This creates neural connections only if the activity is clear (versus confusing or fuzzy). It must be challenging and done for brief segments. Keeping it short, 12 to 20 minutes, is important to avoid overloading the hippocampus, which has limited short-term storage. Use your most effective, reliable, and actionable feedback tools: observable body language; student strategy, effort, and attitude; or the three questions (*"Where am I right now?"* *"Where am I going?"* and *"How do I get there?"*).

Some call this process *rigor*. Others call it *productive struggle.* I also like the term *healthy friction.* There must be constraints; when the task is too easy, the brain gets bored. Remember our motto: *Harder makes us smarter.* Your content? Use problem solving, creativity challenges, chess, writing code, playing a musical instrument, theater, and problem-based learning.

Keep challenging students as they progress, using repetition. One-time learning associations are likely to lose their detailed representations (Yang et al., 2016), and your students may forget what they seem to have learned. Four to six repetitions will keep the brain dependent on the hippocampus and allow learning to remain stable over time. Retrieval repetition (versus review) with novelty works best. In this method, students work with a partner to retrieve learning, then create a memory device for next time.

3. Utilize emotional "lock-ins" as rewards for learning. For example, "If most or all of your answers were correct, raise your hand and say, 'Oh yeah!'" Another time, replace the affirmation with an identity statement, such as "I'm an emerging scholar!" Remember to use quick celebrations and rewards when a successful small chunk of learning is done (Nielson & Bryant, 2005). Use these about once or twice an hour; avoid overdoing it. Novelty works, so rotate your affirming catchphrases. Celebrations may seem corny, but brain growth depends on a stream of intermittent rewards (Li, Long, Chen, & Li, 2019).

4. Ensure downtime with breaks, partner walks, or naps right after the brief learning segments for rapid neural consolidation. Your brain has two opposing networks involved in learning: (1) your *task-linked* networks, which are recruited during interactions on the learning task, and (2) your *default-mode* network, or "downtime," operating on internal representations. You're either (1) doing the inputting and processing *or* (2) consolidating the information and recording the memories, *but not both at the same time.*

As your brain decouples from the learning task, your default brain networks support the consolidation of durable episodic memories (Sneve et al., 2017). This "downtime" helps foster the long-term memory (Dudai, Karni, & Born, 2015). With any fresh, new learning, just a few minutes for consolidation helps (Bönstrup et al., 2019; Cohen, Pascual-Leone, Press, & Robertson, 2005). When you pile on too much content at once, your brain ruins memory, and the content may be lost.

I am amused when teachers tell me, "I don't have time for downtime breaks!" Gee, most teachers sure have time for reteaching. Set five minutes of mandatory downtime after intense new learning. How? At the secondary level, breaks between classes can work. Make an effort to build in breaks or take walks around the classroom. Do "silence challenges" with teams; they score points for every minute that every student says nothing. The goal is seven minutes, but start with two minutes. At the K–3 level, use brief quiet breaks or naps.

5. Include mental training, or visualization with practice, with your skill building if students are mature enough to go ahead. Why is that? The adolescent brain's hippocampus produces thousands more new neurons daily than the adult brain, yet many of these neurons die within weeks of their generation. The evidence is strong that pre-learning and post-learning visualization can reduce this loss (Curlik & Shors, 2013). The core feature of this strategy is the capacity to learn mentally with only your trained imagination. Learning new associations and skills can increase the new cell survival (Dalla, Bangasser, Edgecomb, & Shors, 2007). Classroom teaching strategies such as these are just one of many factors that separate teachers who struggle from those who succeed.

Seven Ways High-Poverty Schools Can Build Stronger Brains

Effective teaching in a high-poverty classroom always begins with equity. What matters most? Begin with positivity, high expectations, and creating an equitable in-group in your classroom. Next up, an important focus is relevance, rigor, and relationships. Include and engage your students' cultures in any of these activities. Students need to see that they fit within what you're proposing. The research is rock-solid in its support of these approaches. Now we start asking, how do we deal with an event, a topic, or a textbook in a way that builds brains? Figure 8.2 summarizes some key ideas.

How could you apply these ideas at your school? Let's cover how these seven options are being used at high-performing Title I schools. With each option, there are ways you can apply what you have learned. For example, each of the options has that *productive struggle*, or what I call *healthy friction*, when something is hard, but there's a clear *why*, a clear path, and actionable feedback.

Keep in mind that we educators should prepare the student for the student's future and no one's past. For example, start up a computer coding class after school. Apps like Code.org are free online, and the

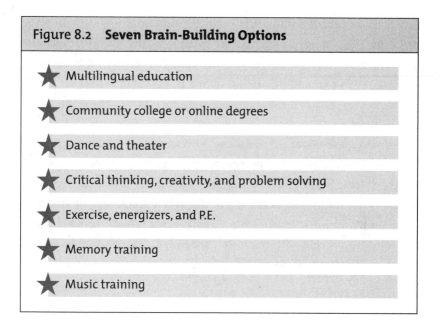

Figure 8.2   **Seven Brain-Building Options**

⭐ Multilingual education

⭐ Community college or online degrees

⭐ Dance and theater

⭐ Critical thinking, creativity, and problem solving

⭐ Exercise, energizers, and P.E.

⭐ Memory training

⭐ Music training

early skills can be learned by 2nd graders. With a high school diploma and savvy skills, your kids can start off with a six-figure salary. Following are a few other ideas for brain-building.

Multilingual Education

Counter the bias of "They don't know our language." Any teacher who checks the recent research on multilingual learners may be in for a surprise. In school and out, switching back and forth between languages *contributes to cognition* (Kang et al., 2017). Overwhelming evidence suggests that multilingualism is a core way to build brains faster (Buchweitz & Prat, 2013). In five years, most teachers *will still be fluent in only one language,* but many of their students *will be fluent in two languages.* Who's the faster learner now?

Community College or Online Degrees

Counter the bias of "They are not ready for college." Give the high school students who feel ready for college your blessing and high expectations. Studies show that your support matters a lot in their success. Consider dual graduation, which means enabling secondary students to take both community college classes and their typical classes. This can allow some students to graduate with both a high school diploma and an associate degree, which saves money on a college education.

Remember the nearly free option at uopeople.org? It's the first nonprofit, U.S.-accredited, online university dedicated to opening access to higher education globally. Degrees start at $5,000, and there are scholarships available. Most additional education, even online, has been shown to affect both brain structure and cognitive level. Even better, some colleges will provide scholarships, and the credits earned can save the family money if the student decides to complete a four-year degree.

Dance and Theater

Counter the bias of "Performing arts are not rigorous college-prep learning." Actually, dance and theater are very rigorous. Any staff member who thinks these subjects are simply not relevant is biased or way behind in the research. Researchers who study dance notice structural brain changes, including increased hippocampal volume, gray matter volume, and white matter integrity. Functional changes included improved cognitive function in memory and attention, plus body balance (Teixeira-Machado, Arida, & de Jesus, 2019). Theater practice also works magic. For example, after four weeks of instruction, older adults given theater training made significantly greater gains than did a control group on both cognitive and psychological well-being measures (Noice, Noice, & Staines, 2004).

Critical Thinking, Creativity, and Problem Solving

Counter the bias of "This is not in our curriculum." Simply use the existing curriculum and go deeper. Remember the high school study from earlier in this chapter? IQ showed a documented 10- to 15-point increase in three years as a result of teaching rigorous creative problem solving (Stankov & Lee, 2020). Recent evidence shows a connection between divergent thinking and functional brain connectivity. Translated, this study shows the power of creativity in initiating better calming states for learning and, conversely, potentially higher-order paths for intelligence (Cousijn, Zanolie, Munsters, Kleibeuker, & Crone, 2014).

Remember, *easy makes kids queasy,* and *harder makes them smarter.* Ask more difficult questions and follow up answers with additional questions. Allow students to collaborate in small groups. Focus on rigor and relevance daily. One of the reasons teachers struggle is that when they read about what fosters better brains, a bias kicks in. "Well, I wish I had the time." Notice those biases. You *do* have the time. Stop doing things that lack efficacy and *foster more of what builds brains.*

Exercise, Energizers, and P.E.

Counter the bias of "We don't have time for it." Physical activity, especially aerobic exercise, greatly increases the number of new neurons that are produced in the hippocampus, the structure highly involved in declarative memory. Additionally, mental training via skill learning increases the numbers of new neurons that *survive,* particularly when the training goals are challenging (Curlik & Shors, 2013). The research evidence is clear that healthier learners learn better (Basch, 2011a) and that students of color in particular do better academically with physical activity at school (Basch, 2011b).

Schools that use more movement and energizers find that students learn and behave better. Their brains are better regulated (Erwin, Fedewa, Beighle, & Ahn, 2012). A high school in Illinois has found a way to use movement to boost students' math scores and get students reading a year and a half ahead of their peers. Overall, the academic performance of students at this high school placed them among the top five countries in the world (Ratey, 2008). The secret is simple. The staff set the class schedule so that students took a P.E. class *immediately before their most challenging subject.* It is well researched that students who are physically active within an hour before learning demonstrate better long-term memory retrieval than those who did not exercise (Pontifex, Gwizdala, Parks, Pfeiffer, & Fenn, 2016). Seriously? Exercise is that good? Yes. And now it's about time for the biases to kick in: "I just don't have the time," or "They won't let us do that." I hope you're connecting the dots by now.

Memory Training

Counter the bias of "We don't do memorization; how could it be important?" Surprisingly, working memory is a *greater predictor of student success* in school than even IQ (Alloway & Alloway, 2010). Working memory training using current curriculum is correlated with greater plasticity and connectivity in brain regions that are thought to be critical in learning (Caeyenberghs, Metzler-Baddeley, Foley, & Jones, 2016). Other researchers have clarified that this memory training has *near transfer* (transfer within the given subject matter) and very little *far transfer* (applied to random items such as commercials, phone numbers, or general daily life). We do know that nearly every cognitive skill engages working memory. Its training promotes both brain plasticity and behavioral gains (Pappa, Biswas, Flegal, Evans, & Baylan, 2020). Learn more about how to teach it via a no-cost webinar at www.jensenlearning.com/workingmemory.

Music Training

Counter the bias of "We can't afford any music teachers or music programs." Playing an instrument is a well-researched way to build the brain. Long-term musical training improves the ability to ignore irrelevant stimuli, and it shortens tactile and multisensory reaction times (Landry & Champoux, 2017). It improves executive function on critical tasks like processing and retaining information, controlling behavior, making decisions, and solving problems. Musical training can improve memory, listening skills, and attention, and strengthen executive functioning in school-age kids (D'Souza, Moradzadeh, & Wiseheart, 2018).

Emerging Equity Tools to Embrace

Make the following affirmation for yourself: "This week I will cultivate a slightly different role at school. My new identity choices include 'I am a cognitive brain builder. I foster rigor, relevance, and repetition daily.'" This week, share narratives and stories that highlight and foster your students' strengths to succeed. Commit to sharing school and personal narratives that create agency, enthusiasm, and results. As you debunk false biases, you will find that your stories become more hopeful and uplifting.

To achieve your goals, build social support. Ask yourself, "Who have I or will I connect with this week about this book I'm reading? What can I share? What am I still uncertain about? Avoid setting a goal to form a new habit—instead, just do it. Remember, your ultimate identity goal is to *become a daily change agent who fosters equity and excellence.*

Chapter in a Nutshell

Earlier, you were reminded that brains can grow and change. Intelligence is modifiable, not fixed. The seven approaches you just read about are examples of course offerings at schools that fit the mold of *high-poverty and high-performing schools.* My experience in visiting and working with *lower-performing* schools is there is always a long list of excuses. One claim is that there is no money. If that's true, you could write a grant, appeal to wealthy community donors, or start crowdfunding. The point is, stop the excuses. Just. Go. Do. It.

Another excuse is that there is no one to run the program. Investigate in your community: Do you have retired athletes, musicians, or artists? Begin small. The seven items in this group are all massive brain boosters. It takes someone to assume the initial leadership until others rise up. Is this hard? Of course! Remember, *harder makes us smarter.*

Revisit the Student Questions

The key to your understanding and implementation of effective new tools is first, the power of peer support. We saw this in the story about the calculus students. Then we saw the power of role modeling for your own students. Finally, we saw the seven paths that work in schools. What they all have in common is *rigor*. Now we circle around and come back to you. Review the student questions from the start of the chapter.

➤ *"If I struggle, is my teacher culturally and cognitively competent enough to help me succeed?"*

➤ *"If I make mistakes, will my teacher still believe in me?"*

➤ *"Can my teacher make changes for the better, and help me and my fellow students improve as well?"*

The good news is that you can generate the affirmative answers for your students on those questions. You now have the intention, the de-biasing, the narrative, and the identity to move forward.

Before the Next Chapter

I have developed a nine-step process I refer to as my "air-tight" habit builder that is the most complete way to change a habit because it covers all the needs of your brain. What habits do you need to form to ensure the change begins as intended? It's simple. This nine-step habit builder appears in Chapter 9 (see Figure 9.4, p. 184) and is available for download at www.jensenlearning.com/equity-resources.

If this habit-building process sounds a bit lengthy, don't worry: You'll be able to fill in all these numbered items in 15 minutes or less. In time, you'll get pretty quick at doing these habit formers. Walk through the process verbally with your colleagues to troubleshoot it and tweak for excellence. Set up a simple accountability system where you check in daily. Do this in person, with a text, or by email. Meet weekly to review progress or improve the process.

Will you use this simple habit builder? I hope so. Hard work is inevitable when you grow. The successful teachers who grow and love their job are playing the long game. Those who keep trying to negotiate ways to avoid the hard work want a shortcut. But most shortcuts in life will leave you short in life. Teachers who seek shortcuts allow their biases to run their life; they tell themselves stories about the impossibility of the kids and their job. And, of course, they'll carry that to the other jobs they have for the rest of their lives. Be different; be the teacher that your students need in order to succeed.

9

The Emerging You

Student Questions
➤ *"Is my teacher robust or fragile?"*
➤ *"Is my teacher an expert at anything?"*
➤ *"Does my teacher admit mistakes and demonstrate continuous growth?"*
➤ *"Can my teacher change for the better and adopt a new behavior?"*

This chapter is about growth and how to make it happen. It is about making changes you can live with. The primary focus is about *the new emerging you,* because what's really required in your current role is to become effective at your job. It will take thoughtfulness and effort. It will also take some change tools. But it will be worth it.

I have met many struggling teachers over the years. One dominant mindset these teachers share is the need to fit in with their herd. We are social creatures, and that's expected. If most of the school staff is struggling academically with kids, it often becomes socially acceptable for an individual teacher to struggle. We fool ourselves into believing that being average or even below proficiency is acceptable. But I hope you now know better. Mediocrity is the choice of failures. Nobel laureate Dr. Richard Feynman (2015) said, "The first principle is that you must not fool yourself—and you are the easiest person to fool" (p. 345). The topics we will explore in this chapter are:

- "Me, Change? I'm Just Fine the Way I Am!"
- Connections to Poverty
- You Go First: Lead by Example
- Defining the Change Process
- Two Change Tools to Embrace: Go Personal, Go Professional
- Foster the Growth of Your Dreams

"Me, Change? I'm Just Fine the Way I Am!"

The room was boisterously engaged and supremely positive. Evaluations were through the roof. I had been invited to do a two-day training for more than 400 new teachers on the campus of a large teachers college. Most of the attendees were getting their first exposure to different ways of teaching students from poverty. My self-talk was, "I can do this; it is right up my alley."

Nearby school principals were also invited. There was high activity and engagement, and attendees connected with the content. As a trainer, I felt good that the event was well received. Several principals came up to me afterward and told me this was a breath of fresh air. Another principal from a nearby elementary school that gets new teachers from this university every summer said that he had a 50 percent staff turnover every year. He was glad that finally his new teachers would have a better chance of succeeding, and maybe next time they would renew their contracts instead of leaving.

While I was wrapping my head around an annual 50 percent turnover, another principal came up and said his nearby elementary school had an *80 percent* annual turnover rate. Imagine having to hire 80 percent of a faculty every single year. My head was spinning! For new teachers, both of these elementary schools were the end of the teacher prep pipeline: a paying job in teaching. *And then they quit.*

When the dean of education came up at the end to thank me, I asked how this event might be blended with what the university's professors were already doing. The dean looked me in the eye and said, "Oh, I'm sure they're already doing a lot of this stuff." If the dean had actually followed up with nearby schools, she would have discovered that the university's own teacher prep program was partly responsible for poor new teacher preparation. The professors were actually *increasing* the likelihood that new teachers would quit the profession. For a moment, I felt smug. "At least I am giving the staff the real tools they need," I thought.

A moment later, another realization hit me. There I was (again), pointing fingers. This time, it was at the "poor" university preparation that many new teachers were getting. That's when I started asking more and better questions *about my own work*. What am I missing? What could I do differently? I finally concluded that many of my own assumptions about equity, learning, poverty, and habit change were flat-out wrong. I felt ashamed.

I was asking others to change, but I was an amateur at it. I decided, "Go back to square one. Restart with more humility. Every day, learn, grow, change, and share. Determine what teachers need, not what I want to tell them. Support their personal lives. Never stop improving; the status quo is rarely acceptable. The finish line is . . . there isn't one. Yesterday was the last easy day. *Harder makes me smarter.* Learn more!" That was the impetus to start this book.

Debrief Time

Reflect on your response to any bias you spot in the previous vignette. One possible bias begins with, "It's not my fault—it's them." In short, most of us tend to claim full credit and assert genius when our students do well or things go better than expected. But do you also claim ownership when the reverse happens? The more biases you uncover and debunk, the better you get. The less pride and the more humility, the better. Hiding your mistakes fosters cognitive and emotional fragility. I forgot my humility at the training that day. The more you're willing to be wrong and own your mistakes, biases, and misdeeds, the better your chances for career success. Owning and correcting your errors replaces fragility with strength. Process this in a brief writing assignment or in a discussion with a partner.

Connections to Poverty

At schools with more than 75 percent of students eligible for free or reduced-price lunch, almost two-thirds of the students agreed with the statement "There are tenured teachers who deliver poor instruction." And a whopping 84 percent said school leaders were a problem. Children from poverty, who need strong teachers and leaders the most, are the least likely to get them (Weisburg, Sexton, Mulhern, & Keeling, 2009).

Do you recall the Emerging Scholars program for the Black calculus students in the previous chapter? Apparently not much has changed among educators. Many still believe falsehoods expressed by university professors more than 40 years ago. Instead of checking their own biases, engaging cultural responsiveness, and reducing discrimination with equitable practices, many educators still blame the same old culprits. The excuses I hear most often from teachers of struggling students are a supposed lack of student motivation, bad genes, and poor parenting. But this widespread teacher response is perpetuated not by data but by biases, narratives, and stories. It's time. Be different; change the stories, and you change hearts and minds. Especially those of your colleagues and yourself.

You Go First: Lead by Example

You may recall that I asked at the beginning of Chapter 1, "How has that 'grab and go' approach been working out for you and your students?" For most teachers, not so well. You'll never have a better class, with better-behaved kids, who score at or above proficiency, until you make *personal changes* in sync with your *professional changes*. Choose to grow and lead your students by example, not through rules, tricks, or threats.

One study (Duckworth, Quinn, & Seligman, 2009) assessed hundreds of new teachers who had come through Teach for America—which trains teachers specifically to work in high-poverty schools—before and after a year of teaching. Teachers who scored high in "life satisfaction" were 43 percent more likely to produce high-performing students than their less-satisfied colleagues were. Maybe their engagement, zest, and enthusiasm for life were contagious. Does that help you understand why I beg you to work on yourself first?

Overall, teachers and administrators in high-poverty schools are happiest when they feel they are making progress and making a difference. If you organize and lead a successful program that gets tangible results, that matters, too. It gives you a sense of control, autonomy, and mission. Even small steps toward meaningful goals work well; it is enough to feel progress toward overcoming challenges (Amabile & Kramer, 2011).

How do you lead by example? You'll want to examine your intention, biases, stories and narratives, identities, and context. Then be a role model so your students see how well life can be lived.

Any one of the three steps in the growth process shown in Figure 9.1 is a great place to start. Ideally, though, you'll start at the bottom

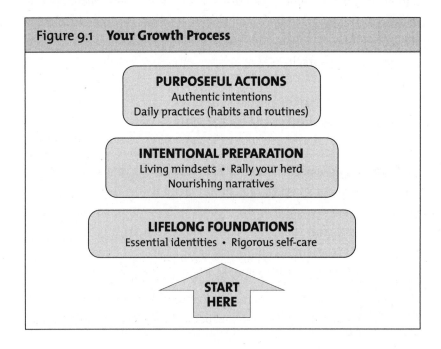

Figure 9.1   **Your Growth Process**

PURPOSEFUL ACTIONS
Authentic intentions
Daily practices (habits and routines)

INTENTIONAL PREPARATION
Living mindsets • Rally your herd
Nourishing narratives

LIFELONG FOUNDATIONS
Essential identities • Rigorous self-care

START HERE

(Lifelong Foundations) and grow upward. Then, add what you can when you can. Is it worth it? Yes. I use each of the disciplines outlined in the three steps, and I am still a work in progress. How about you? Are you done with learning in your profession, or are you ready to grow into an educator who has a great year, every year?

Maybe you believe that this is a bit intrusive; after all, it's your personal life. I am sorry about that. After all, in many professions, your personal life is nobody's business. But in education, it is everybody's business. Students have a right to see *viable role models* for adulthood. And they have a right to have access to *teachers who are active learners* with a healthy sense of well-being. Your students need to see that life can be good and that it is worth living. Many kids lack that option at home, and it's a critical part of growing up healthy.

Defining the Change Process

Surprisingly, many staff are unaware (before they start) that teaching well in a high-poverty school is doable. It simply requires a specific set of strengths. You might hold the bias that success could be hard work and maybe it won't pay off quickly. That's true on both counts. But as you grow, you will better withstand the tough days, chaos, and disruptions that, for some, would cause a complete breakdown. You may face a long list of mishaps. But then you'll bounce back the next day.

You'll learn to start applying the equitable and culturally responsive tools you've read about. Growth is now at the top of your list. Your students need to get a year and a half's worth of gains every school year. Being merely "OK" at your job is a disaster for your students' scholastic careers. Your job demands that you be not just a hungry learner, but also one who applies your learning immediately. Time is of the essence.

Most educators lack a reliable internal system for growth. What follows is a simple but challenging pathway. I have uncovered these tools piecemeal over the last 20 years, and together they revisit what you've been reading about throughout this book. Every item on this list has passed my evidence-based test and is necessary, but by itself insufficient, for miracles. But working with multiple tools gives you a superpower. The three steps in the growth process are Lifelong Foundations, Intentional Preparation, and Purposeful Actions. Remember your "why" for each of them. Then I'll show you how to plug in your changes. If you are ready to become *the best teacher your students ever had,* let's get started.

Step One: Lifelong Foundations

You would probably say your character and your health are pretty important. Yet do your daily actions match up with your beliefs? No matter how many strategies you learn, unless you have good physical, mental, and emotional health, they'll never get implemented. And unless a new strategy fits into your identity (the "hats" you wear), it's unlikely you'll embrace the idea and stay with it. Let's start by exploring the power of identity.

Essential identities: Embrace and affirm your multiple hats. In large-scale societies, the signals of integration into each new culture require different identities (Smaldino, 2019). This goes way back in time to when human tribes sought labels to distinguish attributes (Moffett, 2013). Today, we see the value in wearing multiple "hats" that announce new identities. Your work colleagues may assign you an identity by saying, "You are our best with the kids who . . . ." Today, you may go to a sports event with your child and wear a cap with a team logo, affirming the identity "I am a big _____ fan." You may go out for a power walk with friends and affirm, "I'm fit and I never quit."

Today's roles at both home and school require that you wear more hats than ever (Albalooshi, Moeini-Jazani, Fennis, & Warlop, 2020). That means you'll have roles such as "I am an engaging, relentless equity builder every day." These roles are essential and need special attention. Create a list of who you need to be over a week's time. Write out all the identities. Keep the ones you want to add to your daily reads. By reading your list of identity statements, you'll make the identities more and more familiar and easier to transition into and out of. This process is woven into my own daily story, so the process takes me just 45 seconds each day.

Rigorous self-care: Remain calm in the storm. Self-care at its best is you looking after yourself and managing the key indicators of well-being. It is any activity that you do purposefully to take care of your mental, emotional, and physical health. It is restorative; it refuels you and improves well-being. Some self-care activities you may want to consider are identified in Figure 9.2.

Rigorous self-care is an aggregate of dominant, relevant skill sets operating in a complex system that is full of interdependencies. Your skill sets enable you to flourish, even in chaos (Aven, 2018). Crucially, this means you'll want to learn to love errors—the type you learn and grow from as you get better. Avoid playing the victim or playing the blame game. Embrace the unfamiliar and charge ahead daily; lead with boldness, setting an example for your students.

Figure 9.2   Better Stress Regulation Gives You Your Life Back

INCREASE CONTROL:

Do daily habits, tiny actions that put you back in control. Take a walk, write in your journal, talk with a good friend, do a workout, take a Pilates or yoga class, or clean your classroom or kitchen.

The source of your stress is all within. When you face an aversive situation or person and you perceive little or no control, your brain stresses. Decrease the perception of relevance and boost control.

DECREASE RELEVANCE:

Shift your perception of what's relevant. Watch less news and more inspiring documentaries. Use the one-week rule: if it won't matter in a week, walk away. Begin delegation of less critical tasks and cross more off your to-do list.

At the crux of this is continuous improvement generated from volatility, randomness, and stressors. There is continuous strengthening from the new habits you take on. Without rigorous self-care, most teachers in a high-poverty school have a low chance for success. You want to be calm and focused in the middle of a storm; that's what you're prepared for, and it's both a mindset *and* a skill set.

To foster rigorous self-care,

- Keep up with all necessary planned checkups or visits to the doctor.
- Eat a nutritious diet that is high in vegetables; include healthful grains, proteins, water, and tea. Eat less sugar and less of what comes in a box, frozen, or in a can; eat more of what's fresh. The health of your gut influences your stress regulation and immune system (Rea, Dinan, & Cryan, 2016).
- Become relentless at managing your stress. You can improve your awareness, prevention, resistance, and resilience by starting habits to lower your stress. A simple example is to embrace a common stress reducer to inoculate your body and brain. It could be an intensive exercise routine or a cold shower. Get started and download "15 Ways to De-Stress" at www.jensenlearning.com/equity-resources.
- Get enough sleep. Adults usually need seven to eight hours of sleep each night. Make your bedroom dark or wear a sleep mask, and keep the temperature at 65–68 degrees if possible. Ingest no alcohol or caffeine for three hours before bedtime.
- Exercise five to six times per week. Choose a form of exercise that you like. The slower the activity, the longer time you need per day. Shorter, high-intensity workouts are my favorite.
- Use relaxation exercises or practice meditation.
- Spend daily downtime with your loved ones.
- Do at least one relaxing or fun activity every day, such as cooking, going for a walk, or talking with a friend or family member.
- Away from work, foster supportive partners and friends. Life can be tough without that emotional sounding board and backstop.

- Ensure you have access to supportive professional networks. These connections are linked to higher levels of teacher efficacy (Moolenaar, Sleegers, & Daly, 2012) and lower levels of burnout (Lim & Eo, 2014).
- Become a guru at saying no to things that feel like time wasters. For example, avoid attending gatherings you dislike or spending time with "friends" who are no longer friends; turn off your phone when you're busy.

Step Two: Intentional Preparation

Intentional preparation is the middle step in our pathway for growth. Once you've laid a solid foundation, you'll be ready to plan for purposeful action. During this stage, you'll foster and model a living growth mindset, garner strong social support from your herd, and create nourishing narratives that sustain you every day.

Living mindsets: Recognize your biases and commit to growth. Although the word *mindset* has become popular lately, there's a problem. Teachers know the definition of the word, but until the growth mindset is actually lived (versus talked about), they will struggle. Successful teachers in high-poverty schools question their own biases as they engage in the growth process. Learn to uncover biases like a detective without hurting others' feelings. Be a role model for "living" the growth mindset so that students want to be like you.

Biases are cognitive shortcuts that save you time but distort reality. There are about a dozen biases that are very common in our profession, and more than 100 additional biases pop up less often. Until you learn to recognize them and de-bias yourself over time, you'll struggle. Some of the most common classroom biases are the *bandwagon effect, blind spot bias, confirmation bias, familiarity bias,* and *stereotype bias.*

One I am personally grappling with now is the *time-discounting bias.* This occurs when we value future time less than the present. We are thinking we can "do something later" with little or no loss. I also call it the *mañana effect.* It's as if time tomorrow is on sale. That misperception can lead you to put something off forever.

The core mindset we need is the growth mindset. This mindset says that intelligence, skills, and attitudes can be improved. We all have the capacity to grow into a better version of ourselves. One of the reasons that studies have found students to be more successful in growth-mindset classrooms than in typical classrooms is that the teachers not only teach their kids about the growth mindset but also practice what they preach. Unless you walk the walk with your growth-mindset talk, students may tune you out.

There is a de-bias tool in Appendix C and at www.jensenlearning.com/equity-resources to help you defuse your biases. Adopt the mindset that much of what you perceive is likely to be biased. Unless your biases continue to be named and maimed, your goal of equity hangs precariously in the balance.

Now you know why I have been nudging you to consider engaging the *living growth mindset.* Unless you're willing to grow, your students will find someone else to follow. Every semester or school year, dedicate yourself to growing in a new area. Share the goal, the steps, the milestones, and the evidence of growth with your class. As students see you moving forward, you will become more authentic in engaging them to move forward, too.

Rally your herd: Work in teams with students, partners, and colleagues. Each of us has an opportunity to spend more time alone or more time with others. Having said that, the road is more easily traveled with collegial support. In fact, social collaboration is a powerful way to learn, grow, and feel supported, especially when you are teaching students who are different from you (Stearns, Banerjee, Mickelson, & Moller, 2014). Working in collegial teams can bring impressive results to your school. The effect size for collective teacher efficacy is 1.23 (J. Hattie, personal communication, May 23, 2017). This translates to more than double the typical yearly rate of student learning.

If the social support is not there within your school, consider teaming up with a close friend, colleague, or partner. Quality social support means you prioritize two things that may not be on your list at the moment: deep-dive discussions (including evidence) and support for emotional well-being. Set up a weekly meeting where each of you can share progress on projects and be an ally who is truthful and supportive. Insist that each member of your collegial support team hold the others accountable.

Nourishing narratives: Inspire and build a productive life. The brain is a story junkie. Our stories are the single best predictors of our behaviors. We fabricate and confabulate them endlessly. Stories reinforce our biases, identities, and values. To change your life, change your stories. We all start with the facts, yet we can choose our intentions, framing, biases, and the narrative we create around those facts. You can hear these when you listen to others' stories.

If you lived through a horrible car crash and lost a limb, what's the story you tell? Are you a horribly unfortunate person who became disabled? Or are you one of the luckiest people alive because you avoided a midlife funeral and have your whole life in front of you, starting today? Your story is up to you.

Our brains create stories constantly. They are automatically generated because they help us survive. They are easy to remember, and they transmit information from one person, one culture, or one generation to the next. Stories glue our biases together (Suzuki et al., 2018). Our brains continually turn events, conversations, and one-liners into stories. It's usually easy on the brain, which makes us underestimate the falsehoods that may be produced in the process. Be mindful and skeptical of the blurbs you hear at school (e.g., "The apple doesn't fall far from the tree" or "Like mother, like daughter"). These statements are convenient, packaged biases. You're a better person than that, true? Or am I overestimating you? I think not.

Stop and listen to your own stories. Do they excite and energize you, or make excuses for mediocrity? Create stories about how you are *now succeeding with equity*. Sculpt and read your positive stories daily. Feed your brain the mental foods of the great minds of our time. Your stories and the narratives you extract from them can foster clarity, intention, mindset, identity, and skill sets. Every day, I read the narratives that best support my life. It takes me about 45 seconds. Is a "better you" worth 45 seconds a day? Learn the system I have used for years. The best people in their fields have learned to sculpt their stories carefully in ways that support a balanced, healthy, and productive life. Go to www.jensenlearning. com/equity-resources and download "Your Personal Daily Story."

Step Three: Purposeful Actions

Planning and preparation are a solid, necessary step in any success process. But as you know, what gets results is always the "doing." Here we focus on what you actually do every day. We begin with authentic intentions and finish with our daily practices.

Authentic intentions: Create a system. Let's begin with a common perception among teachers: "If I am really psyched about a relevant, fresh idea (from an online source, a book, a colleague, or professional development), then that will usually translate into classroom changes."

Sorry, you're likely off on that one. *Intention* to make a change is just one part of the process. Intention is a good thing; I discussed its power in the first chapter of this book. Yet alone, it has an effect size of 0.38, which translates into only about a 22 percent chance of your implementing change (Webb & Sheeran, 2006). That means that if intention is the only link in the chain of implementation, your odds of success are low.

Let's do a simple thought experiment. How good a teacher would you be if you had implemented *even half* of all the great ideas you had ever been exposed to? For most, that's a serious "Oops" realization.

Anytime throughout the day, starting when you rise in the morning, pause and ask yourself, "What do I ideally intend to have happen? What am I really after?" This will keep you on task and focused on the goal. Your students want to know whether you're authentic. So, how do you become more authentic? It's not luck, or gritting your teeth. Create a system.

For me, what works is a two-fold plan of reading daily, authentic intentions and making a brief list. I start my day with a reading of my daily affirmations of intention. If you refuse to create a system for daily intentions, you may get the same ol', same ol'. If you really have an intention to succeed, get serious. Use simple affirmations: "When X occurs, I will do Y." For example, you might say, "Today, anytime I see energy drop in my students, I will use an energizer, then increase relevance to get buy-in." Or if you sense a potential disruption in your class, "I will take a slow breath and pause. Next, I will connect with and affirm my student so they know I am listening." Write the affirmation on a sticky note or send yourself a text. Then, start your intentional habit.

Daily practices: Deepen your skill sets with habits. During the course of this book, I have invited you to turn a notion, an idea, or a concept into action. Of course, we want to avoid a "one-shot" stab at success. The genuine success is the formation of a habit. *Daily practices* means you take what needs to be done and turn each step into a replicable (and modifiable) tiny step of growth. You can do this using affirmations, authentic intentions, positive narratives, or the nine-step habit builder shared in Chapter 8 and again up ahead (see Figure 9.4, p. 184). The reality is many strategies can be a great idea. But to become a great teacher, you want to foster the habits that repeat the great ideas, day after day.

Some teachers are known schoolwide for connecting with people. Others have skill sets in organizing and planning lessons. Some are amazing team builders. And others have highly specific teaching skill sets—for example, repairing students' reading problems. The simple but rare skill of knowing how to build new habits has been introduced earlier in this book. We'll return to it before we finish up.

Two Change Tools to Embrace: Go Personal, Go Professional

Let's roll up our sleeves and decide which changes you'll begin with. I suggest you choose one personal-care change and one professional change. Why? If you're falling apart mentally, physically, or emotionally, your teaching will be a disaster. And the converse is true: If your health is great but you continue to do the same ol', same ol', things will remain the same or go downhill. Remember, personal and professional go together. Read on for the two lists to choose from.

Go Personal: Robust Self-Care Habit Choices

Be open to a new habit. Be the one who takes care of yourself. Be the one who greets kids with a smile and handshake every day. And support your own students by giving them more control over their daily lives.

The bottom line is this: If you choose to ignore your self-care and you're miserable at work, what's the message your kids are getting? To me, it sounds like they're getting a daily dose of, "If life is bad for my teacher, what chance do I have?"

Choose one action to get started:

- ☐ **Use the one-week rule:** If whatever is stressing you out now will not matter a week from now, let it go; make it irrelevant. Some things are just the noise of the day.
- ☐ **Redirect your attention and move on.** Learn to pivot in conversations that are going badly. "Oops, I gotta go. I'm running late. Catch you tomorrow."
- ☐ **Write it down for later;** keep a small notepad or use your mobile device to offload an action step when you have time.
- ☐ **Go for five minutes without complaining,** and then increase the length of time every week. It's not easy.
- ☐ **Practice mindfulness or meditation;** start up with apps. When you feel a new stress coming on, say to yourself, "I've got this. I am resilient and I can run my brain."
- ☐ **Talk it over with a friend or partner.** Get and give hugs often.
- ☐ **Reframe the experience:** "I learned something; I learned what *not* to do," or "That gave me a practice run."
- ☐ **Burn off energy with play or exercise.** Go for a walk or a run, take your kids to a park, play with your pet, or take a daily swim.

If this sounds like too much, pause for a moment. Start small. Take tiny steps. My own self-care process started more than 15 years ago. First, I began by defining a new identity: "I am one who values fitness and health." I started going to the gym. Then I started swimming. I kept at my habit. Last year, I swam more than 32 miles underwater, holding my breath for every pool length. No, I am not bragging. I say this because you need to know that I only ask others to do something I have already done and continue to do. My self-care habits have helped me regain the robust health I had decades ago. It is hard work, yet it's doable. Anything of value in life is like that. I started slowly, adding one tiny habit every month. Now I ask you to take on one new personal change.

Start here: In my own words, what change (that is an action step) am I choosing? _____

_____

Did I choose it, value it, and see the urgency? _____

_____

When will I start, and where? _____

_____

How will I track the habit and reward myself? _____

_____

Go Professional: Engaging with Classroom Equity

Many teachers will complain about their students, but never develop the expertise or daily habits to do anything about it. Take on a change. Be the one who is indispensable to your school. The bottom line is this: If you choose *not* to become really good at anything at work, what's the message you are sending to your students and colleagues?

Most of the educators I've met never develop a specific expertise, even after 20, 30, or 40 years in their profession. Imagine doing something for *a third of a century* and still having zero expertise. Yes, you've become older and more experienced. But are you any better? If you were, your student proficiency scores would be going up *every year.*

Become an expert with powerful habits. Nearly everyone has habits in their life. The question is, Will doing that habit today, and moving forward for the next five years, change anything?

Choose one action to get started:

☐ **Begin with yourself.** Purposefully choose your higher intentions, debunk one core bias per week, generate better stories, and foster a healthier identity.

☐ **Be culturally responsive.** Engage student voice, choice, and vision. Use verbal examples and materials that connect culturally. Ensure that every child's culture is respected and included.

☐ **Foster relationships.** Be an ally, not an adversary. See your students' faces, listen to them, believe in their ability to succeed, and tell them often. Be empathetic. When student behaviors need a pivot, remember the role of culture, stressors on the body, and the stereotype biases you may have. Use each student's name often.

☐ **Create equitable environments.** Be fair, positive, and challenging. Foster a safe in-group with 100 percent inclusion. Treat every student with the highest respect.

☐ **Teach with much higher expectations,** encouraging big goals and providing micro-feedback along the path. Be a role model by sharing your own high expectations for yourself.

☐ **Use the core rapid brain-builder rules.** Help students get smarter using rigor, engagement, relevance, and feedback.

Start here: In my own words, what action am I choosing? _____

_____

When will I start, and where? _____

_____

What's my trigger to start? _____

_____

How will I reward myself each time I complete the emerging habit? __

_____

Foster the Growth of Your Dreams

Most teachers see themselves as a Jack or Jill of all trades and master of none. That mindset is ineffective in a high-poverty school. School leaders often carelessly ask the staff to "do this and do that." Over a few years' time, teachers have been asked to do countless things, but rarely does a leader sit with the staff at the start of the year and have a conversation about "becoming an expert." Staff members who have no expertise are often considered more replaceable. I have discovered that being expert in a few important skills is far more valuable to your students and your colleagues than having busy hands with a busy calendar and being exhausted over fighting daily fires.

Forty percent of your day is spent following habits you already have (Wood, Quinn, & Kashy, 2002). Leaders in every industry rose to prominence by forming strong personal and workplace habits that drive health, relationships, and success. Figure 9.3 identifies how forming new habits helps change your mindset.

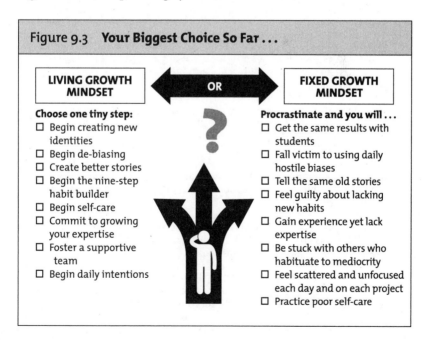

Figure 9.3   Your Biggest Choice So Far . . .

LIVING GROWTH MINDSET ← OR → **FIXED GROWTH MINDSET**

Choose one tiny step:
- ☐ Begin creating new identities
- ☐ Begin de-biasing
- ☐ Create better stories
- ☐ Begin the nine-step habit builder
- ☐ Begin self-care
- ☐ Commit to growing your expertise
- ☐ Foster a supportive team
- ☐ Begin daily intentions

Procrastinate and you will . . .
- ☐ Get the same results with students
- ☐ Fall victim to using daily hostile biases
- ☐ Tell the same old stories
- ☐ Feel guilty about lacking new habits
- ☐ Gain experience yet lack expertise
- ☐ Be stuck with others who habituate to mediocrity
- ☐ Feel scattered and unfocused each day and on each project
- ☐ Practice poor self-care

There are many, many ways to change habits. The simplest habit change tool is to create a cue to initiate the habit, define the behavior (with a plan B), and create a small, fun reward. The more thorough the process, the greater the likelihood it will succeed. I would rather you do that than nothing. So, if you're really ready to go, let's charge ahead with one final change tool: the "Nine-Step, Crush-It Habit Builder." Just write down the new habit you'd like to begin and complete the form in Figure 9.4.

Figure 9.4 Nine-Step, Crush-It Habit Builder

1. **Choice:** What is the action you chose that you want to become a habit? Ensure that it is your own idea.

2. **Buy-in:** Why is it important to you to begin this new action now? What makes it urgent?

3. **Shift and ensure your identity:** What identity do you need to have to guard and affirm this habit? "I am one who does …"

4. **Craft and shrink the change:** What starting step could you begin with that would get this habit going? Start with a 30-second to 3-minute change.

5. **Obstacles:** What obstacles may disrupt optimal implementation, and how can you mitigate them? This is your Plan B. Make plans to counter the potential problems, such as a fire drill, a visitor, or interruptions. Write them out and plug them in to the next step.

6. **Mentally walk through each step of the activity.** Have other staff members review the process so they can make sense of it, too. Revise any steps needed to ensure that the new habit works.

7. **Create a cue or trigger for the habit:** A simple cue could be an alert on your smartphone, the time on your classroom clock, a sticky-note reminder, the end of another action or habit, an action by a student or staff member, or even a bell.

8. **Create a tracking tool:** How will everyone keep track of accountability and rewards as they are making the changes? Examples include a calendar, peg marks, or a scale to weigh yourself.

9. **Set up rewards:** Simply marking progress can work as a reward—for example, making checks on a paper calendar or moving tokens from one jar to another. Some people like stickers or digital icons. If a sweet treat works, go for it. Or use your students' applause.

You can download a copy of this form at www.jensenlearning.com/ equity-resources. Retype it so you can edit it for clarity, change a word here and there, and make it your own. Fill out two copies, one for personal growth and one for professional growth. Post it up where you'll read it. It's time for you to get started.

Chapter in a Nutshell

I am a hopeful person. I am hoping that you become the kind of educator who catches yourself when you point fingers, and then owns your experience and the opportunities to change. I am hoping you foster equity because you realize that maybe your teaching was on autopilot and your biases needed debunking. I am hoping that every time you're tempted to blame another, you instead hold up a mirror. I am hoping you have allowed yourself to grow by broadening your identities. Trust me; I've faced all these challenges, and I am better off for doing it. Many people say, "Hope is not a strategy." I understand that. But hope must be in place *before you choose your strategy.*

Revisit the Student Questions

At the start of this chapter, the student questions seemed demanding. In retrospect, yes, they are.

> *"Is my teacher robust or fragile?"*

> *"Is my teacher an expert at anything?"*

> *"Does my teacher admit mistakes and demonstrate continuous growth?"*

> *"Can my teacher change for the better and adopt a new behavior?"*

I am hoping you're still with me and see and believe that these questions are critical. When students get affirmative answers, they are more than on your side; they'll do anything for you.

Our Journey Ends and Begins

I wrote this book to encourage you to take stock of your career. Educators rarely take the time to think critically about *their* lives, passions, and values. Most educators seem to prefer to go with the flow and take life as it comes. I understand that. I have been there. So why start the change? For me, it took hitting rock bottom. Most of the happiest people will tell you their life is full of little things that took time to build, often from the bottom up. That was me.

How do you want to spend the rest of your time on this planet? That decision can only be made by you. Clarity can power up your life. You'll never have to apologize for the people or things you love. Are you now walking the right path? Sometimes your view of the path ahead will seem hazy, but be patient. Maybe if you reread certain sections in this book, you'll find that your path reveals itself.

I hope to meet you someday at your school and see the excitement in your eyes and sense the spark in your heart. You know you'll be ready. I have faith in you. Just wake up fresh. Practice your habits. Have one good day. Then repeat. Again. And again . . . until next time.

Appendix A
10 Discovery Questions: What's True About Poverty?

(T/F) 1. The neighborhood that kids live in and the classroom teachers they have in school are two of the biggest influences on students' lifelong success.

True. Although many other factors also matter, research shows that both of these factors have a major influence on low-income students' success. Neighborhoods matter because they carry more than a dozen contributing factors: noise, safety, pollution, law enforcement, landlord pricing, property taxes, open spaces, community, and so on (Chetty, Hendren, Kline, & Saez, 2014). And teachers matter a great deal, too (Gordon, Kane, & Staiger, 2006; Wenglinsky, 2002).

(T/F) 2. Children from low-income families start school with smaller and less-complex vocabularies than their middle-income or high-income peers. There's a 30-million-word gap.

False. This one is complicated. First, the evidence is robust that the ideal time for fostering a rich vocabulary is in the early years (Golinkoff, Hoff, Rowe, Tamis-LeMonda, & Hirsh-Pasek, 2019). However, researchers (Adair, Sánchez-Suzuki Colegrove, & McManus, 2017) disagree about whether to make broad assumptions about the "30-million-word gap," a number that was first identified in Betty Hart and Todd R. Risley's 1995 study of just 43 children of one ethnicity (Black) in one geographic area. That's far too small a sample to generalize across the millions of children living in poverty. Multiple studies have failed to corroborate this "language gap" of 20–30 million words (Purpura, 2019; Sperry, Sperry, & Miller, 2019a; Sperry, Sperry, & Miller, 2019b). Some researchers, though, are concerned that questioning the size of the language gap will diminish policy change.

(T/F) 3. Students from poverty have typical brain development. They just fall behind because of lack of motivation or parental support. Unfortunately, once a student from poverty enters school one to three years behind, there is little hope.

False. There are two parts to this statement. First, regarding brain development, evidence from large samples of children from low-income households shows nontypical (atypical) brain development (Noble et al., 2015). This lag occurs in multiple crucial brain areas, including total gray matter, the temporal and frontal lobe, and the hippocampus (Hair, Hanson, Wolfe, & Pollak, 2015). The brain regions responsible for higher cognitive functioning continue to mature throughout childhood and adolescence (Sowell et al., 2003), meaning that the opportunity for change parallels the school years. The brain has a robust capacity for change.

The second part of this statement clearly suggests that teachers make little difference. Additionally, it suggests that the early brain is fixed. Both suggestions are false. When students from poverty are given above-average teachers (those whose average students gain at least 1.5 years' worth of learning every year), evidence shows that these students can gain two full standard deviations in scores between 1st grade and graduation (Ferguson, 1998).

The UTD Texas Schools Project (which observed more than a half-million students in multiple cohorts in grades 3–7 in more than 1,000 schools) found that teachers do make a difference. With higher-quality teachers, students from poverty outperformed their peers (Rivkin, Hanushek, & Kain, 2005). Another study found that replacing the lowest-performing 5–8 percent of teachers in the United States with average teachers would put the nation's schools' scores among the top three countries in the world, compared with number 17 currently (Hanushek, 2011). The data are unequivocal. Teachers matter (Chetty, Friedman, & Rockoff, 2011).

(T/F) 4. Even if you're poor in the United States, you're still doing pretty well. Poor people often have cell phones, name-brand shoes, and big-screen TVs.

False. Sometimes the visible stuff, such as showy "bling" or the latest tech gadgets, seems significant. But it's what you *don't* see that matters. The same poor families with those supposed "frills" may also be unable to afford a vacation, pay all their monthly bills, upgrade to a safer car, get air conditioning or heating for their homes, build up savings, own real estate, or start planning for retirement. They don't have enough money in their accounts to contract with an investment advisor to build a portfolio and get their money working for them.

If you criticize low-income parents who have cell phones (which are almost a must-have to get and keep a job) or buy their teenagers name-brand shoes (which are a low-cost way of showing social status), you're not looking in the right places. Yes, teenagers in middle and upper-income families also have those things. But for many who live in poverty, decisions are driven by the dual impact of threat and deprivation. Those two factors trigger a regulatory shift toward the present and the focus of cognitive skills on immediate wants and needs (Sheehy-Skeffington, 2020).

(T/F) 5. The United States' education system is mostly equal and fair, partly because we live in a meritocracy (a system based on effort and achievement).

False. The U.S. education system is choking with ethnic and socio-economic bias favoring middle-income and upper-income Whites and Asians. Not surprisingly, economic mobility patterns differ by race; Black Americans have much worse mobility patterns than White

Americans. In general, social and economic class is a far better pre-dictor than education level of where someone ends up in society (Harding, Jencks, Lopoo, & Mayer, 2005). For example, 54 percent of children born in the bottom quintile (one-fifth) income level *who do not get a high school diploma* remain on the bottom rung as adults. But among those born in the top income quintile, almost as many *remain on the top rung* (14 percent) as fall to the bottom (16 percent) (Reeves & Sawhill, 2014).

(T/F) 6. Poor people value education about the same as middle-income people do.

True. On the surface, poor people may appear to value education less. Family members from poverty often show up at fewer school functions because of extended work hours, transportation scarcity, and babysit-ting issues. That can create the illusion that they don't care. But the reality is that most (not all) students living in poverty attend schools with fewer resources, less-qualified teachers, and marginal leaders. Their parents have seen their children held to low expectations, sub-jected to discriminatory academic policies, and disciplined harshly. Yet in spite of that, most families in poverty do value education (Compton-Lilly, 2003).

(T/F) 7. It's cheaper to be poor. Poor people don't have to pay for a lot of things that middle-income and wealthy people have to pay for.

False. In poor neighborhoods, the nearest grocery store (via walking or public transportation) is often a high-priced mini mart. Those stores lack a wide selection of healthful foods, such as fresh vegetables. Poor families may not be able to afford an internet connection or a home lap-top, making it hard for them to research the best deals or lowest prices for consumer items. They may not be able to get the credit needed on short notice to take advantage of sales.

With little or no savings, poor families can be blindsided by unex-pected expenses (to repair a car, pay for a wedding or funeral, pay a security deposit of first and last month's rent on a new apartment, etc.). They may need to meet these emergencies by selling something or borrowing money. If they sell something, it's usually done at a pawn shop where they get a terrible price. If they borrow, it is usually at steep, unsecured interest rates, and the payments get harder and harder to make. In contrast, middle-income and wealthy families can often borrow cheaply from a home equity loan or use their savings (Board of Governors of the U.S. Federal Reserve, 2018).

(T/F) 8. Most poor people are unmotivated and lack ambition. They are more likely to be substance abusers than middle-income and wealthy people are.

False. On average, poor people work about the same number of hours per week as middle-income people do. The overwhelming majority of SNAP (food stamp) recipients who can work do work (Rosenbaum, 2013). In fact, 2019 data showed that in the year after receiving SNAP benefits, more than 70 percent of SNAP recipients worked. The great majority of children receiving SNAP benefits lived in households with at least one working adult (Center on Budget and Policy Priorities, 2019).

Regarding substance abuse, the data show that middle- and upper-income people have more access to drugs (cannabis, alcohol, opioids, meth, and prescriptions) and more money to spend on them (Diala, Muntaner, & Walrath, 2004; Lyman & Luthar, 2014). But what about actual usage? Drug and alcohol abuse are clearly more prevalent among wealthy people than among poor people (Galea, Ahern, Tracy, & Vlahov, 2007; Jones, 2015).

(T/F) 9. African Americans in poverty have higher rates of suicide, depression, and drug use and lower rates of college attendance and completion than those in any other racial or economic category.

False. *Native Americans* have the highest incidence of dropouts, domestic violence, substance abuse, and depression (Center for Behavioral Health Statistics and Quality, 2016; Eitle & Eitle, 2013; Libby,

Orton, Beals, Buchwald, Manson, & AI-SUPERPFP Team, 2008; Substance Abuse and Mental Health Services Administration, 2015). They have the highest school dropout rates at 37 percent, and the lowest percentage of college attendance. They also have the highest death rates from obesity, homicide, suicides, unintentional accidents, and injuries (Tomayko et al., 2017; Williams et al., 2018).

(T/F) 10. Poor people get more government handouts than nonpoor people do.

False. People from every socioeconomic level of society (more than 90 percent of all Americans) are beneficiaries of various government programs. Programs like Medicare, Social Security, and unemployment insurance are not limited to people living in poverty (Moses, 2011).

Many government benefits take the form of tax breaks that are not available to poor people: for example, tax deductions on home mortgage interest, business deductions, use of offshore financial accounts, and such wealth-building tools as trusts. People living in poverty pay less in federal income tax, but only because they don't earn enough to qualify. They do pay sales tax and payroll tax, and inequitable tax structures in the great majority of states mean that low- and middle-income families pay a much greater share of their income in taxes than wealthy families do. One study found that "On average, the lowest-income 20 percent of taxpayers face a state and local tax rate more than 50 percent higher than the top 1 percent of households. The nationwide average effective state and local tax rate is 11.4 percent for the lowest-income 20 percent of individuals and families, 9.9 percent for the middle 20 percent, and 7.4 percent for the top 1 percent" (Wiehle et al., 2013).

Appendix B
Questions That Students from Poverty May Ask (but Never Out Loud)

Begin to care about what students think about, ask, and worry about. Until you can wrap your head around the world that your students live in, you'll always struggle. Many researchers have asked students core questions: "What matters to you? What do you care about?"

Why ask students? *That's who we serve.* Here are their questions.

➢ *"Who is my teacher, and what does my teacher believe?"*

➢ *"Does my teacher respect and support me, or will I be marginalized again?"*

➢ *"Is my teacher an ally or an adversary?"*

➢ *"Does my teacher see, hear, and respect me with empathy and show that they care about how I am doing?"*

➢ *"Does my teacher have high expectations and truly believe in me?"*

➢ *"Is my teacher willing to challenge me to get better?"*

➢ *"Do I belong in this challenging academic environment, and can I succeed at this subject/in this class?"*

➢ *"Am I in the in-group or not? Is my culture respected?"*

➢ *"Will my voice be heard?"*

➢ *"Are my classroom and my school safe places to be myself and be free from harm?"*

➢ *"Does this work have real value (relevance), and does my teacher share the why with me every day?"*

➤ *"Will my teacher keep me connected, captivated, and engaged?"*

➤ *"Will I be bored and tired or energized and celebrated each day in class?"*

➤ *"Where am I right now?"*

➤ *"Where am I going?"*

➤ *"How do I get there?"*

➤ *"Does my teacher understand where I'm coming from? Will my teacher keep class culturally responsive, fair, and just?"*

➤ *"Can my teacher use whole-class student awareness to create a positive climate?"*

➤ *"If I struggle, is my teacher culturally and cognitively competent enough to help me succeed?"*

➤ *"If I make mistakes, will my teacher still believe in me?"*

➤ *"Can my teacher make changes for the better, and help me and my fellow students improve as well?"*

➤ *"Is my teacher robust or fragile?"*

➤ *"Is my teacher an expert at anything?"*

➤ *"Does my teacher admit mistakes and demonstrate continuous growth?"*

➤ *"Can my teacher change for the better and adopt a new behavior?"*

Sources for the Student Questions

The following surveys were used to gather and aggregate the questions listed at the start of each chapter. The results, from tens of thousands of students, show highly predictive student outcomes.

1. www.TripodProject.org
2. www.YouthTruthSurvey.org
3. www.ResonantEducation.com (formerly mystudentsurvey.org)
4. Farrington, Roderick, Allensworth, Nagaoka, Johnson, Keyes, & Beechum, 2012
5. Kirabo Jackson, 2012

Appendix C
How to De-Bias for Equity

Let's dig into *de-biasing*. This process is part of learning to run your own brain better. That means you'll discover how to manage or outsmart your brain's box of biases. In addition to a lack of awareness of the impact of our own biases in the classroom, educator overconfidence is a huge issue in de-biasing (Berner & Graber, 2008). Even those who are aware of the potential impact of biases on workplace judgment may not believe that they themselves are vulnerable to them (that's another bias). In short, there's a lot of work to do.

Seven Steps to Debunk the Bias

You'll want to be willing to challenge yourself with these steps. Since reading about it will not put it in action, be willing to engage the growth mindset and de-bias identity with just a few steps. There are only seven steps. Ready? Go!

☐ **Notice your own bias** when it occurs. Recognize your stereotypic response. ("Oops. I just caught myself using an *us vs. them* bias.") What was the bias? _____

☐ **Ask yourself,** "What's my intention in this conversation or analysis? Is it to finish up fast, or to thoughtfully examine the next steps?" Your response is: _____

☐ **Recheck and broaden your intended "identity"** in this situation. ("I am a thoughtful educator, fully committed to equity.") Restate your identity regarding this bias: _____

☐ **Reexamine full evidence.** Your own experiences need enriching from wider and deeper sources. *Ask others for counterevidence* or research online through free databases (e.g., eric.ed.gov or pubmed. ncbi.nlm.nih.gov). Spend time with a person different from you. Consider options for countering your bias, such as having conversations with teachers of a different ethnicity. Imagine out-group examples counter to your first stereotypic response. Your de-bias decision is: _____

☐ **Recall the trigger** (person, questions, event, etc.) and consider next-time readiness. ("I got upset. Next time that happens, I'll take a slow breath first.") Your new response is: _____

☐ **Tie up any loose ends** (is an apology needed?). Make contact with the person you had the stereotypic response with and learn a new perspective from conversations. ("I apologize to you. I never meant to marginalize another.") Your response is: _____

☐ **Apply a new decision:** Replace the bias with a fresh response (double-check for a new bias first) and follow it through. Find, start, and share positive success stories. Trigger a motivator to correct it and use a tool to change it. ("I believe in equity, and I choose to embody that belief every day.") Your new decision is: _____

Follow-Through Is Simple

☐ **For the next week:** Consider eliminating the elements that triggered the bias (redesign the working environment, rearrange teams or roles, or check workload fatigue at the time of the bias comment). Which one will you do? _____

☐ **For the long term, start these:** Switch perception from a stereotypic response to a more personalized response. ("This person is/was . . . .") Temporarily adopt the perspective of the other individual. (Don't assume that you know; if you don't, ask politely.) When you can empathize, you're on the right track toward success. Then take on the challenge of using de-bias steps for the other issues. Which one will you begin? _____

Sources on the De-Bias Process

- "Overconfidence as a Cause of Diagnostic Error in Medicine," by E. S. Berner & M. L. Graber, 2008. *American Journal of Medicine, 121*(5 Suppl), pp. S2–23.
- "Cognitive Debiasing 1: Origins of Bias and Theory of Debiasing," by P. Croskerry, G. Singhal, & S. Mamede, 2013a. *BMJ Quality & Safety, Suppl 2,* pp. ii58–ii64.
- "Cognitive Debiasing 2: Impediments to and Strategies for Change," by P. Croskerry, G. Singhal, & S. Mamede, 2013b. *BMJ Quality & Safety, Suppl 2,* pp. ii65–ii72.
- "Long-Term Reduction in Implicit Race Bias: A Prejudice Habit-Breaking Intervention," by P. G. Devine, P. S. Forscher, A. J. Austin, & W. T. L. Cox, 2012. *Journal of Experimental Social Psychology, 48,* pp. 1267–1278.
- "Cognitive Interventions to Reduce Diagnostic Error: A Narrative Review," by M. L. Graber, S. Kissam, V. L. Payne, A. L. Meyer, A. Sorensen, N. Lenfestey, et al., 2012. *BMJ Quality & Safety, 21,* pp. 535–557.
- "Before You Make That Big Decision," by D. Kahneman, D. Lovallo, & O. Sibony, 2011. *Harvard Business Review, 89,* pp. 50–60.

Appendix D
Suggested Booklist for Teaching with Poverty and Equity in Mind

Before you begin checking out the list, remember that poverty and racism are two separate issues. Yes, they overlap, but never assume that becoming engaged in just one of the two areas will meet all your students' needs. That being said, many students would find that teachers even going halfway would be a refreshing change.

Specifically for White Teachers
- *Between the World and Me* by Ta-Nehisi Coates
- *Caste* by Isabel Wilkerson
- *The New Jim Crow: Mass Incarceration in The Age of Colorblindness* by Michelle Alexander
- *The Sum of Us* by Heather McGee
- *White Fragility* by Robin DiAngelo

Specifically for Teachers of Black Students
- *About Centering Possibility in Black Education* by Chezare A. Warren
- *Strong Black Girls: Reclaiming Schools in Their Own Image* by Danielle Apugo, Lynnette Mawhinney, and Afiya Mbilishaka

Specifically for Teachers of Latino Students
- *Reaching Out to Latino Families of English Language Learners* by David Campos, Rocio Delgado, and Mary Esther Soto Huerta

Specifically for Teachers of Asian Students

+ *Unraveling the "Model Minority" Stereotype: Listening to Asian American Youth* by Stacey J. Lee

Specifically for Teachers of Native American Students

+ *Indian Education for All: Decolonizing Indigenous Education in Public Schools* by John P. Hopkins

Teaching Students of Multiple Ethnicities

+ *Becoming the Educator They Need: Strategies, Mindsets, and Beliefs for Supporting Male Black and Latino Students* by Robert Jackson
+ *Critical Race Theory in Teacher Education: Informing Classroom Culture and Practice* by Keonghee Tao Han and Judson Laughter
+ *Cultural Competence Now: 56 Exercises to Help Educators Understand and Challenge Bias, Racism, and Privilege* by Vernita Mayfield
+ *Culturally Responsive Teaching and the Brain: Promoting Authentic Engagement and Rigor Among Culturally and Linguistically Diverse Students* by Zaretta Hammond
+ *The Equity & Social Justice Education 50: Critical Questions for Improving Opportunities and Outcomes for Black Students* by Baruti K. Kafele
+ *Equity in School-Parent Partnerships: Cultivating Community and Family Trust in Culturally Diverse Classrooms* by Socorro G. Herrera, Lisa Porter, and Katherine Barko-Alva
+ *Generation Mixed Goes to School: Radically Listening to Multiracial Kids* by Ralina L. Joseph and Allison Briscoe-Smith
+ *The Innocent Classroom: Dismantling Racial Bias to Support Students of Color* by Alexs Pate
+ *Keeping It Real and Relevant: Building Authentic Relationships in Your Diverse Classroom* by Ignacio Lopez
+ *Racial Microaggressions: Using Critical Race Theory to Respond to Everyday Racism* by Daniel G. Solórzano and Lindsay Pérez Huber

References

Adair, J. K., Sánchez-Suzuki Colegrove, K., & McManus, M. E. (2017). How the word gap argument negatively impacts young children of Latinx immigrants' conceptualizations of learning. *Harvard Educational Review, 87,* 309–334.

Ainsworth, M., & Bowlby, J. (1991). An ethological approach to personality development. *American Psychologist, 46,* 333–341.

Albalooshi, S., Moeini-Jazani, M., Fennis, B. M., & Warlop, L. (2020). Reinstating the resourceful self: When and how self-affirmations improve executive performance of the powerless. *Personality and Social Psychology Bulletin, 46,* 189–203.

Alloway, T., & Alloway, R. (2010). Investigating the predictive roles of working memory and IQ in academic attainment. *Journal of Experimental Child Psychology, 106,* 20–29.

Amabile, T. M., & Kramer, S. J. (2011). The power of small wins. *Harvard Business Review, 89*(5), 70–80.

Ames, D. R., & Kammrath, L. K. (2004). Mind-reading and metacognition: Narcissism, not actual competence, predicts self-estimated ability. *Journal of Nonverbal Behavior, 28*(3).

Anderson, B. A. (2019). Neurobiology of value-driven attention. *Current Opinion in Psychology, 29,* 27–33.

Anderson, K. B., & Graham, L. M. (2007). Hostile attribution bias. *Encyclopedia of Social Psychology* (pp. 446–447). SAGE Publications.

Anderson, S. (2019, October 14). Immigrant Nobel Prize winners keep leading the way for America. *Forbes Magazine.* www.forbes.com/sites/stuartanderson/2019/10/14/immigrant-nobel-prize-winners-keep-leading-the-way-for-america

Atwell, M. N., Balfanz, R., Bridgeland, J., & Ingram, E. (2019). *Building a grad nation: Progress and challenge in raising high school graduation rates: Annual update 2019.* Johns Hopkins University School of Education. www.americaspromise.org/2019-building-grad-nation-report

Aven, T. (2018). Reflections on the use of conceptual research in risk analysis. *Risk Analysis, 38,* 2415–2423.

Azzam, A. (2007). Why students drop out. *Educational Leadership, 64*(7), 91–93.

Balfanz, J., Byrnes, V., & Fox, J. (2015). Sent home and put off track: The antecedents, disproportionalities, and consequences of being suspended in the 9th grade. In D. J. Losen (Ed.), *Closing the school discipline gap: Equitable remedies for excessive exclusion* (pp. 17–30). Teachers College Press.

Barros, R. M., Silver, E. J., & Stein, R. E. (2009). School recess and group classroom behavior. *Pediatrics, 123,* 431–436.

Basch, C. E. (2011a). Healthier students are better learners: High-quality, strategically planned, and effectively coordinated school health programs must be a fundamental mission of schools to help close the achievement gap. *Journal of School Health, 81,* 650–662.

Basch, C. E. (2011b). Physical activity and the achievement gap among urban minority youth. *Journal of School Health, 81,* 626–634.

Bates, T. C., Lewis, G. J., & Weiss, A. (2013). Childhood socioeconomic status amplifies genetic effects on adult intelligence. *Psychological Science, 24,* 2111–2116.

Benner, A. D., & Mistry, R. S. (2007). Congruence of mother and teacher educational expectations and low-income youth's academic competence. *Journal of Educational Psychology, 99*(1), 140–153.

Benson, B. (2016, September 1). Cognitive bias cheat sheet [blog post]. *Better Humans.* https://betterhumans.pub/cognitive-bias-cheat-sheet-55a472476b18

Berner, E. S., & Graber, M. L. (2008). Overconfidence as a cause of diagnostic error in medicine. *American Journal of Medicine, 121*(5 Suppl), S2–23.

Bernstein, M. J., & Claypool, H. M. (2012). Social exclusion and pain sensitivity: Why exclusion sometimes hurts and sometimes numbs. *Personality and Social Psychology Bulletin, 38,* 185–196.

Biswas, S. (2019, October 15). Abhijit Banerjee and Esther Duflo: The Nobel couple fighting poverty. *BBC News.* www.bbc.com/news/world-asia-india-50048519

Board of Governors of the U.S. Federal Reserve. (2018). *Report on the economic well-being of U.S. households in 2017.* Author.

Bonilla, E. (2008). Evidence about the power of intention. *Investigacion Clinica, 49*(4), 595–615.

Bönstrup, M., Iturrate, I., Thompson, R., Cruciani, G., Censor, N., & Cohen, L. G. (2019, April 22). A rapid form of offline consolidation in skill learning. *Current Biology, 29*(8), 1346–1351.

Boser, U., Wilhelm, M., & Hanna, R. (2014). *The power of the Pygmalion effect.* Center for American Progress.

Bottiani, J. H., Bradshaw, C. P., & Mendelson, T. (2016). Inequality in Black and White high school students' perceptions of school support: An examination of race in context. *Journal of Youth and Adolescence, 45*(6), 1176–1191.

Brown, C. S., & Chu, H. (2012). Discrimination, ethnic identity, and academic outcomes of Mexican immigrant children: The importance of school context. *Child Development, 83*(5), 1471–1485.

Brown, C. S., & Stone, E. A. (2016). Gender stereotypes and discrimination: How sexism impacts development. *Advances in Child Development and Behavior, 50,* 105–133.

Bruner, J. S. (2001). Self-making and world-making. In J. Brockmeier & D. Carbaugh (Eds.), *Narrative identity: Studies in autobiography, self and culture* (pp. 25–36). John Benjamins.

Buchweitz, A., & Prat, C. (2013). The bilingual brain: Flexibility and control in the human cortex. *Physics of Life Reviews, 10,* 428–443.

Burns, R. D., Brusseau, T. A., Fu, Y., Myrer, R. S., & Hannon, J. C. (2016). Comprehensive school physical activity programming and classroom behavior. *American Journal of Health Behavior, 40*(1), 100–107.

Buzzai, C., Sorrenti, L., Tripiciano, F., Orecchio, S., & Filippello, P. (2020). School alienation and academic achievement: The role of learned helplessness and mastery orientation. *School Psychology, 36*(1), 17–23.

Caeyenberghs, K., Metzler-Baddeley, C., Foley, S., & Jones, D. K. (2016). Dynamics of the human structural connectome underlying working memory training. *Journal of Neuroscience, 36,* 4056–4066.

Carey, R. L. (2019). Imagining the comprehensive mattering of Black boys and young men in society and schools: Toward a new approach. *Harvard Educational Review, 89*(3), 370–396.

Center for Behavioral Health Statistics and Quality. (2016). *2015 National survey on drug use and health: Detailed tables.* Substance Abuse and Mental Health Services Administration.

Center on Budget and Policy Priorities. (2019, June 25). *Policy basics: The Supplemental Nutrition Assistance Program (SNAP)*. www.cbpp.org/research/food-assistance/the-supplemental-nutrition-assistance-program-snap

Chetty, R., Friedman, J. N., & Rockoff, J. E. (2011). *The long-term impacts of teachers: Teacher value-added and student outcomes in adulthood* (NBER Working Paper 17699). National Bureau of Economic Research.

Chetty, R., Hendren, N., Kline, P., & Saez, E. (2014). Where is the land of opportunity in the United States? The geography of intergenerational mobility in the U.S. *Quarterly Journal of Economics, 129*(4), 1553–1623.

Children's Defense Fund. (2020). *The state of America's children 2020. Table 2: Poor children in America in 2018—A portrait*. www.childrensdefense.org/policy/resources/soac-2020-child-poverty-tables

Cohen, D. A., Pascual-Leone, A., Press, D. Z., & Robertson, E. M. (2005). Off-line learning of motor skill memory: A double dissociation of goal and movement. *Proceedings of the National Academy of Sciences of the United States of America, 102*, 18237–18241.

Compton-Lilly, C. (2003). *Reading families: The literate lives of urban children*. Teachers College Press.

Conway-Hicks, S., & de Groot, J. M. (2019). Living in two worlds: Becoming and being a doctor among those who identify with "not from an advantaged background." *Current Problems in Pediatric and Adolescent Health Care, 49*(4), 92–101.

Cook, D. A., & Artino, A. R., Jr. (2016). Motivation to learn: An overview of contemporary theories. *Medical Education, 50*, 997–1014.

Cooper, C. R., Domínguez, E., Cooper, R. G., Higgins, A., & Lipka, A. (2018). Capital, alienation, and challenge: How U.S. Mexican immigrant students build pathways to college and career identities. *New Directions for Child and Adolescent Development, 160*, 75–87.

Cooperative Children's Book Center, School of Education, University of Wisconsin, Madison. (2020). *Book by and/or about Black, Indigenous, and People of Color (all years)*. https://ccbc.education.wisc.edu/literature-resources/ccbc-diversity-statistics/books-by-about-poc-fnn

Cornelius-White, J. (2007). Learner-centered teacher-student relationships are effective: A meta-analysis. *Review of Educational Research, 77*, 113–143.

Cousijn, J., Zanolie, K., Munsters, R. J., Kleibeuker, S. W., & Crone, E. A. (2014). The relation between resting state connectivity and creativity in adolescents before and after training. *PLOS ONE, 9*(9), e105780.

Creamer, J. (2020, Sept. 15). *Inequities persist despite decline in poverty for all major race and Hispanic origin groups*. U.S. Census Bureau. www.census.gov/library/stories/2020/09/poverty-rates-for-blacks-and-hispanics-reached-historic-lows-in-2019.html

Croskerry P., Singhal, G., & Mamede, S. (2013a). Cognitive debiasing 1: Origins of bias and theory of debiasing. *BMJ Quality & Safety, Suppl 2*, ii58–ii64.

Croskerry, P., Singhal, G., & Mamede, S. (2013b). Cognitive debiasing 2: Impediments to and strategies for change. *BMJ Quality & Safety, Suppl 2*, ii65–ii72.

Curlik, D. M., & Shors, T. J. (2013). Training your brain: Do mental and physical (MAP) training enhance cognition through the process of neurogenesis in the hippocampus? *Neuropharmacology, 64*(1), 506–514.

Dalla, C., Bangasser, D., Edgecomb, C., & Shors, T. J. (2007). Neurogenesis and learning: Acquisition and asymptotic performance predict how many new cells survive in the hippocampus. *Neurobiology of Learning and Memory, 88*(1), 143–148.

Darley, J. M., & Gross, P. H. (2000). A hypothesis-confirming bias in labelling effects. In C. Stangor (Ed.), *Stereotypes and prejudice: Essential readings* (p. 212). Psychology Press.

Davis, H. A. (2013). Teacher-student relationships. In J. Hattie & E. M. Anderman (Eds.), *International Guide to Student Achievement* (pp. 221–223). Routledge.

Dee, T. S., & Penner, E. K. (2017). Causal effects of cultural relevance: Evidence from an ethnic studies curriculum. *American Educational Research Journal, 54*, 127–166.

De Houwer, J. (2019). Implicit bias is behavior: A functional-cognitive perspective on implicit bias. *Perspectives on Psychological Science, 14*, 835–840.

Devine, P. G., Forscher, P. S., Austin, A. J., & Cox, W. T. L. (2012). Long-term reduction in implicit race bias: A prejudice habit-breaking intervention. *Journal of Experimental Social Psychology, 48*, 1267–1278.

Dewar, D. (2020). Recognizing white privilege. *Canadian Family Physician, 66*, 879–882.

D'Hondt, F., Eccles, J. S., Houtte, M. V., & Stevens, P. A. (2016). Perceived ethnic discrimination by teachers and ethnic minority students' academic futility: Can parents prepare their youth for better or for worse? *Journal of Youth and Adolescence, 45*(6), 1075–1089.

Diala, C. C., Muntaner, C., & Walrath, C. (2004). Gender, occupational, and socioeconomic correlates of alcohol and drug abuse among U.S. rural, metropolitan, and urban residents. *American Journal of Drug and Alcohol Abuse, 30*(2), 409–428.

Dimitroff, S. J., Kardan, O., Necka, E. A., Decety, J., Berman, M. G., & Norman, G. J. (2017). Physiological dynamics of stress contagion. *Scientific Reports, 7*, 6168.

Domínguez, D. J. F., Lewis, E. D., Turner, R., & Egan, G. F. (2009). The brain in culture and culture in the brain: A review of core issues in neuroanthropology. *Progress in Brain Research, 178*, 43–64.

Downer, J. T., Sabol, T. J., & Hamre, B. (2010). Teacher–child interactions in the classroom: Toward a theory of within- and cross-domain links to children's developmental outcomes. *Early Education and Development, 21*, 699–723.

Draganski, B., Gaser, C., Busch, V., Schuierer, G., Bogdahn, U., & May, A. (2004). Neuroplasticity: Changes in grey matter induced by training. *Nature, 427*, 311–312.

Driscoll, K. C., & Pianta, R. C. (2010). Banking time in head start: Early efficacy of an intervention designed to promote supportive teacher-child relationships. *Early Education and Development, 21*, 38–64.

D'Souza, A. A., Moradzadeh, L., & Wiseheart, M. (2018). Musical training, bilingualism, and executive function: Working memory and inhibitory control. *Cognitive Research: Principles and Implications, 3*, 11.

Dubol, M., Trichard, C., Leroy, C., Sandu, A. L., Rahim, M., Granger, B., et al. (2018). Dopamine transporter and reward anticipation in a dimensional perspective: A multimodal brain imaging study. *Neuropsychopharmacology, 43*, 820–827.

Duckworth, A. L., Quinn, P. D., & Seligman, M. E. P. (2009). Positive predictors of teacher effectiveness. *Journal of Positive Psychology, 4*(6), 540–547.

Dudai, Y., Karni, A., & Born, J. (2015). The consolidation and transformation of memory. *Neuron, 88*, 20–32.

Dumont, H., Protsch, P., Jansen, M., & Becker, M. (2017). Fish swimming into the ocean: How tracking relates to students' self-beliefs and school disengagement at the end of schooling. *Journal of Educational Psychology, 109*, 855–870.

Efferson, C., Lalive, R., & Fehr, E. (2008). The coevolution of cultural groups and ingroup favoritism. *Science, 321*, 1844–1849.

Eitle, D. J., & Eitle, T. M. (2013). Methamphetamine use among rural White and Native American adolescents: An application of the stress process model. *Journal of Drug Education, 43*, 203–221.

Erwin, H., Fedewa, A., Beighle, A., & Ahn, S. (2012). A quantitative review of physical activity, health, and learning outcomes associated with classroom-based physical activity interventions. *Journal of Applied School Psychology, 28*, 14–36.

Eryilmaz, H., Rodriguez-Thompson, A., Tanner, A. S., Giegold, M., Huntington, F. C., & Roffman, J. L. (2017). Neural determinants of human goal-directed vs. habitual action control and their relation to trait motivation. *Scientific Reports, 7*, 6002.

Essa, H. (2016). *Teach us your name.* Kindle Direct Publishing.

Evans, G. W., Gonnella, C., Marcynyszyn, L. A., Gentile, L., & Salpekar, N. (2005). The role of chaos in poverty and children's socioemotional adjustment. *Psychological Science, 16,* 560–565.

Evans, G. W., & Kim, P. (2012). Childhood poverty and young adults' allostatic load: The mediating role of childhood cumulative risk exposure. *Psychological Science, 23,* 979–983.

Evans, G. W., Li, D., & Whipple, S. S. (2013). Cumulative risk and child development. *Psychological Bulletin, 139,* 1342–1396.

Evans, G. W., Swain, J. E., King, A. P., Wang, X., Javanbakht, A., Ho, S. S., et al. (2016). Childhood cumulative risk exposure and adult amygdala volume and function. *Journal of Neuroscience Research, 94,* 535–543.

Ewing, J. (2020). *Math for ELLs: As easy as uno, dos, tres.* Rowman and Littlefield.

Fabelo, T., Thompson, M. D., Plotkin, M., Carmichael, D., Marchbanks, M. P., III, & Booth, E. A. (2011). *Breaking schools' rules: A statewide study of how school discipline relates to students' success and juvenile justice involvement.* Council of State Governments Justice Center. https://csgjusticecenter.org/publications/breaking-schools-rules

Farrington, C. A., Roderick, M., Allensworth, E. A., Nagaoka, J., Johnson, D. W., Keyes, T. S., & Beechum, N. (2012). *Teaching adolescents to become learners: The role of noncognitive factors in academic performance: A critical literature review.* Consortium on Chicago School Research.

Felitti, V. J., Anda, R. F., Nordenberg, D., Williamson, D. F., Spitz, A. M., Edwards, V., et al. (1998, May). Relationship of childhood abuse and household dysfunction to many of the leading causes of death in adults. The Adverse Childhood Experiences (ACE) Study. *American Journal of Preventive Medicine, 14*(4), 245–258.

Ferguson, R. (1998). Can schools narrow the test score gap? In C. Jencks & M. Phillips, Eds., *The black-white test score gap: Why it persists and what can be done* (pp. 318–374). Brookings Institution.

Ferguson, R. F. (2003). Teachers' perceptions and expectations and the black-white test score gap. *Urban Education, 38,* 460–507.

Feynman, R. (2015). *The quotable Feynman.* Princeton University Press.

Flowerday, T., & Schraw, G. (2000). Teacher beliefs about instructional choice: A phenomenological study. *Journal of Educational Psychology, 92,* 634–645.

Forgiarini, M., Gallucci, M., & Maravita, A. (2011). Racism and the empathy for pain on our skin. *Frontiers in Psychology, 2,* 108.

Frazier, P., Gabriel, A., Merians, A., & Lust, K. (2019, October). Understanding stress as an impediment to academic achievement. *Journal of American College Health, 67*(6), 562–570.

Frías-Lasserre, D., Villagra, C. A., & Guerrero-Bosagna, C. (2018). Stress in the educational system as a potential source of epigenetic influences on children's development and behavior. *Frontiers in Behavioral Neuroscience, 12,* 143.

Fullilove, R. E., & Treisman, P. U. (1990). Mathematics achievement among African-American undergraduates at the University of California, Berkeley. *Journal of Negro Education, 59,* 463–478.

Galea, S., Ahern, J., Tracy, M., & Vlahov, D. (2007). Neighborhood income and income distribution and the use of cigarettes, alcohol, and marijuana. *American Journal of Preventive Medicine, 32,* 195–202.

Gershenson, S., Hart, C. M. D., Lindsay, C. A., & Papageorge, N. W. (2017). *The long-run impacts of same-race teachers* (Working Paper 25254). National Bureau of Economic Research. www.nber.org/system/files/working_papers/w25254/w25254.pdf

Gershenson, S., Holt, S. B., & Papageorge, N. W. (2016, June). Who believes me? The effect of student-teacher demographic match on teacher expectations. *Economics of Education Review, 52,* 209–224.

Gershenson, S., & Papageorge, N. (2021). The power of teacher expectations. *Education Next, 18*(1). www.educationnext.org/power-of-teacher-expectations-racial-bias-hinders-student-attainment

Gibbs, B. G. (2010). Reversing fortunes or content change? Gender gaps in math-related skill throughout childhood. *Social Science Research, 39,* 540–569.

Glock, S., Kovacs, C., & Pit-ten Cate, I. (2019). Teachers' attitudes towards ethnic minority students: Effects of schools' cultural diversity. *British Journal of Educational Psychology, 89*(4), 616–634.

Goldhaber, D., Theobald, R., & Tien, C. (2019). Why we need a diverse teacher workforce. *Phi Delta Kappan, 100*(5), 25–30.

Golinkoff, R. M., Hoff, E., Rowe, M. L., Tamis-LeMonda, C. S., & Hirsh-Pasek, K. (2019). Language matters: Denying the existence of the 30-million-word gap has serious consequences. *Child Development, 90*(3), 985–992.

Gordon, R., Kane, T. J., & Staiger, D. O. (2006). *Identifying effective teachers using performance on the job* (Discussion Paper No. 2006-01). Brookings Institution.

Graber, M. L., Kissam, S., Payne, V. L., Meyer, A. L., Sorensen, A., Lenfestey. N., et al. (2012). Cognitive interventions to reduce diagnostic error: A narrative review. *BMJ Quality & Safety, 21,* 535–557.

Greene, R. W. (2016). *Lost and found: Helping behaviorally challenging students.* Jossey-Bass.

Gupta, R. (2019). Positive emotions have a unique capacity to capture attention. *Progress in Brain Research, 247,* 23–46.

Hagoort, P. (2020). The meaning-making mechanism(s) behind the eyes and between the ears. *Philosophical Transactions of the Royal Society B: Biological Sciences, 375*(1791).

Hair, N. L., Hanson, J. L., Wolfe, B. L., & Pollak, S. D. (2015). Association of child poverty, brain development, and academic achievement. *JAMA Pediatrics, 169*(9), 822–829.

Hammond, Z. (2015). *Culturally responsive teaching and the brain.* Corwin.

Hanson, J. L., Chandra, A., Wolfe, B. L., & Pollak, S. D. (2011). Association between income and the hippocampus. *PLOS ONE, 6*(5), e18712.

Hanushek, E. A. (2011). The economic value of higher teacher quality. *Economics of Education Review, 30,* 466–479.

Harding, D. J., Jencks, C., Lopoo L., & Mayer, S. (2005). The changing effects of family background on the incomes of American adults. In S. Bowles, H. Gintis, & M. Osborne Groves (Eds.), *Unequal chances: Family background and economic success* (pp. 100–144). Russell Sage Foundation.

Hardt, J., & Rutter, M. (2004). Validity of adult retrospective reports of adverse childhood experiences: Review of the evidence. *Journal of Child Psychology and Psychiatry, 45,* 260–273.

Hart, B., & Risley, T. R. (1995). *Meaningful differences in the everyday experience of young American children.* Paul H. Brookes.

Hart, W., Albarracin, D., Eagly, A. H., Brechan, I., Lindberg, M. J., & Merrill, L. (2009). Feeling validated versus being correct: A meta-analysis of selective exposure to information. *Psychological Bulletin, 135,* 555–588.

Hattie, J. A. (2012). *Visible learning for teachers: Maximizing impact on learning.* Routledge.

Hattie, J. A. (2022). *Visible learning MetaX database.* Corwin Visible Learning Plus. www.visiblelearningmetax.com/Influences

Hattie, J. A., & Timperley, H. (2007). The power of feedback. *Review of Educational Research, 77,* 81–112.

Hattie, J. A., & Yates, G. (2013). *Visible learning and the science of how we learn.* Routledge.

Hegelund, E. R., Gronkjaer, M., Osler, M., Dammeyer, J., Flensborg-Madsen, T., & Mortensen, E. L. (2020, January). The influence of educational attainment on intelligence. *Intelligence, 78,* 101419.

Hofstetter, S., Tavor, I., Moryosef, S. T., & Assaf, Y. (2013). Short-term learning induces white matter plasticity in the fornix. *Journal of Neuroscience, 33*(31), 12844–12850.

Hollis, J. F., Gullion, C. M., Stevens, V. J., Brantley, P. J., Appel, L. J., Ard, J. D., et al. (2008). Weight loss during the intensive intervention phase of the weight-loss maintenance trial. *American Journal of Preventative Medicine, 35*(2), 118.

Hsen-Hsing, M. (2009). The effect size of variables associated with creativity. *Creativity Research Journal, 21*(1), 30–42.

Hughes, J. N. (2011). Longitudinal effects of teacher and student perceptions of teacher–student relationship qualities on academic adjustment. *Elementary School Journal, 112,* 38–60.

Hughes, M., & Tucker, W. (2018). Poverty as an adverse childhood experience. *North Carolina Medical Journal, 79,* 124–126.

Hus, Y. (2001). Early reading for low-SES minority language children: An attempt to "catch them before they fall." *Folia Phoniatrica et Logopaedica, 53,* 173–182.

Hussar, B., Zhang, J., Hein, S., Wang, K., Roberts, A., Cui, J., et al. (2020). *The condition of education 2020.* National Center for Education Statistics, U.S. Department of Education. https://nces.ed.gov/pubs2020/2020144.pdf

Ingersoll, R. M., Merrill, E., Stuckey, D., & Collins, G. (2018). *Seven trends: The transformation of the teaching force—Updated October 2018 (#RR 2018-2).* Consortium for Policy Research in Education, University of Pennsylvania. https://repository.upenn.edu/cgi/viewcontent.cgi?article=1109&context=cpre_researchreports

Jacob, A., & McGovern, K. (2015). *The mirage: Confronting the hard truth about our quest for teacher development.* TNTP. http://tntp.org/assets/documents/TNTP-Mirage_2015.pdf

Jednoróg, K., Altarelli, I., Monzalvo, K., Fluss, J., Dubois, J., Billard, C., et al. (2012). The influence of socioeconomic status on children's brain structure. *PLOS ONE, 7*(8), e42486.

Jeon, Y. K., & Ha, C. H. (2017). The effect of exercise intensity on brain derived neurotrophic factor and memory in adolescents. *Environmental Health and Preventive Medicine, 22*(1), 27.

Jones, E. E., Carter-Sowell, A. R., Kelly, J. R., & Williams, K. D. (2009). "I'm out of the loop": Ostracism through information exclusion. *Group Processes and Intergroup Relations, 12,* 157–174.

Jones, J. M. (2015, July 27). *Gallup poll: Drinking highest among educated, upper-income Americans.* https://news.gallup.com/poll/184358/drinking-highest-among-educated-upper-income-americans.aspx

Juárez Ramos, V. (2019). *Analyzing the role of cognitive biases in the decision-making process.* IGI Global.

Kaba, A. (2020). MacArthur Fellows, 1981–2018: Gender, race and educational attainment. *Sociology Mind, 10,* 86–126.

Kahneman, D. (2011). *Thinking, fast and slow.* Farrar, Straus & Giroux.

Kahneman, D., Knetsch, J. L., & Thaler, R. H. (1991). Anomalies: The endowment effect, loss aversion, and status quo bias. *The Journal of Economic Perspectives, 5,* 193–206.

Kahneman, D., Lovallo, D., & Sibony, O. (2011). Before you make that big decision. *Harvard Business Review, 89,* 50–60.

Kaiser Family Foundation. (2019). *State health facts: Poverty rate by race/ethnicity.* www.kff.org/other/state-indicator/poverty-rate-by-raceethnicity

Kang, C., Fu, Y., Wu, J., Ma, F., Lu, C., & Guo, T. (2017). Short-term language switching training tunes the neural correlates of cognitive control in bilingual language production. *Human Brain Mapping, 38,* 5859–5870.

Kanherkar, R. R., Bhatia-Dey, N., & Csoka, A. B. (2014). Epigenetics across the human lifespan. *Frontiers in Cell and Developmental Biology, 2,* 49.

Karlsson, N., Loewenstein, G., & Seppi, D. (2009). The ostrich effect: Selective attention to information. *Journal of Risk and Uncertainty, 38,* 95–115.

Kendi, I. X. (2019). *How to be an antiracist.* Random House.

Kenrick, D. T., Neuberg, S. L., Griskevicius, V., Becker, D. V., & Schaller, M. (2010). Goal-driven cognition and functional behavior: The fundamental-motives framework. *Current Directions in Psychological Science, 19,* 63–67.

Kidd, C., & Hayden, B. Y. (2015). The psychology and neuroscience of curiosity. *Neuron, 88*(3), 449–460.

Kidwell, S. L., Young, M. E., Hinkle, L. D., Ratliff, A. D., Marcum, M. E., & Martin, C. N. (2010). Emotional competence and behavior problems: Differences across preschool assessment of attachment classifications. *Clinical Child Psychology and Psychiatry, 15,* 391–406.

Kiecolt-Glaser, J. K., Gouin, J. P., & Hantsoo, L. (2010). Close relationships, inflammation, and health. *Neuroscience and Biobehavioral Reviews, 35,* 33–38.

Kirabo Jackson, C. (2012). *Non-cognitive ability, test scores, and teacher quality: Evidence from 9th grade teachers in North Carolina.* (NBER Working Paper 18624). National Bureau of Economic Research. www.nber.org/papers/w18624

Kitayama, S., & Uskul, A. K. (2011). Culture, mind, and the brain: Current evidence and future directions. *Annual Review of Psychology, 62,* 419–449.

Knowles, M. L., Lucas, G. M., Molden, D. C., Gardner, W. L., & Dean, K. K. (2010). There's no substitute for belonging: Self-affirmation following social and nonsocial threats. *Personality and Social Psychology Bulletin, 36,* 173–186.

Kong, F., Ma, X., You, X., & Xiang, Y. (2018). The resilient brain: Psychological resilience mediates the effect of amplitude of low-frequency fluctuations in orbitofrontal cortex on subjective well-being in young healthy adults. *Social Cognitive and Affective Neuroscience, 13,* 755–763.

Korn, C. W., Rosenblau, G., Rodriguez Buritica, J. M., & Heekeren, H. R. (2016). Performance feedback processing is positively biased as predicted by attribution theory. *PLOS ONE, 11*(2), e0148581.

Landry, S. P., & Champoux, F. (2017). Musicians react faster and are better multisensory integrators. *Brain and Cognition, 111,* 156–162.

Leitch, L. (2017). Action steps using ACEs and trauma-informed care: A resilience model. *Health Justice, 5,* 5.

Lewis, G. M. (2014). Implementing a reform-oriented pedagogy: Challenges for novice secondary mathematics teachers. *Mathematics Education Research Journal, 26,* 399–419.

Li, H. X., Long, Q. S., Chen, A. T., & Li, Q. (2019). The influence of reward motivation on emotion regulation. *Sheng Li Xue Bao, 71,* 562–574.

Libby, A. M., Orton, H. D., Beals, J., Buchwald, D., Manson S. M, & AI-SUPERPFP Team (2008). Childhood abuse and later parenting outcomes in two American Indian tribes. *Child Abuse & Neglect, 32*(2), 195–211.

Lim, S., & Eo, S. (2014). The mediating roles of collective teacher efficacy in the relations of teachers' perceptions of school organizational climate to their burnout. *Teaching and Teacher Education, 44,* 138–147.

Lindebaum, D., & Geddes, D. (2016). The place and role of (moral) anger in organizational behavior studies. *Journal of Organizational Behavior, 37,* 738–757.

Losen, D. J., & Martinez, T. E. (2013). *Out of school and off track: The overuse of suspensions in American middle and high schools.* Civil Rights Project.

Lyman, E. L., & Luthar, S. S. (2014). Further evidence on the "costs of privilege": Perfectionism in high-achieving youth at socioeconomic extremes. *Psychology in the Schools, 51,* 913–930.

Mackey, A. P., Singley, A. T. M., Wendelken, C., & Bunge, S. A. (2015). Characterizing behavioral and brain changes associated with practicing reasoning skills. *PLOS ONE, 10*(9).

Maier, S. F., & Seligman, M. E. (2016). Learned helplessness at fifty: Insights from neuroscience. *Psychological Review, 123,* 349–367.

Maier, S. F., & Watkins, L. R. (2010). Role of the medial prefrontal cortex in coping and resilience. *Brain Research, 1355,* 52–60.

Malle, B. F. (2011). Attribution theories: How people make sense of behavior. In D. Chadee (Ed.), *Theories in social psychology* (pp. 72–95). Wiley-Blackwell.

Martinez, F. (2021, September 30). Latinx files: The six Latinx "geniuses." *Los Angeles Times.* www.latimes.com/world-nation/newsletter/2021-09-30/latinx-files-macarthur-genius-fellows-latinx-files

Marzano, R. J. (2003). Building classroom relationships. *Educational Leadership, 61*(1), 6–13.

Marzano, R. J., Marzano, J. S., & Pickering, D. J. (2003). *Classroom management that works.* ASCD.

Masten, C. L., Telzer, E. H., & Eisenberger, N. I. (2011). An FMRI investigation of attributing negative social treatment to racial discrimination. *Journal of Cognitive Neuroscience, 23,* 1042–1051.

Masuda, N., & Fu, F. (2015). Evolutionary models of in-group favoritism. *F1000prime Reports, 7*(27).

Mayfield, V. (2020). *Cultural competence now: 56 exercises to help educators understand and challenge bias, racism, and privilege.* ASCD.

McAdams, D. P., & Guo, J. (2015). Narrating the generative life. *Psychological Science, 26*(4), 475–483.

McCormick, M. P., O'Connor, E. E., Cappella, E., & McClowry, S. G. (2013). Teacher–child relationships and academic achievement: A multilevel propensity score model approach. *Journal of School Psychology, 51,* 611–624.

McCoy, H. (2020, October). Black lives matter, and yes, you are racist: The parallelism of the twentieth and twenty-first centuries. *Child & Adolescent Social Work Journal, 37,* 463–475.

McIntosh, P. (1989). *White privilege: Unpacking the invisible knapsack.* https://psychology.umbc.edu/files/2016/10/White-Privilege_McIntosh-1989.pdf

McKinnon, R. D., Friedman-Krauss, A., Roy, A. L., & Raver, C. C. (2018). Teacher-child relationships in the context of poverty: The role of frequent school mobility. *Journal of Children and Poverty, 24,* 25–46.

McLaughlin, K. A., Weissman, D., & Bitrán, D. (2019). Childhood adversity and neural development: A systematic review. *Annual Review of Developmental Psychology, 1,* 277–312.

Meeusen, R. (2005). Exercise and the brain: Insight in new therapeutic modalities. *Annals of Transplantation, 10,* 49–51.

Mergelsberg, E. L. P., Mullan, B. A., Allom, V., & Scott, A. (2020, June 17). An intervention designed to investigate habit formation in a novel health behaviour. *Psychology & Health,* 1–22.

Merrick, M. T., Ford, D. C., Ports, K. A., & Guinn, A. S. (2018). Prevalence of adverse childhood experiences from the 2011–2014 behavioral risk factor surveillance system in 23 states. *JAMA Pediatrics, 172,* 1038–1044.

Mezulis, A. H., Abramson, L. Y., Hyde, J. S., & Hankin, B. L. (2004). Is there a universal positivity bias in attributions? A meta-analytic review of individual, developmental, and cultural differences in the self-serving attributional bias. *Psychological Bulletin, 130,* 711–747.

Miasnikov, A. A., Chen, J. C., Gross, N., Poytress, B. S., & Weinberger, N. M. (2008). Motivationally neutral stimulation of the nucleus basalis induces specific behavioral memory. *Neurobiology of Learning and Memory, 90,* 125–137.

Milne, S., Orbell, S. & Sheeran, P. (2002). Combining motivational and volitional interventions to promote exercise participation: Protection motivation theory and implementation intentions. *British Journal of Health Psychology, 7(Pt. 2)*, 163–194.

Moffett, M. W. (2013). Human identity and the evolution of societies. *Human Nature, 24*, 219–267.

Moolenaar, N. M., Sleegers, P. J., & Daly, A. J. (2012). Teaming up: Linking collaboration networks, collective efficacy, and student achievement. *Teaching and Teacher Education, 28*(2), 251–262.

Morewedge, C. K., & Kahneman, D. (2010). Associative processes in intuitive judgment. *Trends in Cognitive Science, 14*, 435–440.

Moses, J. (2011, December). *The facts about Americans who receive public benefits.* Center for American Progress.

Nadal, K. (2018). *Microaggressions and traumatic stress: Theory, research, and clinical treatment.* American Psychological Association.

Nation's Report Card. (2019). *NAEP reading: National student group scores and score gaps.* www.nationsreportcard.gov/reading/nation/groups?grade=4

Nelson, B. D., & Hajcak, G. (2017). Defensive motivation and attention in anticipation of different types of predictable and unpredictable threat: A startle and event-related potential investigation. *Psychophysiology, 54*(8), 1180–1194.

Niehaus, K., Rudasill, K. M., & Rakes, R. (2012). A longitudinal study of school connectedness and academic outcomes across sixth grade. *Journal of School Psychology, 50*, 443–460.

Nielson, K. A., & Bryant, T. (2005). The effects of non-contingent extrinsic and intrinsic rewards on memory consolidation. *Neurobiology of Learning and Memory, 84*, 42–48.

Noble, K. G., Houston, S. M., Brito, N. H., Bartsch, H., Kan, E., Kuperman, J. M., et al. (2015). Family income, parental education and brain structure in children and adolescents. *Nature Neuroscience, 18*(5), 773–778.

Noble, K. G., Houston, S. M., Kan, E., & Sowell, E. R. (2012). Neural correlates of socioeconomic status in the developing human brain. *Developmental Science, 15*, 516–527.

Noice, H., Noice, T., & Staines, G. (2014). A short-term intervention to enhance cognitive and affective functioning in older adults. *Journal of Aging and Health, 16*, 562–585.

Olejnik, S., & Algina, J. (2000). Measures of effect size for comparative studies: Applications, interpretations, and limitations. *Contemporary Educational Psychology, 25*, 241–286.

Ortega, L., Lyubansky, M., Nettles, S., & Espelage, D. L. (2016). Outcomes of a restorative circles program in a high school setting. *Psychology of Violence, 6*, 459–468.

Ortiz, R. (2019). Building resilience against the sequelae of adverse childhood experiences: Rise up, change your life, and reform health care. *American Journal of Lifestyle Medicine, 13*, 470–479.

Ozubko, J. D., & Fugelsang, J. (2011). Remembering makes evidence compelling: Retrieval from memory can give rise to the illusion of truth. *Journal of Experimental Psychology: Learning, Memory, and Cognition, 37*(1), 270–276.

Pappa, K., Biswas, V., Flegal, K. E., Evans, J. J., & Baylan, S. (2020). Working memory updating training promotes plasticity & behavioural gains: A systematic review & meta-analysis. *Neuroscience & Biobehavioral Reviews, 18*, 209–235.

Parker, E. A., Feinberg, T. M., Lane, H. G., Deitch, R., Zemanick, A., Saksvig, B. I., et al. (2020). Diet quality of elementary and middle school teachers is associated with healthier nutrition-related classroom practices. *Preventive Medicine Reports, 18*, 101087.

Patall, E. A., Cooper, H., & Robinson, J. C. (2008). The effects of choice on intrinsic motivation and related outcomes: A meta-analysis of research findings. *Psychological Bulletin, 134*, 270–300.

Plomin, R., & Deary, I. J. (2015). Genetics and intelligence differences: Five special findings. *Molecular Psychiatry, 20*, 89–108.

Pohl, R. F. (Ed.) (2004). *Cognitive illusions: A handbook on fallacies and biases in thinking, judgement and memory.* Psychology Press.

Pontifex, M. B., Gwizdala, K. L., Parks, A. C., Pfeiffer, K. A., & Fenn, K. M. (2016). The association between physical activity during the day and long-term memory stability. *Scientific Reports, 6*, 38148.

Powers, J. T., Cook, J. E., Purdie-Vaughns, V., Garcia, J., Apfel, N., & Cohen, G. L. (2016). Changing environments by changing individuals: The emergent effects of psychological intervention. *Psychological Science, 27*, 150–160.

Pronin, E., Lin, D. Y., & Ross, L. (2002). The bias blind spot: Perceptions of bias in self versus others. *Personality and Social Psychology Bulletin, 28*, 369–381.

Purpura, D. J. (2019, October). Language clearly matters; Methods matter too. *Child Development, 90*(6), 1839–1846.

Quaedflieg, C., & Schwabe, L. (2018, March). Memory dynamics under stress. *Memory, 26*(3), 364–376.

Quevedo, K., Waters, T. E., Scott, H., Roisman, G. I., Shaw, D. S., & Forbes, E. E. (2017). Brain activity and infant attachment history in young men during loss and reward processing. *Development and Psychopathology, 29*, 465–476.

Raphael, D. (2011). Poverty in childhood and adverse health outcomes in adulthood. *Maturitas, 69*, 22–26.

Ratey, J. J. (2008). *Spark: The revolutionary new science of exercise and the brain.* Little, Brown and Company.

Rea, K., Dinan, T. G., & Cryan, J. F. (2016). The microbiome: A key regulator of stress and neuroinflammation. *Neurobiology of Stress, 4*, 23–33.

Reeves, R. V., & Sawhill, I. V. (2014). *Equality of opportunity: Definitions, trends, and interventions.* Conference paper presented at the 58th Economic Conference, Federal Reserve Bank of Boston, October 2014. www.bostonfed.org/inequality2014/papers/reeves-sawhill.pdf

Ritchie, S. J., & Tucker-Drob, E. M. (2018). How much does education improve intelligence? A meta-analysis. *Psychological Science, 29*, 1358–1369.

Rivkin, S. G., Hanushek, E. A., & Kain, J. F. (2005, March). Teachers, schools, and academic achievement. *Econometrica, 73*(2), 417–458.

Robinson-Cimpian, J. P., Lubienski, S. T., Ganley, C. M., & Copur-Gencturk, Y. (2014). Teachers' perceptions of students' mathematics proficiency may exacerbate early gender gaps in achievement. *Developmental Psychology, 50*, 1262–1281.

Roebroeks, W., & Soressi, M. (2016). Neanderthals revised. *Proceedings of the National Academy of Sciences of the United States of America, 113*, 6372–6379.

Roorda, D. L., Koomen, H. M. Y., Spilt, J. L., & Oort, F. J. (2011). The influence of affective teacher-student relationships on students' school engagement and achievement: A meta-analytic approach. *Review of Educational Research, 81*(4), 493–529.

Roos, L. E., Knight, E. L., Beauchamp K. G., Berkman, E. T., Faraday, K., Hyslop, K., & Fisher, P. A. (2017). Acute stress impairs inhibitory control based on individual differences in parasympathetic nervous system activity. *Biological Psychology, 125*, 58–63.

Rosenbaum, D. (2013). *The relationship between SNAP and work among low-income households.* Center on Budget and Household Priorities.

Rudasill, K. M. (2011). Child temperament, teacher–child interactions, and teacher–child relationships: A longitudinal investigation from first to third grade. *Early Childhood Research Quarterly, 26*, 147–156.

Rutter, M., Moffitt, T. E., & Caspi, A. (2006). Gene-environment interplay and psychopathology: Multiple varieties but real effects. *Journal of Child Psychology and Psychiatry, 47*(3–4), 226–261.

Schlegel, A. A., Rudelson, J. J., & Tse, P. U. (2012). White matter structure changes as adults learn a second language. *Journal of Cognitive Neuroscience, 24,* 1664–1670.

Schwanhäusser, B., Busse, D., Li, N., Dittmar, G., Schuchhardt, J., Wolf, J., et al. (2011). Global quantification of mammalian gene expression control. *Nature, 473,* 337–342.

Schweiger, G. (2019). Ethics, poverty and children's vulnerability. *Ethics & Social Welfare, 13,* 288–301.

Shaffer, M. L. (2019). Impacting student motivation: Reasons for not eliminating extracurricular activities. *Journal of Physical Education, Recreation & Dance, 90,* 8–14.

Sheehy-Skeffington, J. (2020). The effects of low socioeconomic status on decision-making processes. *Current Opinion in Psychology, 33,* 183–188.

Slater, J., Strait, D. L., Skoe, E., O'Connell, S., Thompson, E., & Kraus, N. (2014). Longitudinal effects of group music instruction on literacy skills in low-income children. *PLOS ONE, 19*(11), e113383.

Smaldino, P. E. (2019). Social identity and cooperation in cultural evolution. *Behavioural Processes, 161,* 108–116.

Sneve, M. H., Grydeland, H., Amlien, I. K., Langnes, E., Walhovd, K. B., & Fjell, A. M. (2017). Decoupling of large-scale brain networks supports the consolidation of durable episodic memories. *Neuroimage, 153,* 336–345.

Sowell, E. R., Peterson, B. S., Thompson, P. M., Welcome, S. E., Henkenius, A. L., & Toga, A. W. (2003). Mapping cortical change across the human life span. *Nature Neuroscience, 6,* 309–315.

Sperry, D. E, Sperry, L. L, & Miller, P. J. (2019a). Language does matter: But there is more to language than vocabulary and directed speech. *Child Development, 90*(3), 993–997.

Sperry D. E., Sperry, L. L., & Miller, P. J. (2019b). Reexamining the verbal environments of children from different socioeconomic backgrounds. *Child Development, 90*(4), 1303–1318.

Spilt, J. L., & Koomen, H. M. (2009). Widening the view on teacher-child relationships: Teachers' narratives concerning disruptive versus nondisruptive children. *School Psychology Review, 38,* 86–101.

Sripada, R. K., Swain, J. E., Evans, G. W., Welsh, R. C., & Liberzon, I. (2014). Childhood poverty and stress reactivity are associated with aberrant functional connectivity in default mode network. *Neuropsychopharmacology, 39,* 2244–2251.

Stallen, M., De Dreu, C. K., Shalvi, S., Smidts, A., & Sanfey, A. G. (2012). The herding hormone: Oxytocin stimulates in-group conformity. *Psychological Science, 23,* 1288–1292.

Stankov, L., & Lee, J. (2020). We can boost IQ: Revisiting Kvashchev's experiment. *Journal of Intelligence, 8*(4), 41.

Stanley, D. A., & Adolphs, R. (2013). Toward a neural basis for social behavior. *Neuron, 80*(3), 816–826.

Stearns, E., Banerjee, N., Mickelson, R., & Moller, S. (2014). Collective pedagogical teacher culture, teacher-student ethno-racial mismatch, and teacher job satisfaction. *Social Science Research, 45,* 56–72.

Stein, G. L., Supple, A. J., Huq, N., Dunbar, A. S., & Prinstein, M. J. (2016). A longitudinal examination of perceived discrimination and depressive symptoms in ethnic minority youth: The roles of attributional style, positive ethnic/racial affect, and emotional reactivity. *Developmental Psychology, 52,* 259–271.

Steinert, Y., O'Sullivan, P. S., & Irby, D. M. (2019). Strengthening teachers' professional identities through faculty development. *Academic Medicine, 94,* 963–968.

Stemmann, H., & Freiwald, W. A. (2019). Evidence for an attentional priority map in inferotemporal cortex. *Proceedings of the National Academy of Sciences, 116,* 23797–23805.

Stillman, T. F., Baumeister, R. F., Lambert, N. M., Crescioni, A. W., DeWall, C. N., & Fincham, F. D. (2009). Alone and without purpose: Life loses meaning following social exclusion. *Journal of Experimental Social Psychology, 45,* 686–694.

Substance Abuse and Mental Health Services Administration. (2015). *Treatment episode data set (TEDS): 2003–2013: National admissions to substance abuse treatment services.* Author.

Suzuki, W. A., Feliú-Mójer, M. I., Hasson, U., Yehuda, R., & Zarate, J. M. (2018). Dialogues: The science and power of storytelling. *Journal of Neuroscience, 38,* 9468–9470.

Taylor, J., Roehrig, A. D., Soden Hensler, B., Connor, C. M., & Schatschneider, C. (2010). Teacher quality moderates the genetic effects on early reading. *Science, 328,* 512–514.

Teixeira-Machado, L., Arida, R. M., & de Jesus, M. J. (2019). Dance for neuroplasticity: A descriptive systematic review. *Neuroscience & Biobehavioral Reviews, 96,* 232–240.

Thomas, C. R., & Gadbois, S. A. (2007). Academic self-handicapping: The role of self-concept clarity and students' learning strategies. *British Journal of Educational Psychology, 77,* 101–119.

TNTP. (2018). The opportunity myth: What students can show us about how school is letting them down—and how to fix it. https://tntp.org/publications/view/student-experiences/the-opportunity-myth

Tomalski, P., Moore, D. G., Ribeiro, H., Axelsson, E. L., Murphy, E., & Karmiloff-Smith, A. (2013). Socioeconomic status and functional brain development—Associations in early infancy. *Developmental Science, 16*(5), 676–687.

Tomayko, E. J., Mosso, K. L., Cronin, K. A., Carmichael, L., Kim, K., Parker, T., et al. (2017). Household food insecurity and dietary patterns in rural and urban American Indian families with young children. *BMC Public Health, 30,* 611.

Tucker-Drob, E. M. (2012). Preschools reduce early academic-achievement gaps: A longitudinal twin approach. *Psychological Science, 23,* 310–319.

Tucker-Drob, E. M., & Bates T. C. (2016). Large cross-national differences in gene × socioeconomic status interaction on intelligence. *Psychological Science, 27,* 138–149.

U.S. Census Bureau. (2020, Sept. 15). Income, poverty, and health insurance coverage in the United States. www.census.gov/newsroom/press-releases/2020/income-poverty.html

U.S. Department of Education Office for Civil Rights. (2018). *2015–16 Civil Rights Data Collection: School Climate and Safety.* Author.

Voss, J. L., Gonsalves, B. D., Federmeier, K. D., Tranel, D., & Cohen, N. J. (2011). Hippocampal brain-network coordination during volitional exploratory behavior enhances learning. *Nature Neuroscience, 14,* 115–120.

Vrtička, P., & Vuilleumier, P. (2012). Neuroscience of human social interactions and adult attachment style. *Frontiers in Human Neuroscience, 17,* 212.

Wallace, J. M., Jr., Goodkind, S., Wallace, C. M., & Bachman, J. G. (2008). Racial, ethnic, and gender differences in school discipline among U.S. high school students: 1991–2005. *Negro Educational Review, 59,* 47–62.

Walton, G. M., & Cohen, G. L. (2011). A brief social-belonging intervention improves academic and health outcomes of minority students. *Science, 331,* 1447–1451.

Webb, T. L., & Sheeran, P. (2006). Does changing behavioral intentions engender behavior change? A meta-analysis of the experimental evidence. *Psychological Bulletin, 132,* 249–268.

Wei, P., & Kang, G. (2014, June). Task relevance regulates the interaction between reward expectation and emotion. *Experimental Brain Research, 232*(6), 1783–1791.

Weisburg, D., Sexton, S., Mulhern, J., & Keeling, D. (2009). *The widget effect: Our national failure to acknowledge and act on differences in teacher effectiveness.* TNTP.

Wenglinsky, H. (2002). How schools matter: The link between teacher classroom practices and student academic performance. *Education Policy Analysis Archives, 10,* 1–30.

Wentzel, K. R. (2012). Teacher-student relationships and adolescent competence at school. In T. Wubbels, P. den Brok, & J. van Tartwijk (Eds.), *Interpersonal Relationships in Education* (pp. 19–36). Sense Publishers.

West, R. F., Meserve, R. J., & Stanovich, K. E. (2012). Cognitive sophistication does not attenuate the bias blind spot. *Journal of Personality and Social Psychology, 103*(3), 506–519.

White, S. F., Voss, J. L., Chiang, J. J., Wang, L., McLaughlin, K. A., & Miller, G. E. (2019, December). Exposure to violence and low family income are associated with heightened amygdala responsiveness to threat among adolescents. *Developmental Cognitive Neuroscience, 40,* 100709.

Wiehle, M., Davis, A., Davis, C., Gardner, M., Gee, L. C., & Grundman, D. (2013). *Who pays? A distributional analysis of the tax systems in all 50 states.* Institute on Taxation & Economic Policy. https://itep.org/whopays/

Wiliam, D., & Thompson, M. (2008). Integrating assessment with learning: What will it take to make it work? In C. A. Dwyer (Ed.), *The Future of Assessment: Shaping Teaching and Learning* (pp. 53–82). Routledge.

Williams, A. S., Ge, B., Petroski, G., Kruse, R. L., McElroy, J. A., & Koopman, R. J. (2018). Socioeconomic status and other factors associated with childhood obesity. *Journal of American Board of Family Medicine, 31,* 514–521.

Wilson, D., Jones, D., Bocell, F., Crawford, J., Kim, M. J., Veilleux, N., et al. (2015). Belonging and academic engagement among undergraduate STEM students: A multi-institutional study. *Research in Higher Education, 7,* 750–776.

Wisniewski, B., Zierer, K., & Hattie, J. (2020). The power of feedback revisited: A meta-analysis of educational feedback research. *Frontiers in Psychology, 10,* 3087.

Wood, W., Quinn, J. M., & Kashy, D. A. (2002). Habits in everyday life: Thought, emotion, and action. *Journal of Personality and Social Psychology, 83,* 1281–1297.

Yang, J. J., Zhan, L. X., Wang, Y. Y., Du, X. Y., Zhou, W. X., Ning, X. L., et al. (2016). Effects of learning experience on forgetting rates of item and associative memories. *Learning & Memory, 23,* 365–378.

Yeager, D. S., Purdie-Vaughns, V., Garcia, J., Apfel, N., Brzustoski, P., Master, A., et al. (2014). Breaking the cycle of mistrust: Wise interventions to provide critical feedback across the racial divide. *Journal of Experimental Psychology: General, 143,* 804–824.

Yeager, D. S., Purdie-Vaughns, V., Hooper, S. Y., & Cohen, G. L. (2017). Loss of institutional trust among racial and ethnic minority adolescents: A consequence of procedural injustice and a cause of life-span outcomes. *Child Development, 88,* 658–676.

Yeager, D. S., & Walton, G. (2011). Social-psychological interventions in education: They're not magic. *Review of Educational Research, 81,* 267–301.

Yeates, P., Woolf, K., Benbow, E., Davies, B., Boohan, M., & Eva, K. (2017). A randomised trial of the influence of racial stereotype bias on examiners' scores, feedback and recollections in undergraduate clinical exams. *BMC Medicine, 15,* 179.

Yoon, J. S. (2002). Teacher characteristics as predictors of teacher-student relationships: Stress, negative affect, and self-efficacy. *Social Behavior and Personality, 30,* 485–493.

Zuckerman, M., & Tsai, F. F. (2005). Costs of self-handicapping. *Journal of Personality, 73,* 411–442.

Zwosta, K., Ruge, H., Goschke, T., & Wolfensteller, U. (2018). Habit strength is predicted by activity dynamics in goal-directed brain systems during training. *Neuroimage, 165,* 125–137.

Index

About the Author

Eric Jensen is a former teacher who grew up in San Diego, California. Jensen's academic background includes an MA in Organizational Development and a PhD in Human Development. He embraces evidence-based practices from neuroscience to the classroom. Jensen cofounded the first and largest brain-compatible learning program, held in 14 countries with more than 80,000 graduates. He has written more than 30 books, including *Engaging Students with Poverty in Mind, Teaching with the Brain in Mind, Brain-Based Learning, Enriching the Brain,* and *Poor Students, Rich Teaching.*

Dr. Jensen is a member of the invitation-only Society for Neuroscience and is listed among the Top 30 Global Gurus in Education at www.globalgurus.org. Jensen is a mentor and trainer for many professional developers throughout the world. Currently, he provides professional development on equity, student engagement, brain-based learning, and the change process. To get in touch, visit www.jensenlearning.com or email info@jensenlearning.com.

Related ASCD Resources

At the time of publication, the following resources were available (ASCD stock numbers appear in parentheses).

Print Products

Becoming the Educator They Need: Strategies, Mindsets, and Beliefs for Supporting Male Black and Latino Students by Robert Jackson (#119010)

Cultivating Joyful Learning Spaces for Black Girls: Insights into Interrupting School Pushout by Monique W. Morris (#121004)

Cultural Competence Now: 56 Exercises to Help Educators Understand and Challenge Bias, Racism, and Privilege by Vernita Mayfield (#118043)

Culture, Class, and Race: Constructive Conversations That Unite and Energize Your School and Community by Brenda CampbellJones, Shannon Keeny, and Franklin CampbellJones (#118010)

Engaging Students with Poverty in Mind: Practical Strategies for Raising Achievement by Eric Jensen (#113001)

The Equity and Social Justice Education 50: Critical Questions for Improving Opportunities and Outcomes for Black Students by Baruti K. Kafele (#121060)

The Handbook for Poor Students, Rich Teaching by Eric Jensen (#319078)

The Innocent Classroom: Dismantling Racial Bias to Support Students of Color by Alexs Pate (#120025)

Literacy Is Liberation: Working Toward Justice Through Culturally Relevant Teaching by Kimberly N. Parker (#122024)

Relationship, Responsibility, and Regulation: Trauma-Invested Practices for Fostering Resilient Learners by Kristin Van Marter Souers with Pete Hall (#119027)

Restoring Students' Innate Power: Trauma-Responsive Strategies for Teaching Multilingual Newcomers by Louise El Yaafouri (#122004)

Teaching and Supporting Students Living with Adversity (Quick Reference Guide) by Debbie Zacarian and Lourdes Alvarez-Ortiz (#QRG120035)

Teaching Students from Poverty (Quick Reference Guide) by Eric Jensen (#QRG118041)

Turning High-Poverty Schools into High-Performing Schools, 2nd Edition by William H. Parrett and Kathleen M. Budge (#120031)

Uprooting Instructional Inequity: The Power of Inquiry-Based Professional Learning by Jill Harrison Berg (#121016)

Your Students, My Students, Our Students: Rethinking Equitable and Inclusive Classrooms by Lee Ann Jung, Nancy Frey, Douglas Fisher, and Julie Kroener (#119019)

For up-to-date information about ASCD resources, go to **www.ascd.org.** You can search the complete archives of *Educational Leadership* at **www.ascd.org/el.**

ASCD myTeachSource®

Download resources from a professional learning platform with hundreds of research-based best practices and tools for your classroom at http://myteachsource.ascd.org/.

For more information, send an email to member@ascd.org; call 1-800-933-2723 or 703-578-9600; send a fax to 703-575-5400; or write to Information Services, ASCD, 2800 Shirlington Road, Suite 1001, Arlington, VA 22206 USA.

THE WHOLE CHILD

The ASCD Whole Child approach is an effort to transition from a focus on narrowly defined academic achievement to one that promotes the long-term development and success of all children. Through this approach, ASCD supports educators, families, community members, and policymakers as they move from a vision about educating the whole child to sustainable, collaborative actions.

Teaching with Poverty and Equity in Mind relates to the **safe, engaged, supported, and challenged** tenets.

For more about the ASCD Whole Child approach, visit ***www.ascd.org/wholechild.***

WHOLE CHILD
TENETS

1 HEALTHY
Each student enters school healthy and learns about and practices a healthy lifestyle.

2 SAFE
Each student learns in an environment that is physically and emotionally safe for students and adults.

3 ENGAGED
Each student is actively engaged in learning and is connected to the school and broader community.

4 SUPPORTED
Each student has access to personalized learning and is supported by qualified, caring adults.

5 CHALLENGED
Each student is challenged academically and prepared for success in college or further study and for employment and participation in a global environment.